DATE DUE			

BOULEZ

BOULEZ

Joan Peyser

SCHIRMER BOOKS

A Division of Macmillan Publishing Co., Inc.
NEW YORK

Collier Macmillan Publishers
LONDON

Schirmer Books
A Division of Macmillan Publishing Co., Inc.
866 Third Avenue, New York, N.Y. 10022

Collier Macmillan Canada, Ltd.

Library of Congress Catalog Card Number: 76-20884

Printed in the United States of America

printing number   1   2   3   4   5   6   7   8   9   10

Library of Congress Cataloging in Publication Data

Peyser, Joan.
  Boulez.

   Includes index.
   1. Boulez, Pierre, 1925-   2. Composers--
France--Biography. 3. Conductors (Music)--France--
Biography.
ML410.B773P5   780'.92'4 [B]   76-20884
ISBN 0-02-871700-7

COPYRIGHT ACKNOWLEDGMENTS

   Excerpts from Pierre Boulez, Boulez on Music Today, Harvard University Press, 1971, reprinted by permission of Faber and Faber Ltd and Harvard University Press. Copyright © Pierre Boulez 1971.
   Columbia Records for English translations of "Le Visage Nuptial," "Le Soleil des Eaux," "Pli Selon Pli," Mallarmé "Sonnets."
   Editions Gallimard for permission to reprint the Mallarmé "Sonnets" and René Char "Le Visage Nuptial," "Complainte du Lézard Amoureux" (extracted from "Les Matinaux") and "La Sorgue" (extracted from "Fureur et Mystère"), Copyright © Editions Gallimard and René Char.
   Editions Gallimard for permission to reprint Henri Michaux, "Poésies pour Pouvoir" extracted from Face aux Verrous, copyright 1954 Editions Gallimard.
   Music Faculty of the University of Montreal for "Interview with Pierre Boulez," by Maryvonne Kindirgi from Les Cahiers Canadiens de musique (The Canadian Music Books), vol. 2, spring 1971.
   The New York Times for Joan Peyser, "A Fighter From Way Back," January 1961 and "Bringing 'em Back to Life?" June 1971 © 1969/1971 by The New York Times Company. Reprinted by permission.
   Louise Varèse for English translation of "Poésies pour Pouvoir."

for Jeanne Boulez

the source

Contents

Introduction

On June 1, 1969, the New York Philharmonic announced the appointment of Pierre Boulez as its music director. He was to succeed Leonard Bernstein, the ebullient, gifted musical personality who had begun his career in the 1940s as the protégé of Serge Koussevitzky. For Bernstein, the first American to assume the post, it was very definitely a step up in prestige. For Boulez it was, in some people's view, a step down. As a critic, an organizer of musical thought, Boulez had no equal in the 1950s. And as a member of the postwar avant-garde, he had led the way to a new musical grammar that had been accepted by many of the most talented and aggressive composers in the world.

Boulez built his conducting career in the 1960s when aleatory music threatened the idea in which he believed. Composer Olivier Messiaen, Boulez's teacher at the Paris Conservatoire, suggests what lies behind his virtual shift of profession: "Boulez is a great composer. He is also a very intelligent man. He understands all the changes and they make him suffer. There are people who go unperturbed through change. Like Bach. Like Richard Strauss.

"But Boulez cannot. He thinks that advancing the language is all. He feels he must be in the advance guard and he doesn't like what is happening there."

The desire to escape from the severe discipline into which Boulez's idea had led moved whole sections of the new music world toward what he viewed as theatrical gimmickry and nihilism. Boulez accepted the Philharmonic post primarily to attack this situation. His purpose was to promote his own cause, to make familiar to large audiences the modern language in which he believed, in which form exercised a centripetal role.

When he accepted the job, Boulez planned several innovations. First, he would concentrate his initial season in Philharmonic Hall on the works of Franz Liszt and Alban Berg. In doing that, he said he would follow the precept of the Museum of Modern Art—which proselytized, twenty-five years ago, for late nineteenth- and early twentieth-century art, setting a model that other museums quickly followed. Second, he would devote entire evenings at the Juilliard School to the analysis of crucial twentieth-century works. Finally, he would preside over evenings in Greenwich Village where he would present recently composed "documents." There, in an informal atmosphere, members of the New York Philharmonic would play new works which would be discussed by the composer, the listeners, and Boulez.

Boulez designed this plan with one purpose in mind: to narrow the gap between composer and listener that had begun in 1912 with Schoenberg's *Pierrot Lunaire*. That gap was widened ten years later with the "revelation" by Schoenberg of the laws of dodecaphony and has shown no signs of diminishing since. This is intellectual music, art that obeys integral laws of musical structure, and no one in the performing world understands it better than Boulez. If he could focus on this particular repertoire with the best orchestra in the most powerful city in the world, that would provide the ultimate test: is this music just seductive to the eye because of the relations a musician reads in the score, or does it finally appeal to something more that makes it memorable and even moving in some way? If the latter proved to be true, then serialism would displace tonality and provide the musical vocabulary for a long time to come.

Boulez's commitment allows for no shift in taste. He personifies the control of mind over body, just as Bernstein personifies the reverse. Bernstein reportedly loses seven pounds a performance because he perspires so freely. Boulez rarely perspires at all. Bernstein has a family and a highly styled social life. Boulez lives only for his work, and he lives alone. Bernstein says "I love you" to those he meets in corridors. There's no evidence that Boulez has ever said "I love you" in his life.

Thus it is fitting that Boulez—not anyone else—promulgate the most crucial musical idea of the century, one that replaces tonality, the traditional method of composition in Western civilization, with a

2

newly created scheme. New York was the place and the 1970s the time for him to make his point momentously. Because of Boulez's talent, his energy, his position, and his devotion to that language he was better suited to test it than any other musician in the world.

Before beginning Boulez's story, I think it might prove useful for the reader to know something of my own route to new music as well as the tug of war between Boulez and me that lies behind this history.

I grew up in Manhattan in a middle class family. My mother was an amateur musician and I began to play the piano at five, studying with a teacher who supplemented my work with instruction in harmony. Often I went to recitals at Carnegie Hall. The fare was heavily weighted with Bach, Mozart, Beethoven, and Liszt. I played and heard pieces up to but not beyond Debussy, Stravinsky and early Satie.

Concentration on the music of the past continued through my education at the High School of Music and Art, and Smith and Barnard Colleges. During my graduate training in musicology at Columbia, I moved even further back in time and wrote a thesis on the sixteenth century French chanson. It was only after I left Columbia and began to publish articles about music, that I was struck by how our time differs from all other times in its access to the music of earlier periods. Until recently an age had only its own art; now listeners are exposed to old music as never before through live programming, their own record collections, and radio stations' record collections. Today's composers must compete with Beethoven and Bach.

To do what I could toward making contemporary music at least understandable to the non-specialist, I wrote a book on the early twentieth century: *The New Music: the Sense behind the Sound*, and in the Sunday *New York Times* I published interviews with dozens of composers ranging from the traditionalists, Benjamin Britten and Hans Werner Henze, to Elliott Carter and Luciano Berio. I also wrote essays on the work being done at the Columbia Princeton Electronic Music Center in New York and at Bell Laboratories in New Jersey, for technology had begun to provide many new tools.

At the end of 1968 I received a press release that Boulez was to be a guest conductor at the New York Philharmonic in the spring of '69. I recalled an issue of *The Musical Quarterly*, devoted to contemporary music in Europe, in which the French musicologist Antoine Golea referred to Boulez as "the prototype and guiding light of his whole generation" and went on to make the striking comment that Boulez and his associates were engaged in nothing less than "the dismantling of music and its total reconstruction under new laws."

3

The issue appeared in January 1965 and must have made a strong impression on me then, for I remembered it four years later when I learned Boulez was touring the United States. I reread the issue and searched out more Boulez. The New York Public Library was stocked not only with his early scores but also with *La Nouvelle Revue Française*, *Contrepoint*, and *Le Revue Musicale*, in which he propounded his aesthetics of new music. There were also European recordings of some of his early works. All of it convinced me Boulez was a genius, an heir to Schoenberg, Stravinsky, Webern, and Berg, and I began to cultivate the idea of replacing Bernstein, a nineteenth-century man, with a man who was genuinely twentieth-century. It was then I interviewed Boulez for the first time.

We met for lunch at the Ritz-Carlton Hotel in Boston. Boulez was congenial and polite. He spoke kindly of his parents and teachers, undermining the prevailing image of him as the *enfant terrible* of the new-music world. When I finished my lunch I put my notebook away, thanked Boulez for his time, but told him that he had given me nothing that would justify an article in Section 2 of the *Times*.

Boulez ordered another beer, I another cup of coffee. I asked if he had read my interview with the American composer Milton Babbitt which had appeared in the *Times* a short while before. Boulez said he had been in Chicago at the time but that someone had quoted to him Babbitt's remark that a performance of a Babbitt piece in Lincoln Center was like a philosophy paper being read on the Johnny Carson show. Boulez attacked Babbitt's "ghetto" point of view and then put the knife deeply into America's back. There had been no strong musical personalities in the United States, he said, since World War II. I slipped my notebook out of my purse and took down his comments on my lap. I felt a mixture of triumph and guilt that I had cleverly manipulated Boulez into giving a lively, controversial interview. Since then I have learned that nobody manipulates Boulez into giving anything he does not choose to give.

At the end of our conversation I asked Boulez if he would accept the Philharmonic post if it were offered to him. He ridiculed the notion that he was being considered, but added that he would never accept it. New York has bad musical habits, he said, and to change bad habits one must know them well.

The interview appeared on March 9, just before he began his month-long engagement with the New York orchestra. During the next four weeks Boulez played early twentieth-century music with great elegance and passion, with the perfect balance of excitement and control. The New York critics raved, and on April 1 the board of di-

4

rectors offered him the big job. Although he had recently committed himself for the same period to the BBC Symphony in London, Boulez did not say no to New York. In May he said yes. On June 1 his appointment was announced. The *New York Times* reported the event on page 1, adding that Boulez could not be reached for comment as to why he told the paper only a few months before that he would never accept the prestigious music post.

That summer I was living in the Berkshire mountains and attended a Boulez rehearsal of a Boston Symphony concert at the Tanglewood festival. I was backstage when Boulez stopped for a break. "I have an apology to make," he told me. "I said I wouldn't take it and I took it. The matter was especially complicated," he went on, "and it would not have been discreet for me to discuss it at that time." "Ah," I laughed, "we were collaborators. The only way to land a big job in music in the United States is to proclaim arrogantly that you would never stoop to take it."

In March 1971 my book on early twentieth-century music appeared. I sent it to Boulez, who was then conducting in Cleveland, and wrote that I wanted to concentrate my next book on him. I said I was a friend of Louise Varèse, the widow of the composer Edgard Varèse, and that Mrs. Varèse had told me she was flying to Cleveland the following week to attend his all-Varèse concert there. If he were interested in my project I would accompany her and we could confer then about the book. Boulez sent me a letter which is reproduced here not only to illustrate that part of Boulez that wishes to remain anonymous —there is neither letterhead nor date and the signature bears little resemblance to the letters of his name—but also to reveal how even the simplest message from him is not so simple. He always makes the other person in any dialogue come virtually all the way to him.

In Cleveland we met in Severance Hall and I told Boulez what I planned to do: I would report on all his activities in New York. In my lexicon he was a genuine artist, an ascetic committed to an Idea. I wanted to observe what would go on when he entered New York's show business world. I would follow him like a shadow, reporting everything that was said and done. Therefore the administration would know that if they were to inhibit his desire to program advanced works, at least there would be a chronicle to document what they had done to him.

Boulez agreed to the venture. He said there would be some matters —such as negotiations with the unions—which he would prefer to remain secret. He did not want to jeopardize his success there by re-

Dear Mr. Payne,

Unfortunately, I had no time to answer you sooner.

I phoned the Vance who gave me your phone number.

But I could not reach you.

I can manage an appointment on the morning of the 27th, ca 11:00, at Severance Hall.

Thank you very much for your book. I began to read it during my travelling breaks. I hope to have a good idea of it when you are in Cleveland.

I will try anyway to call you again.

With my best regards

Tony

vealing whatever concessions they would agree to give him. He was then hoping for a bank of rehearsal hours, he explained. If he did not use the time allotted for one program because it contained no new and difficult works, he could add those hours to a more demanding program. (The union never agreed to this plan.) I assured him I would go along with this and added that if he ever said anything to me that he regretted at a later time, he should not hesitate to ask me to strike it from the record. (Boulez never did.) I said the book would be published without his approval and he replied, "Of course. It is your own work." We agreed to begin our new routine when he arrived in New York the following week for his second guest engagement with the orchestra. He was not to start his official tenure for another six months.

When I appeared at the first rehearsal, I was told it was closed. I left word for Boulez that I was upset that he had forgotten to clear the way for me. After the rehearsal Boulez called. He said he was keeping all the rehearsals closed because the musicians required severe discipline and he did not want to humiliate them in front of anyone. I said I did not think the book would work and added that perhaps we should stop now. Boulez suggested I be optimistic and invited me to a rehearsal the next afternoon of a *New and Newer Music* concert at Alice Tully Hall. He said we would dine together afterwards when he would answer any questions on my mind.

That call set the tone for our collaboration. I was not invited to large orchestra rehearsals except on specified, rare occasions. Neither was I invited to programming conferences with management, to composers' conferences on the Village programs, nor to auditions for new players. I did attend recording sessions, rehearsals for the Prospective Encounters, and rehearsals for small chamber groups he would conduct from time to time. We lunched and dined together frequently. At the end of a few months I saw how little solid material I had and decided to write a different kind of book, one that would have its roots in Erik Erikson's concept of psychobiography. I hoped to explain how this formidable talent and extraordinary intellect grew to be the man and the cultural force he became.

But that project, too, proved fraught with frustration. When I told Boulez that I wanted to find out whatever I could about his early life and had therefore planned a trip to his home town, Boulez told me that I must not go there, that nobody there would remember him. But I did go to Montbrison, registered at the hotel in the center of town, and although the concierge did not know the name Boulez, he called the mayor who certainly did. Within minutes the mayor and five citizens were sitting at a table with me, drinking what they think is a typical American drink—Scotch in orange juice—and reminiscing about Boulez and his family. They invited me to tour Boulez's school the following day.

Boulez's record revealed that he had excelled in science and mathematics and had always been exceptionally neat and well-behaved. A priest showed me around. At the chapel door he asked me if what he had been told was true: that Boulez no longer believed in God. I said it was and he replied, "Then I won't show you the chapel where he prayed twice a day between the ages of six and sixteen."

I made three trips to Europe for this book but never met Boulez's mother, although I tried many times. Meanwhile, more casual visitors managed easily. Boulez's mother, according to others, is a simple and garrulous woman. Apparently her son did not want me to hear whatever it was that she had to say. He preferred that I speak with his sister,

7

a vivacious, outgoing, intelligent woman who adores and idealizes her brother. They speak to each other at least once a week. At our first meeting Jeanne Chevalier expressed extreme reservation about the book. She said the story of her brother's life could be told in one paragraph. She repeated this in letters to me and finally wrote she was against the book because she feared it would "reveal my brother naked." I reported this to Boulez who shrugged his shoulders. He always appears invulnerable to anything outside himself. Then too, he knew he would never offer me information with which I could "undress" him.

And so, for the next five years, through hundreds of hours of conversation, Boulez concealed a lot of his life from me. Just before I made my first trip to France I asked him for the address of René Leibowitz, his second and probably most important composition teacher. (Messiaen was his only other.) Boulez said, "Leibowitz is no friend of mine." I explained I was not limiting my interviews to friends. "Of course," he answered, "you are preparing a document." Still, he did not help me to locate Leibowitz, who was then living in an apartment on the Left Bank. When I told Leibowitz my subject was Boulez, he became silent. Only after I explained that I was writing a history of midcentury music, in which Leibowitz had played a large role, did he begin to unfold his own story of the confrontation and terrible trouble with Boulez—including Boulez's efforts to wreck Leibowitz's career.

A few weeks after our long conversation, Leibowitz died at fifty-nine of a heart attack. I wrote his obituary for the New York Times. When I next saw Boulez it was on an airplane bound for Indiana. I was accompanying him on a New York Philharmonic tour. He was reading the obituary as I entered the aircraft. "I see you got to Leibowitz before he died," was all he said.

What Leibowitz told about Boulez was the story of an explosive man, capable of expressing great passion and rage, hardly the man we know today who is so much in control of his feelings and appetites. Only on rare occasions does he lose control. One such incident involved Robert Craft, Stravinsky's amanuensis, who repeatedly attacked Boulez during his early conducting days in New York. Writing in the New York Review of Books, Craft had Stravinsky say that Boulez's major work, Pli Selon Pli, was "pretty monotonous and monotonously pretty" and that his programming in New York would prove to be a bore. Boulez told me he wanted to reply, that he could be "very aggressive" in situations like this. Then, more as a friend than a neutral observer, I counseled Boulez against doing this. I explained that the editor's loyalty would be to Craft who was a regular contributor to the *New York Review*. I assured Boulez a better moment would come.

In the spring of 1971 I wrote an article for the Sunday *Times* describing a typical Boulez day in New York. Craft wrote a letter in response, attacking Boulez's musicianship and my judgment. I told Boulez that if he were waiting for a moment to reply, this was probably as good as any. I assured him that the *Times* would give him whatever space he would need.

Boulez wrote a letter attacking Craft's "sour mixture of incompetence and pedantry" and challenging the authorship of Stravinsky's writings, claiming what has subsequently been charged by others: that, in the later years, they were not only written by Craft but not even reviewed by the aging master. Boulez ended by admonishing Craft to "stop imposing your insipid countenance on the features of a man who has nothing in common with your rancor, your impotence, and—in a word, your nothingness."

Carlos Moseley, the president of the New York Philharmonic, had asked Boulez to send the letter to him first; when he saw it, he refused to send it on to the *Times*. But Boulez never told me that. Instead he wrote me that he had decided not to reply, that Craft was not worth his time. His sister said the same in another letter. Yet I have a copy of the original Boulez letter in my files.

Repeatedly, in connection with specific incidents, Boulez told me the particular version that would project a controlled and powerful image, the only image he wished to project. Boulez would not tolerate a portrait of himself that would reveal a man alternately shy and blunt, friendly and forbidding, vulnerable and steel-like, a believable portrait of the deeply struggling human being he is. When I told him how difficult he was making it for me to write a genuinely good book about him, he insisted he was telling me the truth as he "saw it." On occasion, of course, facts can mislead. But with the Craft letter he was telling a lie. And there were other lies as well.

Often, inconsistencies were never resolved. One involved the composer John Cage, whom Boulez first met in 1949. Their friendship ended in 1952 when Cage announced his own principle of chance, so alien to what Boulez was formulating at the same time. But it exploded in 1957 when Boulez published an article, *Alea*, that not only attacked the principle of free-floating chance which had by then seduced many of Boulez's followers, but substituted in its place his own "controlled" chance. Cage was enraged. He says that the following summer, when he was teaching in Germany, Karlheinz Stockhausen brought Boulez to his hotel room to try to bring about a reconciliation

9

between them. Cage says he refused to open the door. Boulez denies that the incident took place. Stockhausen could clear the matter up but he will not talk to me. Stockhausen and Boulez quarreled in 1972 and have not exchanged any words since then.

Boulez's need to exhibit undaunted strength caused him to present himself as the only leader, as an individual ahead of the crowd, as the sole progenitor with no disciples. His need to be first and never a follower revealed itself in his early adult life in the way he quickly despised those from whom he had learned. It reveals itself today in the way he would rewrite history if he could. Boulez says, for example, that in the first version of *Le Livre pour Cordes*, then called *Le Livre pour Quatuor*, in 1948–49, he intended all along that it should be a series of detachable movements from which the players could select which ones they wished to play. That was well before Cage promulgated his chance philosophy. But the chance aspect of the Boulez work was not stated in the original Heugel publication. Moreover, when the final version was published in the 1960s, the idea of choice was very much in the air. It is impossible to determine with any certainty whether this kind of performer involvement had been part of Boulez's original plan. The facts suggest it was not. Boulez wrote much music in the late '40s and early '50s, and none of it contained any such options. The first work of his that exhibited this principle was the *Third Piano Sonata*, composed in 1957.

The hiding of roots, influences, weakness, and passion that is at the core of the man is also at the core of the music he loves—the highly structured music of the early twentieth century. Boulez was obsessed with this music, and it was this that the Philharmonic did not comprehend. The late David Keiser, then chairman of the orchestra's Music Policy Committee, told me they had selected Boulez because he was a "leader, a top-notch musician, technically a very fine conductor under whom the orchestra plays very well." Keiser added that Boulez had a "fine personality and was in the right age bracket." What Boulez was thinking never entered Keiser's mind. Thus Boulez received his appointment almost by a misconception. Keiser thought he was getting a man of great talent, extraordinary energy, and with an impeccable ear. Of course he was right about that. But he also thought he was getting a forty-four-year-old conductor and he was not quite right about that. The Philharmonic had chosen a forty-four-year-old composer tied to a kind of music that neither Keiser nor his audience wanted or understood, and a conductor with less than ten years experience with large orchestras.

Boulez presented large doses of the music he loves during his guest appearances in 1969 and 1971, and during his first full season in New York, 1971–72. But the audience did not like what it heard and cancelled subscriptions and wrote angry letters. In an almost standard response, Moseley replied that "minute-to-minute" there was no more modern music under Boulez than under Bernstein. To arrive at this estimate, Moseley had to equate such traditionalists as Prokofiev, Copland, and Bernstein himself with Schoenberg, Webern, Berg, and Varèse.

But the subscribers heard the difference and would not allow their protests to be sloughed off. After Boulez's first season of Berg and Liszt he moved backward—under public pressure—to a second season of Haydn and Stravinsky, to a third of "Early and Late Romanticism," and to a fourth of nineteenth-century "Nationalism." In 1975 Tchaikovsky's *First Piano Concerto* was played in the hall, when Boulez was away. "I am not a fascist," Boulez explains. "I hate Tchaikovsky and I will not conduct him. But if the audience wants him, it can have him."

Simultaneous with Tchaikovsky at Lincoln Center, Charles Wuorinen and a colleague introduced into Carnegie Hall "The New Orchestra" which, the flyer announced, "has come into being because of the growing concern of many of our foremost composers and performers over the presentation of twentieth-century orchestra music." The implication of Wuorinen's remark was that Boulez might just as well not have come here at all. But Wuorinen was no more successful than Boulez. The New Orchestra's first concert was its last. There is no doubt in my mind that if anyone were able to make this music work, it would have been Boulez at the helm of the New York Philharmonic. That was the combination behind the impeccable performance of Elliott Carter's extremely complicated *Concerto for Orchestra*. That was the combination behind the first performance of Varèse's *Amériques* in forty-six years.

As we know now, that combination did not work, and when Boulez leaves in 1977 the orchestra's programs will probably become as routine as ever. His successor is the glamorous Zubin Mehta, who specializes in the Romantic period. Still, Boulez refuses to say his mission failed. In this he is unlike Joseph Papp, who in the fall of 1974 acknowledged defeat in bringing new plays into the Vivian Beaumont Theater of Lincoln Center, saying that henceforth he would present only the classics with name performers there. Boulez, on the other hand, continues to claim that the revolution has begun. He has pointed to isolated events—the Mini-Festivals and the Rug Concerts

11

—as evidence to substantiate his claims. But here the success appears to have been personal as well as musical. Students responded not only to the low prices—comparable to movies—but also to Boulez's lack of pretension, absence of pomposity, avoidance of histrionics, as well as to his well-established anti-establishment image, the highly publicized, heroic, iconoclastic *idea* of Boulez. The success cannot be attributed wholly to the "advanced" repertoire. In 1974 Boulez devoted one Mini-Festival to Schubert; the other, on Ives, was a dismal failure. In 1975 the Rug Concerts included Mozart, Mendelssohn, Mahler, and Wagner. Of the forty-two pieces played in ten concerts that spring, almost half were nineteenth century and earlier, and only three were composed after World War II.

Master at keeping two versions of the same story in his head, Boulez was able to play to both sides. In the spring of 1975 he appeared on CBS-TV's *Camera Three* with Moseley, Keiser, and Amyas Ames, all high officials at Lincoln Center, and said there was "absolutely no difference between an establishment and anti-establishment," that they were all working together towards shared aims. Weeks later he did an about-face when he told Nat Hentoff, in a radio interview, that it is better to have courage and stick to your guns and be respected for the facts than it is to end up with everyone thinking you are nice. But Boulez did not stick to his guns and Moseley, Keiser, and Ames ended up thinking him very nice.

The question finally is this: Why did Boulez stay in New York when he could not do what he set out to do, and why did he continue to proclaim that he had done what he set out to do?

There are at least several answers to that, some political, some financial. But I believe the most important one is that the New York position satisfied his quest for fame. It is difficult for anyone to acknowledge such a quest today, for in modern times there is something pejorative in the lust for fame. But this was not always true. In his essay on Freud, the late literary critic Lionel Trilling points out that a love of fame was not only characteristic of Dante, Milton, and Shakespeare, but that it was the "spur to Freud's clear spirit, the intense expression of the sense of self, of the self defined by the thing it makes, which is conceived to be everlasting because it was once a new thing, a thing added to the spirit of man."

What psychoanalytic theory was to Freud, the formulation of a new musical grammar was to Boulez. Here was a syntax that had its roots in a mathematical system, that concentrated on the proliferation of musical material from the smallest possible cell, that juxtaposed tightness and extreme rigidity with invention and flexibility. Here was a grammar to replace tonality, that would bear his recognizable imprint and his name. Through this language Boulez sought immortality—and, while waiting for its arrival, what more appropriate way to spend his time than to retire to public life and exult in the fame that only success can bring?

"Boulez is a prisoner of his brain. He does not have the courage to let his feelings go," says Hilda Strobel, the widow of Heinrich Strobel, a significant person in Boulez's life for more than twenty years.

Boulez's refusal to share facts, thoughts, and feelings is not limited to his relationship with me. Paul Jacobs, the specialist in twentieth century keyboard music who has known Boulez since the mid-50s, says Boulez uses relationships the way other people go to the movies. Boulez would not argue the point. He believes "everyone is replaceable." No one, in any case, knows Boulez well. "Neither I nor anyone," Jacobs maintains, "has ever been able to penetrate Boulez."

A French observer might view Boulez's personality as a matter of "temperament." It was Talleyrand who taught that a diplomat must have the faculty of appearing open while remaining impenetrable, of masking reserve with careless abandon. A psychoanalyst, on the other hand, would probably go along with Frau Strobel and find Boulez a compulsive man with a withdrawn nature who cannot help but behave the way he does, cannot help but correct every mistake—his own as well as those of others, cannot help but continue to revise his scores, and cannot help but withdraw from relationships, particularly from the human interchange that sexuality inevitably brings.

In the United States the man with whom Boulez spends most of his time, outside of Carlos Moseley, is Stephen Jablonsky, an aspiring thirty-three-year-old composer-conductor who first met Boulez at Harvard in 1963. Jablonsky and his wife attend all Boulez concerts, buy Boulez a shirt if he needs a shirt, take him to the movies if he has three unscheduled hours, and are in the Green Room to congratulate him after almost every event. They call for and deliver him to the airport, and that is a time-consuming job. Boulez commutes between New York, London, Paris, and Baden-Baden, rarely staying in one city for more than a few weeks at any time. Boulez's attitude towards cities is the same as towards people: he is uncomfortable being tied to any one. I asked Jablonsky if he and Boulez correspond during the long periods Boulez is away. Jablonsky laughed. "I receive a post card with one line: the date, flight number, and arrival time."

Boulez shares a vacation house at St. Michel de l'Observatoire in the south of France with his sister Jeanne and her family: her husband, son, two daughters, and grandchildren. Until recently he spent little time there. Now he is building his own modern house at the far end of the property. St. Michel must be one of the most beautiful places in the world. High in the French Alps, it is about an hour's drive from Avignon. It seems the perfect setting for Jeanne Chevalier, who runs an orderly and lively household with many visitors, great food and wine. Her husband, a physician, relaxes there, often snoozing under a large straw hat. Her daughters loll about in bikinis, tending to their husbands and naked babies. Boulez remains fully clothed all the time, rarely visiting the pool. Sometimes, when he is in the living room, a baby will crawl in. He regards the child dispassionately. Only if the toddler climbs onto his lap, grabs at a finger or puts an arm around his neck, will he—almost despite himself—break into a smile.

Boulez's personality appears to be more accurately reflected in the large three-story house he rents in Baden-Baden, a town that at various times has housed Brahms, Berlioz, Brecht, Weill, and Hindemith, and one where the rich have been going to die for decades. One visitor says Boulez's house looks like a dentist's waiting room. It is cold, almost antiseptic. Boulez has furnished quarters to his slender, pretty secretary, Astrid Schirmer, and his valet, Hans Messner. The valet occupies a handsome apartment in the basement; the secretary lives on the third floor where she takes all her meals. "What is good about not having a family," Boulez says, "is that one does not have to make conversation at meals. If I am fortunate in not having a family, why should I have to converse with a secretary? From time to time I like being with people, but most of the time I prefer to be alone."

When he is dining with people, Boulez laughs a good deal, but the laughter generally strikes me as forced. Only once can I recall a really raucous laugh that he had difficulty getting under control. He told the story late one night when he was with a few friends: a conductor he knew became interested in a woman he met on a train and went to her compartment to spend the night. On awakening he discovered that the train had uncoupled and that he was miles from his destination— unshaven and without clothes.

Boulez's general approach to life is serious and infuses his attitude toward music. He does not dance. I have never seen him tap his foot, move his body to a lilting rhythm, smile at a melody. Boulez does not own a record player at the present time—not in New York, London, Baden-Baden, or Paris. He once had one in St. Michel, a gift from record executive Ken Glancy, but it was stolen and he did not replace it. "I never play records," he says, "because my reflection comes from reading the score. It is the same with plays. I go sometimes, but I prefer reading them."

A cheerless ambiance pervades Boulez's German house, his primary residence. Miss Schirmer, who takes care of Boulez's scores and his crowded schedule, has confided that she feels isolated there, not only because she has few friends in Germany—she considers London her real home—but also because of Boulez's coldness. She earns a good salary and it comes in German marks.

Hans Messner, whom Boulez hired in the spring of 1972, is his first personal servant and hardly a replica of P. G. Wodehouse's Jeeves. Several motherly figures surrounding Boulez in the United States have expressed dissatisfaction with Hans because he buys frozen shrimp at the A&P, wears dungarees and sleeveless sweaters on the job, and uses Tropicana instead of fresh oranges for juice. But Boulez is more than satisfied with Hans, who quickly developed into a very good cook, and believes that all the criticism stems from Hans's "informality." In New York Boulez puts Hans up at the Empire Hotel, just across the street from his own very handsome highrise apartment. He calls on Hans only when he needs him. When I go to the apartment for a drink, Boulez does everything himself.

Boulez's lack of concern about his valet's attire gives a clue to the absence of that kind of vanity in the man. On occasion small touches appear. When he wears glasses to conduct, he whips them off before turning to take a bow. And he looked into the matter of a hair transplant, but ruled it out when someone told him it had to be repeated every year. Boulez uses any barber around, buys clothes in any store around, leads a very low-key social life. The show business crowd in Bernstein's camp is nowhere in evidence with Boulez. Neither are the intellectuals. Boulez is surrounded by a few adoring people who achieve their status through association with him, as well as several elderly ladies who follow him assiduously like groupies, often flying on the same plane with him. The most prominent of these is Marguerite Staehelin, a wealthy Swiss woman in her seventies who sent him her photograph in a bikini and has seriously proposed marriage. She telephoned me, in fact, with the request to "list Boulez's prospective brides" in my book. Boulez does not cultivate people who would offer competition or argument or press him for a genuine exchange. He has dined at my house at least twenty times and each time I have had different guests. Often I ask him if he met anyone there whom he would like to be with again. Invariably he replies, "It's always very pleasant. Ask whomever you wish."

It is this impersonality that is so striking an aspect of Boulez. The composer Eric Salzman, who has known him for many years, predicted to me at the beginning of Boulez's New York appointment that the public would finally turn from him not because of predominantly modern programs, but because it would sense the truth: that he has absolutely no personal life. Rumors abound but lead nowhere. The only sexual relationship to which Boulez admits—and that only when taken by surprise—was one that took place when he was twenty years old and caused him to set Char's violent love poem for his first important work, *Le Visage Nuptial*. When I mentioned this affair to Boulez's sister, she expressed surprise there had been even that.

Jeanne Boulez Chevalier says that love is the overriding theme of her brother's life. She refuses to elaborate on this except to note that he believes the essence of his life was told over a century ago by Herman Melville in *Pierre or, The Ambiguities*.

Pierre is an allegory, with dark insinuations. The surface level of meaning is simple enough: Pierre, docile, devout, idealistic as a child, comes to an ignoble end, disillusioned and defying God. The road to his destruction begins when he learns that a beautiful and seemingly magical young woman, working as a servant nearby, is his half-sister. Melville's story centers on their incestuous passion.

Jeanne's only son, Pierre, says his mother is as fundamentally "alone" as her brother. The thirty-one-year-old Pierre speaks of the great influence his mother exerted on her brother's early life: she introduced him to certain twentieth-century writers, interested and encouraged him in the piano, and interceded with their father in support of his career in music. Jeanne herself speaks of her collaboration with her brother as a "complicity" between them. In response to my report of his sister's words, Boulez says, "It was the most natural relationship, like brothers and sisters everywhere."

There are no letters or diaries available that might help to establish the nature or intensity of this love. But there can be no doubt that Jeanne has been Pierre's most devoted friend all his life, and that she has always seen him as a Jesus-like figure, an invulnerable knight: pure, ascetic, altogether heroic. She says her brother needs no one and nothing and, without even being challenged, repeatedly claims he never lies. She decorated his room in St. Michel to look like that of a Benedictine monk. As soon as he saw it he changed it. He added an abstract painting someone gave him—even hanging it in the wrong direction

16

because he preferred it that way—and introduced other colorful touches that brought some life to the austere chamber.

Jeanne says that only she knows her brother thoroughly. When I reported to her that he had shared some childhood memories with me —holding his father's hand on the scaffolding of their new house, having his hands tied when he had the chicken pox, and the most extraordinary one of all—seeing his own name on his brother's tiny grave for there had been a Pierre Boulez before he was born—she remarked that he had selected those memories because they were "absolutely meaningless ones and he wished to prevent you from digging further."

Jeanne's severe image of Boulez is the one he has always projected to the world. When those close to him discover that despite his great gifts he is, in the end, a human being and not unlike the rest of us in at least a few ways, they become disillusioned and feel betrayed. An early advocate, Pierre Souvchinsky, shifted to Gilbert Amy. A later one, Strobel, shifted to Stockhausen. But women hold more tenaciously to heroes than do men. They become angry, not disloyal, when disappointment comes.

One such woman was Paule Tévenin, probably Boulez's closest woman friend in his early adult life. Mme Tévenin possessed much in common with Jeanne. A woman of intelligence and vitality, she was also married to a physician and saw Boulez in a heroic light. She befriended him in many ways, entertaining him frequently at her Paris house and publishing his first collected edition of essays. Her "Afterword" to Notes of an Apprentice suggests that she accepted without question whatever he said. She does not appear to have made an effort to maintain any genuine distance from him in order to understand his multifaceted nature. Here is a statement from her published remarks:

> If, for Boulez, acquiring mastery of his technique was an evident necessity, serving an apprenticeship in musical thinking seemed to him no less essential. For that reason, he applied himself to criticism, a criticism sometimes pushed to polemic.

Nowhere does she indicate that she understands his rage is based not on aesthetic issues alone, but that it is invariably directed against those who had immediately preceded him or who had taught him anything.

In time Mme Tévenin became upset, probably by what upsets others who love Boulez: his tendency to rationalize inconvenient facts out of existence, and his habit of filling his time not only with con-

17

ducting assignments but with whatever trivia will keep him from composition. On her last visit to Baden-Baden in 1970 she continually criticized him. After she left, Boulez told Hilda Strobel he would never see Mme Tévenin again, that he could not tolerate her incessant carping. But when I asked him why he broke with her he said, "It was no break. We just live far apart."

To many serious people Boulez is a musical genius, the greatest living composer, and on the basis of his earlier works and long splendid moments in his later ones, I concur with that estimate. Then, too, I admire the man. He is not a complaining hero. He does not chase one exhibitionistic fad after another. His spirit is very strong. Nevertheless, each of us is a prisoner of an earlier time and Boulez's fight against the past is a heroic but hopeless one—in the deepest personal sense. In art he strives to do what is impossible in life.

1

I believe a civilization that conserves is one that will decay because it is afraid of going forward and attributes more importance to memory than the future. The strongest civilizations are those without memory—those capable of complete forgetfulness. They are strong enough to destroy because they know they can replace what is destroyed. Today our musical civilization is not strong; it shows clear signs of withering. . . .

The more I grow, the more I detach myself from other composers, not only from the distant past but also from the recent past and even from the present. Conducting has forced me to absorb a great deal of history, so much so, in fact, that history seems more than ever to me a great burden. In my opinion we must get rid of it once and for all.

——Pierre Boulez, 1975

The art of the past haunts both composer and listener. Even Stravinsky, less than ten years after composing as radical a work as *Le Sacre du Printemps*, was drawn back to music of earlier times. This led him not only to use traditional forms and re-explore tonality, but also to quote from older pieces. In 1920 Stravinsky launched the "neoclassical" movement that dominated music for at least thirty years. Despite his own shift—at sixty-six years old—from neoclassicism to serialism, Stravinsky's bias toward older music remained intact. During the last years of his life he listened to nothing more advanced than Debussy and spent most of his time with recordings of the late Beethoven sonatas and quartets.

Soon after Stravinsky's death, the *Saturday Review* asked Boulez to write a commemorative article. Convention did not prevent Boulez from attacking Stravinsky for quoting old scores, even when done in

19

a spirit of irony. Later, with associates, he embellished his point: "It is not enough to deface the Mona Lisa because that does not kill the Mona Lisa. All the art of the past must be destroyed."

The comment was quoted in the Sunday New York Times, and the media questioned Boulez. To Newsweek he replied, "I must abandon the past. In the beginning in the womb you are tied to an umbilical cord. You're fed through it. Eventually you cut it. You can still love your mother but you have to feed yourself." To Time he revealed his yardstick for art: if a work advances the language, it is good; if it does not, it is bad. "History is much like the guillotine," he said. "If a composer is not moving in the right direction he will be killed, metaphorically speaking. The evolution of music and everything else, for that matter, depends on people who are gifted enough to understand that change is an absolutely irreversible process. You cannot ignore the historical landmarks of music because if you ignore them, then history will ignore you." "The fight," he says, "is a bigger one than getting the audience to cheer. The dilemma of music is the dilemma of our civilization. We have to fight the past to survive."

Thus Boulez promotes Schoenberg, Webern, and Berg because they crystallized the language that moved music in a new direction. And he celebrates Mahler and Wagner, for they are the ones who led the way. But Brahms and Verdi—and particularly Tchaikovsky—go to the guillotine.

Along with the eminent social theorist Theodor Adorno, whom he knew and admired, Boulez was out to kill the musical past because of aesthetic necessity: tonality was exhausted after a few hundred years and a new musical grammar was needed in its place. But Boulez's impassioned assault on the old was imbued with a fanatical fervor, because it stemmed from a need to destroy his own past.

When Boulez was first acclaimed in France as the greatest musical genius since Debussy, a music critic asked him about his youth. "I shall be the first composer in history," he replied, "not to have a biography." His attitude has never altered. He told Newsweek's Hubert Saal, "I have gigantic powers of forgetfulness. I think everyone's childhood is the same. The important decisions are the ones you make when you are no longer a child." "How did you come to be?" asked Mr. Saal. "By myself," Boulez answered. "Neither heredity nor environment played any role at all. It is just a seed," he went on. "The most important things need no explanation."

Adele Siegal, executive secretary of the New York Philharmonic, praised Boulez's meticulous work habits during his first season: "He attends to everything as it comes up. The only occasion I can recall when I had any trouble in this regard involved an entry in a biographical dictionary. Repeatedly I asked him to check this piece about his life, but it remained on his desk, unchecked every day. The evening before he was to return to Europe I explained that if the published article contained errors they would be repeated ad infinitum. Only then did he correct a few minor details and expressed his relief in the margin with 'O.K. Wow!' "

Residents of the French town in which he grew up say that his nature is not typically French. "The French are reserved; Boulez is closed." Like his handwriting, which is so small that it can hardly be read without a magnifying glass, everything serves to hide the ferment inside. In discussing a great work of art Boulez says:

"If it were necessary for me to find a profound motive for such a work, it would be the search for anonymity. Perhaps I can explain it best by an old Chinese story: a painter drew a landscape so beautifully that he entered the picture and disappeared. For me that is the definition of a great work—a landscape painted so well that the artist disappears in it."

Boulez was born on March 26, 1925, in an apartment over a pharmacy on Rue Tupinerie, the main street of the Loire town of Montbrison, which had then a population of seven thousand five hundred and a winding stream that cut through its center. His father, Léon, was an engineer and technical director of a steel factory. He was taller than any of his children are and cut an extremely authoritative figure. Léon had received a strict Catholic upbringing and placed great stress on a structured family life as well as on a classical education for his children. Politics was one of the many subjects not considered suitable for discussion at the dinner table. A rigid but preeminently just man, he prevailed at the top of a tight family pyramid.

Boulez's mother, Marcelle, was, according to her children, "half-Catholic and half-nothing." Her father was an agnostic and a radical socialist, very much a free thinker for his time. She did not move in that direction but was, above all, deferential to her husband. Those who know her describe her as "simple, direct, very talkative . . . like a bull who grabs you by the arm as she talks . . . a woman whom you could never believe would have produced such a son as that!"

The Boulez family is invariably branded as bourgeois by Boulez's contemporaries in a country where the aristocracy passionately promotes the avant-garde, and the avant-garde passionately despises the bourgeoisie. This may, in some measure, explain Pierre Boulez's efforts to erase his historical origins from the face of the map, virtually to "kill off" his contemptible bourgeois past. Boulez's most pejorative comments are reserved for those who, in his words, are afflicted with a "shopkeeper's mentality." But that alone does not explain his refusal to touch on his childhood, his hatred of the way he was as a boy. What he seems to want most to erase is evidence of his former devotion to God and any manifestation of docility before authority.

According to family friends, Pierre was not a strong infant. He didn't walk until he was three, and once, when burned in an accident, his mother rushed him to a priest to be blessed. Perhaps because he was the first boy born after her first son died, Marcelle Boulez seems to have thought that, in the second Pierre, she had produced a special person. She treated him accordingly. In the traditional school system, where winning is the sine qua non, the boy flourished. Freud's statement that "a man who has been the indisputable favorite of his mother keeps for life the feeling of a conqueror, the confidence of success that often induces real success," receives confirmation here.

Of four children, three survived. The original Pierre was born and died in 1920. Jeanne was born in 1922, Pierre in 1925, and Roger in 1936. When Pierre was four the family moved from above the pharmacy to a private house, 46 Rue Alsace Lorraine, a pink building on a tree-lined street. Boulez recalled it being built. With his hand in his father's, he would stand on the scaffolding of the top floor and look down with wonder through the levels below. The house, covered with ivy, had shutters, French windows, and a small garden. In it the family prospered in every way. Neighbors report envy at their admirable state. The Boulezes were united, economically solvent, and generally in excellent health. In 1931 Léon Boulez made his first trip to the United States and brought back a radio. It was the first time Pierre heard orchestral music. Theirs was the simple, provincial life, Boulez emphasizes, with nothing unique about it.

But there was something special in his early life that he did not reveal to me: his knowledge that a brother had died before he was born. When I told him I had learned of this fact, he made the statement, "I have his name." Then he recalled an incident that occurred when he was five years old and visited the town graveyard for the first time. Although he had known the brother had died in infancy, the child had never been referred to by name. At an age when children first become aware of death, Pierre stood at the head of this tiny grave and read on the headstone, *Pierre Boulez*. He spoke of the moment almost in a whisper—but then shook his head, vigorously denying he had been affected by it. "I am a Darwinian," Boulez explained. "I believe I survived because I was the stronger. He was the sketch, I the drawing."

At seven Boulez began his studies at the Institut Victor de la Prade, named for a minor Romantic poet. It was a Catholic seminary, but because there was no lycée in Montbrison, it filled the role of the traditional highly competitive secular high school.

At seven, also, he received his first Communion. His days were devoted to study and prayer. He says he knew nothing at all about sex until well into his adolescence. "Our lives were surrounded by a sense of sin everywhere."

Each morning at 5:40, when it was still completely dark, Pierre made his way down Chemin Charlieu, a winding dirt road, and twenty minutes later arrived at a gray, monastery-like building. There he spent thirteen hours each day. A brilliant student, he remained at the seminary until he was fifteen, when he passed the first part of his baccalaureate. Although he was younger than the minimum age of sixteen, he graduated at the top of his class in physics and chemistry. His teachers report his desk as unfailingly neat, with nothing but his work exposed at any time. According to his childhood associates, he was authoritarian from the time he could talk. Like his father he would brook no argument.

In most solid European bourgeois families, children were given piano lessons, and the Boulez family was no exception to the rule. Pierre's sister Jeanne began to study when she was six and encouraged her younger brother to do the same. Pierre began at the same age and was playing better than his sister within a year. At first he studied with a local teacher, and by nine he was playing difficult Chopin. His musical experience was not limited to the piano. At thirteen he was soprano soloist at the seminary and at fourteen began to make weekly visits to nearby St. Etienne, a much larger town, where he studied with a more sophisticated musician. By then, music was the central fact of his life. Although he excelled in mathematics, he generally hid his grades from his father because he suspected, even then, that he did not want what his father wanted for him—an engineering career. Boulez denies his mathematical gifts today, for his enemies have used his talent in science to attack his "feeling" as a musician.

Boulez disclaims intellectuality. "I am like my peasant grandfather," he says, "my grandfather on my father's side. My sister is the real intellect." Jeanne Chevalier, Boulez's sister, now lives in Roanne, not far from Montbrison, and delights in recalling their childhood days. "Pierre was disciplined in a headstrong way, not in a submissive way.

He was never bad or at all rebellious. When he was struck, he never struck back. He was the best child I ever knew.

"By the time we were fifteen," Mme Chevalier says, "both of us were skeptical about religion. Pierre never liked sports. He didn't like to swim because he hated the spatial limitations of a swimming pool. He showed no important likes or dislikes but he enjoyed vacationing with his family. In those days we toured virtually all of France.

"He had a few comrades at school but friends were not at all important to him. His relations with them were not at all intense. I was the most important person in his life. It was with me that he shared everything—his games, hopes, and deepest dreams. We still travel together—Scotland last year and Mexico this—and we get along very well. He is strong. But I am strong too."

After completing the first part of his baccalaureate, Boulez spent the school year of 1940–41 at the Pensionnat St. Louis at St. Etienne and the next year at the University of Lyon taking courses that would prepare him for an engineering career. Lyon, with a population of one million, was forty-five miles from Montbrison; Pierre would come home every three or four weeks. It was in Lyon that Boulez heard a live orchestra for the first time and attended his first opera, *Boris Godunov*. It was also there that he met a singer, Ninon Vallin, who had performed *Godunov* with Chaliapin. Mme Vallin asked the boy to accompany her in arias from *Aida* and *The Damnation of Faust*. Even then Verdi struck him as "melodramatic"; today he dismisses him as "dum de dum, nothing more." Still, impressed with the boy's musicianship, Mme Vallin persuaded his father to allow him to apply to the Lyon Conservatoire. But the Conservatoire rejected Pierre, supporting the father's assessment of his son's musical gifts. Jeanne Boulez confronted the director and pleaded for a reversal but was unsuccessful.

In the summer of 1942 Jeanne and Pierre made the first decisions that precipitated a separation, both from each other and from their parents. Jeanne met and decided to marry Jack Chevalier, and when Pierre was home for his holiday, interceded with their father in support of a career in music. Pierre wanted an additional year in Lyon, pursuing not engineering but piano, harmony, and counterpoint, with one course in mathematical theory on the side. Mme Vallin recommended a teacher for his musical studies and once again the authoritarian father acquiesced. It was, as Mme Chevalier recalls it, "a clearcut decision against his father." In reconstructing the battle today, Boulez speaks with pride of his own and his sister's strength: "Our parents were strong. But finally we were stronger than they."

24

In the spring of 1940 Germany invaded France, occupying Paris and the north and setting up the Vichy government in the south. Germany took over the south in 1942, when Boulez was in Lyon for his second year. Boulez speaks of the invasion dispassionately, noting simplistically that the French sank their fleet in order not to help the Germans and that, in the spring of 1943, the Germans "decided to have a kind of administration of the south and north." But how is one, on the threshold of manhood and raised in a school system that values the "battle" over everything else, to cope with his country's grotesquely humiliating defeat?

Still, Boulez's subsequent repudiation of France and identification with German culture cannot be attributed to the German victory. Boulez has often said that if you are a sensual person, France may be the country for you, but if you are concerned with more profound matters, France is woefully inadequate. He has been explicit about music in this regard: "From the point of view of form, what influenced me most was German music, in fact what's most German in German music—the continuity, the proliferation of material from a small musical cell. There is also an extraordinary continuity in the rich history of German music, whereas in France there is Rameau, then after a long period Berlioz, then after another long period Debussy."

Boulez saw benefits in the German occupation of Paris. "The theaters were crowded. People could not leave the cities and all of them jammed into concert halls. I went to a concert given by my own piano teacher and could hardly get into it. The Germans virtually brought high culture to France."

Thus, by the time he was eighteen, Boulez had turned against his father, his country, and everything else that had been held up to him as sacred. Indeed, the young man who had "never struck back" struck back with passion. He repudiated Catholicism, spouting Latin obscenities when he was drunk. He flung epithets at France, attacking people in high places. Although he didn't join the Communist party, he attended its meetings, he has said, as a substitute for church-going. He never studied under any one man for any length of time, "detesting the father-son relationship." And as for the musical language itself, he literally tried to kill off the old works by mocking them through distortions at the piano.

When he first heard twelve-tone music in 1945 he found the answer he had been searching for on both aesthetic and psychological grounds. "It was a revelation," he explains. "Here was a music of our time, a language with unlimited possibilities. No other language was possible. It was the most radical revolution since Monteverdi, for all the familiar patterns were now abolished. With it, music moved out of the world of Newton and into the world of Einstein. The tonal idea was based on a universe defined by gravity and attraction. The serial idea is based on a universe that finds itself in perpetual expansion."

Erik Erikson has written that ideas fill the mind and attach themselves to the strongest feelings. "Ideas form systems and systems absorb lives. A believer in a system supports it with all of his instincts. He is no longer alone in his struggle against the world. He has found liberation from uncertainty. . . . With this moral conceit, the idea makes him superior to everyone else."

This is what happened to Boulez, who has devoted his life to forging and implementing an idea. Boulez promulgated this idea as Moses promulgated the idea of one God. And he did it in ways that were familiar to him—rising before dawn and working throughout the day, living the life of the religious celibate, ignoring clothes, entertainment, and food, moving without friends, permitting no dialogue. Boulez says that throughout his life he has refused to define himself through interaction with others. Instead he has defined himself through "personal breaks," breaks that were as filled with rage as the one "against" his father when he was eighteen.

2

There is little to be learned from professors. Personally,
in two years, I learned all I could from teachers. Between the ages of 18 and 21, I discovered the Viennese
school, Stravinsky, and Messiaen—that is to say, I discovered a literature I had no idea existed before I was
17. This discovery was very rapid and that was my good
luck. My choices were led first by instinct, then reason.
Now, more than twenty-five years later, I find those
choices have hardly changed at all. The five or six composers who influenced me most then are still those I
consider the most important of the time. . . .
    It was during those same years that I first saw the
works of Klee, Kandinsky, and Mondrian. Again, I knew
immediately that these figures were the capital ones in
the evolution of painting. They are, in my opinion, still
the most important of that period. . . .
    The same is true of my first encounters with Joyce
and Kafka. I believe I was defined by the period immediately preceding me. What these composers, painters,
and writers did enabled me to move quickly on, because history had been liquidated by them and one had
only to think of oneself.

——Pierre Boulez, 1975

When Boulez arrived in Paris in 1943, the musical climate was much
the same as it had been before the war. Nadia Boulanger, who had
taught neoclassicism in the 1920s and '30s and was the pillar of the
salon of Mme de Polignac, continued to teach neoclassicism then.
Milhaud, Poulenc, Auric, and Honegger still dominated the musical
scene. Henri Sauguet, the only active surviving pupil of Erik Satie, and
the most successful composer of his generation, had adopted the Mil-
haud/Poulenc style. Indeed, in the late 1940s, when Jean-Louis Bar-

27

rault sent Boulez—at that time his music director—to Sauguet's home to pick up scores, Boulez waited outside on the front doorstep, refusing to enter the house on aesthetic grounds.

But one figure emerged in France during the war who was to change the path of music in Europe—René Leibowitz, a composer and conductor of little distinction. Almost singlehandedly he revived twelve-tone writing in Europe, where it had gone underground during the 1930s and early '40s when Hitler was determined to destroy modern art. Leibowitz first heard Schoenberg's *Pierrot Lunaire* in 1932, when he was nineteen, and the work made a formidable impression on him: "I hated it but I could not sleep for two weeks. I tried to reconstruct the entire score in my head. Finally I said, 'If this kind of music can be composed, then I must compose it.'" With a small inheritance from his father, Leibowitz went to Vienna to study with Schoenberg. When he arrived, he learned that Schoenberg had moved to Berlin. So he settled for lessons with Anton Webern, Schoenberg's quiet, submissive pupil. Webern taught Leibowitz harmony and counterpoint. They met twice a week for a year and a half but Webern never displaced Schoenberg in Leibowitz's esteem. Leibowitz found Webern "interesting," but he thought the "universality" was Schoenberg's, that Schoenberg was the great master.

After finishing the course, Leibowitz returned to Paris via Berlin, still determined to meet Schoenberg. Armed with a letter of reference from Webern, he introduced himself to the imperious Viennese, then teaching at the Prussian State Academy of the Arts. Schoenberg invited Leibowitz to attend class for six weeks and allowed him to contribute one composition assignment. "I wrote a tonal song," Leibowitz said, "in the late Romantic idiom. Schoenberg played it on the piano and analyzed it. He made me add another bar, one extra bar before the last. He was exactly right. It had ended too abruptly before that."

On his return to France, Leibowitz studied conducting with Pierre Monteux and played violin in a Paris night club in order to make enough money to buy all the Schoenberg scores he could find. It was then he discovered dodecaphony, for Schoenberg had never discussed the technique in class. He had drawn for examples on eighteenth- and nineteenth-century German and Viennese masters—Bach, Mozart, Haydn, Beethoven, Schubert, Brahms, Reger, and Wagner. As late as 1937 Schoenberg wrote, "I personally hate to be called a revolutionist, which I am not." Indeed, it is important to emphasize here that the innovation of dodecaphony represented to Schoenberg no radical departure from the works that led to it.

To confirm his suspicion that a new system governed the composition of Schoenberg's post-1923 works, Leibowitz consulted Rudolph Kolisch, Schoenberg's brother-in-law and the violinist who premiered many Schoenberg pieces. Kolisch told Leibowitz that when Schoenberg was fifty years old he had evolved a new musical law, a method of composing with twelve tones, each one equal to the other, which he had hoped would displace the old tonal law based on a hierarchical seven-tone scale. Schoenberg's rules were crystal clear: (1) Each row represented an ordered arrangement of all twelve notes of the chromatic scale; (2) each row may be presented in any or all of four ways—original, inverted, backwards, or backwards and inverted; (3) the row may be stated in any of these ways on any degree of the chromatic scale.

Through this technique Schoenberg hoped he had found a melodic way to unify a work that would displace the harmonic way of the past few hundred years. But the melodic way was—to him—an extension of the Austro-German musical language of Brahms and Wagner in whose syntax he was rooted, the language of the chromaticism of the late nineteenth century that had finally burst its tonal seams. Whatever else dodecaphony did, it contributed to a tightening up, to a more secretive, compulsive approach to art that stemmed from its secretive, compulsive originator. It was, above everything else, a strong antidote to Romanticism.

Schoenberg crystallized the rules in 1923. Ten years later he was dismissed from his post at the Prussian State Academy. Forced to flee Berlin because he was Jewish, he first went to Paris, then to Boston, and finally settled in California. During the late 1930s and early '40s his work was rarely performed in the United States and virtually never performed in Europe, where it was branded as decadent. Thus the generation of Leibowitz—and of Boulez and his colleagues—had no opportunity to hear dodecaphonic music.

When World War II broke out, Leibowitz went into hiding in Vichy, then in an apartment in Paris until the Liberation in 1945. Almost immediately he began to conduct the first postwar performances of Schoenberg in Europe and to record Schoenberg works as well. Friendly with the existentialists Merleau Ponty and Jean-Paul Sartre (Sartre wrote the introduction to his book *L'Artiste et sa Conscience*), Leibowitz became famous and important in Paris. Despite the fact that he, a Polish Jew, had an expatriate passport and therefore had difficulty gaining access to the French government radio, Leibowitz gave performances of the Schoenberg school that were important events among the avant-garde. As Boulanger held on to the reins of the dying neoclassical tradition, Leibowitz was celebrated as the father of the New.

In the fall of 1943, when Boulez first arrived from Provence, he moved into a tiny apartment on Rue Beautreillis, near the historic Place des Vosges. A staircase led up six flights to two connecting rooms that had previously been servants' quarters. Because there was no water on the floor, Boulez had to bring it up in buckets from the floor below. A boarder, an elderly lady, helped him in many ways: she prepared a meal for him each day at noon and packed his bag whenever he went away. Charming, intense, with burning eyes, Boulez has never had difficulty finding people willing to help him with the mechanics of daily life.

In his cluttered, tiny rooms he kept his manuscripts rolled up like papyrus on the floor. In addition to the manuscripts there was a narrow bed, a small desk, an electric heater, and several African masks. Reproductions of Paul Klee were on the walls; the works of Rimbaud, Mallarmé, and James Joyce were on the shelves. Boulez had managed to escape military service because before the Occupation he had been too young to serve, and after the Liberation he was exempt; there were no longer any barracks or camps and those born in 1924 and 1925 were excused.

Free to pursue his métier, he enrolled in the Paris Conservatoire, entering the harmony class of Georges Dandelot in the fall of 1943. There he met Arthur Honegger's niece, who led him to Honegger's wife, Andrée Vaurabourg. Mme Honegger taught counterpoint in a small apartment high up on Montmartre. Although counterpoint is taught only after harmony in France, Boulez refused to be bound by this rule, and, in the winter of 1943, he began to take weekly lessons which continued until the fall of 1945. Mme Honegger recalls him as a remarkable student who "always seemed capable of anything at all." The eight-part counterpoint he produced for her still serves as models in her studio.

In the fall of 1944 Boulez entered the advanced harmony class under Olivier Messiaen. Messiaen, one of the most influential composers of his generation, had returned to France in 1942 after having been a prisoner of war. In the early '40s he was the most important teacher at the Conservatoire. Professors there invariably taught from text books; only Messiaen brought music into class, and, what is more, he brought his own newly-composed music. Education in France has generally been the same since the middle of the nineteenth century. It is state-controlled, paid for by taxes, and one can rarely find a job in music unless one possesses a degree from this most conservative Conservatoire.

But Messiaen represented a break from all this. A maverick, he never, for instance, attended the school's committee meetings. Church organist, virtuoso pianist, user of Gregorian melodies, specialist in Asiatic rhythms, fanatical follower of bird songs, Messiaen made a strong impression on his students.

In 1944 when Boulez entered the advanced harmony class, he had heard only Messiaen's *Variations for Violin and Piano*. Boulez admits he was initially awed, but soon the awe turned to disdain. Sometimes he is harsh on Messiaen today: "Messiaen never really interested me. His use of certain Indian and Greek rhythms poses a problem—at least to me. It is difficult to retrieve pieces of another civilization in a work. We must invent our own rhythmic vocabulary, following the norms that are our own. Even in my earliest pieces, I was aware of that."

Messiaen recalls Boulez's dramatic shift in attitude: "When he first entered class, he was very nice. But soon he became angry with the whole world. He thought everything was wrong with music. The next year he discovered the serial language and converted to it with immense passion, judging it the only viable grammar."

In class Boulez exhibited extraordinary facility with the piano, playing works he composed at that time. Messiaen not only taught advanced harmony; he also held a seminar in musical analysis at the home of Guy Bernard Delapierre, an Egyptologist and composer of film music with whom he had been held prisoner in France before being interned in a concentration camp in Germany. The class was held outside the Conservatoire because the Conservatoire limited Messiaen's duties to the most traditional harmony lessons and did not confer upon him a professorship in composition. The analysis class was open to exceptional students. There too Boulez shone. He "discovered" Debussy, studied Schoenberg's early works, and produced a dazzling analysis of *The Rite of Spring* which added considerable information to one Messiaen had produced.

To earn money Boulez played the *ondes martenot*, an electronic keyboard instrument, in a pit orchestra in the Folies Bergères. Messiaen helped him in many ways—even providing him with meals—for Boulez refused to take money from home. "His father," Messiaen recalls, "was very angry when he chose music, and his father was a very severe, very closed man. Today Boulez resembles his father in being exceptionally closed. Even if he is nice and polite there are always hidden things going on. Even if he's smiling, there is more underneath than a smile." But in those days Messiaen could get through to

31

Boulez. After class they would often ride the Metro together. Boulez would say, "Musical aesthetics are being worn out. Music itself will die. Who is there to give it birth?" Messiaen replied, "You will, Pierre."

At the end of the year Boulez earned the Conservatoire's first prize in harmony. Then he moved on to a course in fugue under Mme Simone Plé-Coussade, which he describes as "terrible. After coming from the freedom of Messiaen, I could not stand it. She was unimaginative and the class was dead. That is why I hate all academic teaching. I didn't attend class and received a notice that I would be expelled if I did not change my ways. I said 'Throw me out immediately and perhaps instead of concerning yourself with attendance you will concern yourself with the more important problem of teaching.' That was what gave rise to the petition I organized that Messiaen be given a full professorship in composition." (That petition did not bear fruit until 1949–50.)

During his early student days Boulez wrote several works of which we have no record today—a Sonata for two pianos, a work for *ondes martenot*, and *Oublie Lapide*, a piece for a cappella chorus. The first work which made a mark was the *Trois Psalmodies* for piano, written in 1945. At this time Boulez knew only two early Schoenberg works: *Pierrot Lunaire* and the *Three Pieces for Piano*, *Opus 11*. The *Psalmodies* reflected the early Schoenberg style mixed with a little Honegger. Boulez has said, "While I was writing *Trois Psalmodies* I didn't even know of the existence of serial music but I had a distinct sense of the need for it. And yet now I want to forget these pieces were ever written. They have never been published and they never will be—at least not with my consent."

What Boulez calls "serial" in this instance is the serial treatment of pitch or what is generally referred to as dodecaphony. He says he avoids the term "dodecaphony" both because of its "garden of Greek [i.e. old] roots" as well as "its association with academic techniques." But at bottom, I feel, he avoids it because it was Schoenberg's word, and he was interested in carving a monument that would bear his own word for it.

Here is how Boulez says he came upon the serial idea: "One evening, in 1945, I heard a private performance of Schoenberg's Woodwind Quintet, conducted by René Leibowitz. It was a revelation to me. It obeyed no tonal laws and I found in it a harmonic and contrapuntal richness and a consequent ability to develop, extend, and vary ideas that I had not found anywhere else. I wanted, above all, to know how it was written. Therefore I went to Leibowitz and brought with me other students from Messiaen's harmony class. The first work we analyzed was Webern's *Opus 21 Symphony*. I was very impressed with this and made copies because the score wasn't available at the time. I felt then the significance of this new language."

So, in 1946, Boulez was still under the influence of both Messiaen and Leibowitz. And Messiaen and Leibowitz represented very different worlds. Messiaen was not only a great composer but also a keyboard virtuoso. One day he came to class without the score to Debussy's *Pelléas et Mélisande*, which was scheduled for analysis. Still he sat down at the piano and played it through. Leibowitz could talk analytic rings around Messiaen, who was not very sensitive to pitch or to interval relationships. Messiaen's forte was rhythm and meter.

But the most profound difference between the men can be reduced to national characteristics. Messiaen was part of the French tradition that despised Mahler and Brahms and upheld Debussy against Wagner. Leibowitz, on the other hand, was tied to the Austro-German idea. Thus he used to tell his students that Rameau was to Bach what Debussy was to Schoenberg. Stravinsky, he repeatedly said, was the Telemann of the twentieth century. Indeed he saw the then neoclassic Stravinsky, a product of the Franco-Russian milieu, as his archenemy in his quest for a language derived from Schoenberg. And he acted on his beliefs. During the winter of 1945, when Paris was trying to recover from the Occupation, the city began to celebrate Stravinsky, whose music had been branded decadent by the Nazis. One of the first performances included two works Stravinsky had recently composed in the United States—*Danses Concertantes* and *Four Norwegian Moods*. To the surprise of everyone at the Théâtre des Champs-Elysées the pieces were greeted by prolonged booing from a group of Conservatoire students. Leibowitz was the figure behind this demonstration but Boulez was the young man at the center of things. Thus, at that particular moment, Boulez was following Leibowitz's lead. And the message he proclaimed was this: the musical life of the past would not return, neoclassicism was really dead, the future would take an altogether different turn, and he would take over the quest for the Idea.

In 1946 Boulez engaged in a brief, passionate sexual affair, the only one of his life so far as I know. It was a love-hate relationship so intense and tormented that he has said it could not possibly have gone on. The two joined in a double-suicide pact; Boulez will say nothing more about the affair, not even whether the other person went through with the fatal act. The need for suicide and the release from it proved to be a stimulus of enormous vitality for Boulez. Within the next few years he created a series of wild, courageous works each of which maintained that delicate balance between emotion and intellect. The escape from death—or from the love affair—apparently precipitated a burst of prodigious talent.

Unable to find words to express his deepest feelings, Boulez, throughout his career, has set poems that do exactly that for him. The first poem he chose after the end of this affair was Le Visage Nuptial, by René Char. The form of the music adheres very closely to that of the poem. Today Boulez says it was Char's "condensation" that drew the poet to him, "a contained violence, not a violence of many gestures. What attracted me to Char was not, as many have written, his love of nature, his love of Provence, or his deep understanding of men. Rather was it his extraordinary power to gather together in an extremely concise way a whole universe." (See Appendix.)

Like Boulez's music, Char's poetry is obscure, exceptionally difficult even for a professional to translate. Despite the fact that, in conversation today, Boulez emphasizes his attraction to Char's technique,

Conventions

a) *Pour indiquer les quarts de ton, la convention suivante a été adoptée :*

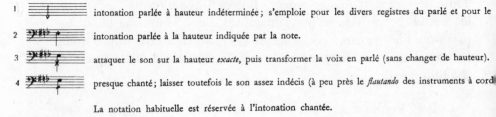

b) *Modifications de l'intonation vocale :*

1 intonation parlée à hauteur indéterminée ; s'emploie pour les divers registres du parlé et pour le

2 intonation parlée à la hauteur indiquée par la note.

3 attaquer le son sur la hauteur *exacte*, puis transformer la voix en parlé (sans changer de hauteur).

4 presque chanté ; laisser toutefois le son assez indécis (à peu près le *flautando* des instruments à cord

La notation habituelle est réservée à l'intonation chantée.

Heugel & Cie, Paris, Publishers

Above, microtonal scheme of Le Visage Nuptial, and following, pages 11 and 12 of the section, Gravité, in which the microtones can be seen.

34

II.. Gravité
L'Emmuré

H. 31.702

he does acknowledge that the violence of the sexual imagery played a role in this particular choice: "It was a strong love poem. It was a good poem for me. It was a meeting with the fancies I was having at that time."

The poem's importance to Boulez can be assessed by two facts. One is that shortly after he began work on it he arranged a visit to Char and then visited him frequently throughout the next ten years. The second is that his original manuscript reads: "*Le Visage Nuptial*, by René Char"; Boulez's own name does not appear anywhere.

Le Visage Nuptial is extraordinarily difficult to perform. To sing and play all the different rhythms accurately and to handle the microtonality with fidelity as well present almost insuperable problems. Indeed, two conductors tried to perform this work in the mid-'50s but gave up. Yet when Boulez himself conducted it in 1957 it was recognized as the beautiful and remarkable work that it is.

Boulez poured forth works in the mid-'40s. His fecundity at this period confirms Schiller's claim that "genius does not proceed by known principles but by feeling and inspiration." By the end of the decade, however, principles superseded feeling and inspiration and Boulez's production began to slow down. The delicate balance between emotion and intellect became weighted in the '50s on the side of intellect.

Le Visage Nuptial was Boulez's first important work with a *text*, but it was not his first important work. Before beginning it, he had composed the *Sonatina for Flute and Piano* and the *First Piano Sonata*.

The *Sonatina* was commissioned by the flutist Jean-Pierre Rampal, who never played it because it was too extreme for his taste. It is a short work and bursts with musical activity. The flute makes frenetic melodic leaps and rhythmic jolts, giving an impression of uncontrolled hysteria. The *First Sonata* is also fast and aggressive. The verbal instructions in the score give a clue to the explosive quality of the piece: "très violent," "brusque, incisif, très fort," "plus animé et plus nerveux," and, for the final chord, "très brutal and très sec."

Boulez says that these pieces—both composed in 1946—were strongly influenced by Schoenberg; he was studying with Leibowitz at the time. "What interested me in the *Sonatina*," he says, "was the metamorphosis of a single theme, and Schoenberg's *Chamber Symphony* is a good example of that. But if one didn't know the influence was Schoenberg, one could never have guessed it, for there is absolutely no similarity from a stylistic point of view. The *Chamber Symphony* is in a post-romantic style, a style that had no effect on me at all."

A.163 bis

Page 29 of the *Sonatina for Flute and Piano*, replete with leaping configurations.

"As for the *First Sonata*, that was influenced by the first pieces in Schoenberg's *Opus 23* as well as the *Opus 11* which I had on my piano for a long time. The third piece of *Opus 11* introduced me to a style of piano writing that was different from anything I had known. There is a great density of texture and a violence of expression that conveys a kind of delirium."

It is in the *First Piano Sonata* that Boulez first works with the serial idea. But even here he did not copy Schoenberg. He did not, in fact, "repeat" anything. On the first page of the score one finds only the first five notes of the row; the remaining seven do not appear until the first bar of the second page. The series appears, ever after, in two parts—one of five notes and the other seven.

Leibowitz recalled the events of 1946 in a conversation several weeks before his death: "Boulez was one of five or six students from the Conservatoire. He was a regular jack-in-the-box. He was also the most arrogant of all.

"I thought he wrote too fast, too carelessly, that he threw in too many notes. When he started his *First Sonata* I told him he knew my address. He should send me the work bit by bit. Then I could help him as he went along. But he brought in the completed manuscript. I didn't like it at all."

With a red pen, Leibowitz began marking up the manuscript, then dedicated to him. Grabbing the score, Boulez fled, shouting at Leibowitz, "Vous êtes merde!" Three years later Boulez's publisher Hervé Dugardin asked him if the dedication should remain on the printed score. As Boulez shouted "Non!" he stabbed the manuscript with a letter opener until it was virtually in shreds. Then he and Dugardin sat on the floor and painstakingly glued the pieces together.

Human actions depend on a mixture of motives. Boulez attributes his break with Leibowitz to his irritation with his teacher for his "pedantry" and for "being imprisoned by academic techniques" that he had distilled from Schoenberg's work. Boulez may have been justified, but that could hardly account for such an eruption of rage. So one must consider the deeper possibility that the student could not bear criticism from the teacher to whom he had just given a part of himself, that he was jealous of Leibowitz's eminence as the leader of a movement he would have as his own, that finally Leibowitz was one more father to whom he had been *le fils mal aimé* and against whom he was driven to rail violently.

Boulez's radical break with Leibowitz afforded him the chance to define himself anew, and, during the next few years, he succeeded in organizing a new musical grammar that conferred upon him the un-

PREMIÈRE SONATE

P. BOULEZ

I

A. 153

First Piano Sonata: the first bar contains the first five notes of
the row. The remaining seven notes appear at the top of page 2.

A.153

Boulez works primarily with the major and minor third. After
presenting the basic cell, he either moves out from it or fills it in.

41

equivocal leadership of the European avant-garde and virtually put Leibowitz out of business. Still he hammered away at Leibowitz, issuing polemical attacks against the man in *Contrepoint* and in *La Nouvelle Revue Française*, France's most prestigious literary magazine.

3

Leibowitz had grown up in the household of Artur Schnabel, the pianist and composer who had been a member of the early Schoenberg circle. Leibowitz's tie to Schoenberg remained firm throughout his life (he even imitated Schoenberg in his devotion to tennis). In 1947 Leibowitz published *Schoenberg et Son Ecole*, probably the first book on twelve-tone music not written in German (German treatises on dodecaphony had appeared in the 1920s). In 1948, he visited Schoenberg in California. Schoenberg, then teaching at USC, told Leibowitz of his great disappointment that, though the war was over, the Germans were still not performing his works.

On his return to Paris in 1948, Leibowitz was invited to conduct and teach at the international school of music in Darmstadt, which had been founded two years before and had focused on European neoclassicism—Stravinsky, Hindemith, and Prokofiev. Leibowitz accepted, but only on the condition that he could conduct a whole Schoenberg program—the *Piano Concerto*, the *Chamber Symphony No. 2*, and the *Five Orchestral Pieces*. Leibowitz delivered eight lectures that summer on the development of music from the turn of the century to the revelation of dodecaphony in 1923. Twenty students attended these talks. None of them had heard this music before, but, by the following summer, Leibowitz claims they knew the literature better than he. Unlike his Conservatoire students, the Germans, with their customary thoroughness, dissected and analyzed the entire repertoire. So Leibowitz, steeped in the German tradition, had his first real success with the Germans themselves. During the summer of 1948 he literally opened the doors to the European adoption of dodecaphony.

But by then Boulez had moved onto something new, to the creation of a new musical grammar that would pass over Schoenberg. Boulez found a "new voice in Webern, one that Leibowitz could not possibly understand because he could see no further than the numbers in a tone row." Boulez also discovered rhythmic patterns in Webern that nourished the discoveries he made under Messiaen. "I had discovered elaborate rhythms," he explains, "through both Messiaen and Stravinsky, whereas Webern thought primarily in terms of pitches. The two things had to be unified." Thus Boulez, in his early twenties, was obsessed with the formulation of a theoretical system that would serve composers in the future as tonality had served them in the past. And he appears to have equated the articulation of this system with the definition of himself as a man. *Le Soleil des Eaux*, a powerful and exciting work, manifests a mélange of Asiatic rhythms and Webern. It was composed in 1947–48. (See Appendix.)

Le Soleil des Eaux was originally a dramatic piece by René Char, which Boulez set to incidental music for a radio performance. In that form the work lasts thirty minutes. It tells of the revolt of fishermen on the Ile sur Sorgue against the installation of a factory that poisoned their water and ruined their livelihood. It is the story of the defense of liberty and is thus connected with Char's own struggle against Nazism and with the part he played in the French Resistance.

Boulez's original score was never sung in full because it was much too long. Boulez first conceived it for voice alone; he wanted to provide "incidental music," with the text having clear priority. The interjections had nothing to do with each other; the work was a kind of collage. In 1950 the composer deleted most of the poem, reducing the final work to ten minutes and treating only those segments that held particular meaning for him: *La Complainte du Lézard Amoureux* and *La Sorgue*. The political ideology disappeared. Boulez describes the poem this way: "La Sorgue deals with human energy. The river comes out completely full grown, like Minerva—abruptly—out of Zeus's head. The river is not obliged to develop; it is already there from the start. There is a big cave, an enormously ebullient source. The Sorgue is the image of strength. It provides a contrast to the first poem which describes the laziness of the country, a country which doesn't have to be busy, as seen through the lizard's eyes."

44

Page 9 from *La Complainte du Lézard Amoureux, Le Soleil des Eaux,* in which the unaccompanied voice is followed by the entrance of the instruments.

45

Page 22 from *La Sorgue, Le Soleil des Eaux*. The declamation of voices together and the dynamics give this part a very aggressive tone.

Le Soleil des Eaux was originally scored for three solo voices and chamber orchestra. In 1958 Boulez made a new version for three soloists, chorus, and full orchestra and revised even that in 1965. *La Complainte du Lézard Amoureux* juxtaposes blocks of music in much the manner of Messiaen and Stravinsky, which must have seemed to Boulez an idiom of an earlier and "lazier" time. It is lightly scored for solo soprano and divided strings with the soprano singing recita- tivelike passages which join one orchestral passage to the next. After the sweetness of the first piece, the aggression of the second stuns the listener. Alternating between contrapuntal violence and ecstatic lyri- cism, *La Sorgue* is filled with agitated vocal lines. A mixed choir speaks at both definite and indefinite pitch, attacks notes at a definite pitch and resolves them into speech, and sings at a half-definite pitch.

Both the words and music of *Le Soleil des Eaux* suggest that Boulez would have preferred to emerge from the womb full grown without the years of immaturity during which he felt impotent against a formidable world. His antipathy to helplessness and passivity (the lizard's love for the goldfinch) and his awe and admiration for the strength of the Sorgue (a river that can rust iron) are themes that recur repeatedly in his conversation. Boulez judges composers on their "strength." He uses the same yardstick in regard to his parents: "They were strong, but we were stronger than they." One wonders what happened in his affair of passion, for here is an area he never entered again.

Along with *Le Soleil des Eaux*, Boulez completed the *Second Piano Sonata* in 1948. Compared with the *First*, all the hesitancy is gone. Boulez knows exactly what he wants—the impression of more vio- lence and more delirium. He also knows how to get what he wants. Whereas the row was divided into two parts in the *First Sonata*, it is divided into four parts in the *Second*. The counterpoint is more elabo- rate, the scale much greater, and the pianism far more percussive than in the *First*. Boulez still calls the piano "my instrument" and his writing for it was pathbreaking.

Because of the frequency with which this work was performed— it became a tour de force for young pianists—Boulez's *Second Sonata* was probably the single most important work from which the post- Webern movement took its cues. Here traditional melody disap- peared. The harmonic system betrayed nothing of the past. Themes played virtually no role at all.

The work is divided into four movements, three of them savage, one (the second) sweet. Once again the verbal instructions denote

47

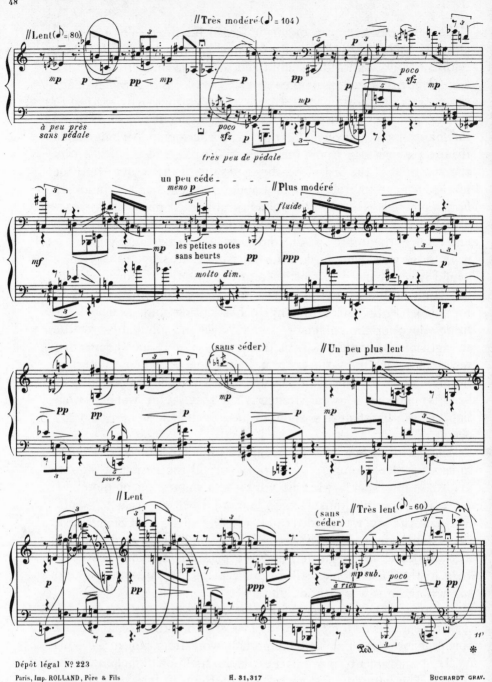

Dépôt légal Nº 223

Paris, Imp. ROLLAND, Père & Fils   H. 31,317   BUCHARDT GRAV.

Heugel & Cie, Paris, Publishers

The last page of the *Second Piano Sonata*. The notes circled are those in tribute to Bach.

the tone: "beaucoup plus rude," "de plus en plus haché et brutal," and even in the lyrical movement, a passage interrupts marked "subito, brèf et violent." Underneath the leaping configurations, the work is organized as precisely as a medieval motet. Two rows are used: one (D, A, D sharp, G sharp, B, E, F sharp, B flat, C, C sharp, F, and G) governs the first and third movements; the other (G, F, G sharp, F sharp, C sharp, C, B flat, B, D, E flat, A, and E) governs the second and fourth. Boulez's testimonial to form is eloquent: an epilogue at the end of the last movement is based on H C A B, the retrograde of B A C H. Bach's use of his own name in *The Art of the Fugue* provided the inspiration for this choice.

In program notes to the early performances, Boulez noted that "all the counterpoints are equally important; there are no principal parts, no secondary parts." In other words, the work has more in common with the polyphony of the late Gothic motet than with the harmonic-melodic music of the intervening eras.

In addition to the increasingly tight treatment of pitch, Boulez turned his attention to rhythm. He says the great distance between the first and second sonatas can be explained by the fact that there was a transitional work, one that is lost. He adds that when he began the *Second Sonata* he had "completely broken with the Schoenbergian concept of the series. What interested me was the manipulation of tones in a functional, not thematic way. This can be seen clearly in the first movement; the series of intervals are tied to certain motives that reappear throughout the section. Then I gradually dissolve the intervallic cells to a point where they have only secondary importance in order to call attention to the rhythmic material."

Boulez's *Second Sonata* appears just as wild as parts of *Le Soleil des Eaux* but here there are no words to suggest the conceptual meaning behind the musical hysteria. The more hidden the meaning the more complex the design. And thus did Boulez begin to move inward.

In 1948–49 Boulez wrote the *Livre pour Quatuor*, a three-movement work he later revised and orchestrated for strings. It is austere, far more restrained than the works preceding it. That may be due to the use of strings which cannot convey the violence or excitement of either a keyboard or chorus. But it may also be due to Boulez's increasing interest in Webern. In 1971 Boulez told a Juilliard audience: "I was attracted by the very small form. What Webern did was very calm, very quiet. It is remarkable to see a face so clearly defined at the beginning of a life. One sees that face in the *Five Pieces*. Of the five, three are slow, only one is very quick. He had in mind the contrast between them, the order and the symmetry. The middle one is the shortest and fastest.

"There Webern's harmony is more complex than simple tonal harmony, more complex than Mahler. The style is still conventional; there are, for instance, still melodic lines. But it's the end of Romanticism. There is an obsession not to repeat. There's a story that Webern, at the end of his life, attended a concert in which a Ravel piece was played. 'Why,' asked Webern, 'does he use so many instruments?'

"With Webern, one instrument can summarize the world. In that, his world is comparable to Paul Klee's. Klee rarely painted a big painting. The world of Klee can be contained in a drop of water. One can see as many faces in a drop of water as in a large landscape. With Webern there is this tense, tight, closed vision with a poetic power that is surprising. There is no aggressiveness here."

But by 1975 even Boulez's attitude toward Webern had changed: "Webern's vocabulary attracted me at the start. I found it very important because it established a grammatic base. But I find that the more Webern went on, the more simple his forms became—too simple, in fact, for my taste. One hearing alone is sufficient to catch the essence of his vocabulary. One does not need a series of readings. It is like a painting by Mondrian. You see the perfection right away and it is very striking, but when you return to it, there is nothing more to take. That is very different from Cézanne, whose paintings I can look at over and over again because of their complexity, because of the infinite detail in design and texture. In that sense Cézanne can be compared to Berg. More and more I am struck by the complexity in Berg—the number of references to himself, the great intricacy of musical construction, the density of the texture. It is a universe in perpetual motion and one that does not stop turning on itself."

Webern drew Boulez in 1948 not only because of the purity of expression but also because of what Boulez sees in him today: that his voice led towards system, not freedom. And system was what Boulez sought. A Webern work, totally organized as to pitch, consists of the unfolding of the original material. The first movement of the Opus 21 Symphony, which Boulez often analyzes for audiences, is a double canon with a retrograde inversion beginning at midpoint. Such systematization was never true of Schoenberg, who wrote music in which the row was not so readily traceable.

Thus Boulez found the control in Webern that he had never found in Schoenberg, and it helped move him into a totally serial world. On an artistic level, strict serialism expressed itself in a master plan in which the composer calculated everything in advance so that nothing unexpected, untoward, could erupt. On a personal level, it must have represented a herculean effort by Boulez to control all those internal forces within himself.

Control is the recurring theme of Boulez's life, and it fit into the temper of the mid-century. The supremacy of intellect over passion, the triumph of mind over physical instinct, began as early as 1920 with neoclassicism and dodecaphony pulling in the reins on the lavish expressionism of pre–World War I days. Stravinsky's *Oedipus Rex* bore the composer's instructions for no movement on stage. It was as far removed from his *Sacre du Printemps* as Schoenberg's *Serenade* was from *Die Glückliche Hand* which even specified lighting effects in the score. Structure had become the order of the day after World War I. After World War II it was elevated to a reigning faith.

In the vacuum of religious belief, in the loss of political faith, Boulez fell in love with an idea, and it filled him as Catholicism and Marxism once had. Because Webern's path led towards order, Webern symbolized that idea. Thus Webern became the idol to Boulez that Schoenberg had been to Leibowitz. That made the confrontation clear. That added psychic energy to the aesthetic fight. If Webern, who had been Schoenberg's pupil, could displace his teacher in worldwide renown, then Boulez would crush *his* teacher, Leibowitz.

Boulez's *Second Sonata* set the tone, an expression of extraordinary temperament and power in deference to the timid, inhibited Webern. This was high-strung, emotional music, anchored by the most precise of pitch plans. This was Boulez at the moment when he began to turn his violent expression into a *technique* for violent expression, into a technique for all composers to use to crush the life out of Romanticism and Schoenberg.

The system, then, underlying the *Second Sonata* was Boulez's antidote to passion unleashed, passion out of control. An admirer of Antonin Artaud, author of the Theater of Cruelty, Boulez had, only a short time before, echoed Artaud in an article published in *Polyphonie*: "I believe that music should be collective hysteria and spells, violently of the present time." But the hysteria and spells were to be brought under the tightest possible control and done so in the name of Webern.

In 1948 Boulez was alone. By 1955, many gifted and tough composers would echo Boulez's praises of the quiet, neglected Webern who was overshadowed and bullied by an imposing master.

Thus Boulez led music at mid-century because aesthetic conditions made it possible. But he did it for his own private reasons as well.

To be free to compose Boulez needed money, and he found work as soon as he left the Conservatoire. In 1946, shortly after Jean-Louis Barrault and Madeleine Renaud separated themselves from the Comédie Française and established an independent company at the Théâtre Marigny, they made plans to stage André Gide's translation of *Hamlet* with incidental music by Honegger. Honegger orchestrated the work for brass, percussion, and *ondes martenot*. To play the electronic keyboard instrument he recommended a counterpoint student who was exceptionally gifted on the instrument, Pierre Boulez. Barrault says that as soon as he met Boulez, he recognized his enormous gifts: "He was aggressive and possessed by music. He had an extraordinary personality, a combination of rage and tenderness. Although he was only twenty years old I made him music director right away. My wife and I became mother and father to him. We remained that way for more than ten years.

"During that time we produced plays with incidental music by Auric, Poulenc, Honegger, Milhaud, Sauguet, and Offenbach, all of which—although Boulez did not like them—he conducted with extreme vigor and authority. He composed prolifically in those early years. But he didn't write incidental music for us; he arranged and conducted what others wrote. Only much later, in 1955, did he agree to compose for our theater. That was for the *Orestes*; he thought he could join the antique theater with the musical language of serialism.

"I remember once, when he first came here, Honegger and Boulez were searching for sounds that could accompany moving stars. Boulez began to joke and improvise at the piano. Soon he was destroying Beethoven and Brahms and all the other classic and romantic composers, both verbally and stylistically. Mme Honegger was there and sighed, 'Poor Boulez! He will have to relive history all by himself.' "

Boulez profited from his experience with Barrault. His experience in the pit put him in contact with musicians and their instruments for the first time. But he is quick to deflate any overblown image: "The title 'Music Director' sounds much more impressive than the job was. Generally I arranged between ten and twelve minutes of music—mostly fanfares and the like—and an occasional half hour of pantomime. Although it brought me to the theater each night, it left me time to compose during the day. The *Orestes*, the only work I set for Barrault, was an important project musically, because there was an opportunity for a lot of music. I was interested in the Japanese

Noh drama at the time and I experimented with that in mind. But the actors were not trained musicians. They could not deliver one simple rhythm. I had to change and simplify so much."

One member of the company reports that Boulez beat the rhythm so violently on her back that she collapsed weeping on the floor. Others say he threw chairs when he lost his temper.

But the Barraults gladly put up with it all. "Behind his savagery, there was an extreme bashfulness, a quivering sensibility, even a secret sentimentality." The surrogate parents loved the son, not only for his great musical talent but also for his special blend of violence and charm.

Boulez always enjoyed polemics, and Paris provided a sympathetic milieu for him with lectures, journals, and an active social and intellectual life. Boulez had been playing ondes martenot not only at the Folies-Bergère and at the Barrault theater, but for a variety of theatrical productions as well. Martenot, its inventor, was grateful for the publicity. To repay Boulez he arranged for a performance of Boulez's First Piano Sonata at his house, with Boulez at the piano, and invited a group of friends that included conductor Roger Desormière, composer Nicolas Nabokov, and composer-critic Virgil Thomson. Afterward Thomson wrote in the New York Herald Tribune that Boulez was "the most brilliant, in my opinion, of all the Paris-under-25s."

One evening in 1948 Boulez attended a lecture in Paris. He doesn't remember who the lecturer was, but afterwards there was a discussion of musical subjects. Desormière spoke. Then he spoke. Afterwards Pierre Souvchinsky introduced himself to Boulez, who describes Souvchinsky as "the last of the conseillers. He had great scope, a very sharp mind. Souvchinsky brought people in contact with one another."

Souvchinsky, an aesthetician and critic of the contemporary world, had a desire to make "discoveries" and to help these new talents to carve out important careers. An elaborate defender of Stravinsky in the 1930s, he helped draft the famous Poetics of Music which Stravinsky delivered at Harvard University in 1940–41. But in 1939 Stravinsky moved permanently to the United States. And in the 1940s he appeared to dry up, devoting his time to the reorchestration of old scores and to unsuccessful attempts to write for Hollywood. This left Souvchinsky hungering for a new talent.

Boulez was the man; and so, immediately after their first meeting, Souvchinsky brought him to Suzanne Tezenas, a charming and cultivated woman. Blond, slender, then in her forties, Mme Tezenas presided over an elegant apartment on Rue Octave Feuillet in the fashionable sixteenth arrondissement. The high-ceilinged apartment was crammed with books piled on tables and lining walls, and abstract paintings mounted Hermitage style and stacked behind every piece of furniture. Two great ceiling-to-floor French windows overlooked carefully ordered gardens. A wood-burning fire, large rubber plants, and small Persian rugs over soft brown carpeting added warmth to Mme Tezenas's pink Venetian living room. Mme Tezenas's money came from her family, steel manufacturers; she contributed generously to the arts.

For years Mme Tezenas had been the constant companion of the novelist Pierre Drieu la Rochelle, a gifted writer and poet and a major spokesman for French Fascism during the 1930s and early '40s. Drieu was a leader of France's largest Fascist party, the Parti Populaire Français. During the German Occupation he actively collaborated with the Nazis. With the departure of Gide and Malraux from *La Nouvelle Revue Française*, Drieu became its editor. The articles he published in the NRF and in avowedly Fascist journals caused many of his countrymen to accuse him of opportunism and treason. At the end of the war he chose to commit suicide rather than stand trial as a collaborator. After the war Mme Tezenas tried to reenter French society. On Sunday evenings she held salons, one for painters (de Staël and Dubuffet were her favorites) and one for writers. But none of these salons achieved any striking success.

When Souvchinsky brought Boulez to her apartment, Mme Tezenas was drawn to him at once. Surely he didn't support Fascism. And she says that while Drieu "always seemed an amateur, Boulez was a strict professional, a man completely apart." Still Boulez did possess qualities in common with Drieu: here was an artist, no doubt about that, one with the faith of a true fanatic; here was a man altogether intolerant of any who disagreed with the way he viewed an idea; here was a man, who, like Drieu, relished confrontation and victory. At their first meeting, three years after Drieu's suicide, Boulez played his *Second Sonata* for her. It was then that Suzanne Tezenas committed herself to the realization of his ideals.

The first of the many Tezenas-Boulez ventures took place in 1949. The evening was devoted not to Boulez himself or to any European avant-garde group but to Boulez's introduction of one American to Paris. John Cage, then thirty-six years old, still virtually unrecognized at home, hoped to take the Old World by storm.

4

There is a strong anti-intellectual streak in America. Nowhere is it more pronounced than in Southern California, where John Cage was born and grew up. It was this anti-intellectualism that finally pulled the rug out from under Boulez.

Cage's father, John Milton Cage, was born in Los Angeles in 1886 and was an inventor of some renown. He repeatedly ran away from home, and he never managed to complete high school. In 1913 he invented a submarine that stayed under water longer than any other in the world. But it ran on a gas engine and left bubbles behind. He had not, his son notes, considered the value of secrecy.

In his early twenties the elder Cage married a woman from a large family in which learning was suspect; only Shakespeare and the Bible were allowed in the home. But she did play the organ in the Episcopal church and hid some other books in her room. Like her husband, she never completed high school. She was divorced twice before marrying Cage. Her son describes the marriage as a "good one between bad people." Then he laughs.

Two boys died before John was born. The first, named Gustavus Adolphus Williamson III after a paternal grandfather, died at birth. The second, Gustavus Adolphus Williamson IV, a "monster with too large a head," died when he was only two weeks old. When the Cages were presented with a third chance, they decided to try to change their fate by naming the boy after his own father. John Milton Cage determined from this that he survived because he possessed his inventor-father's name.

As a boy John studied piano with an aunt, Phoebe James, and with a woman composer of bird songs; he neither heard nor played music by the great artists of the past. After graduating from Los Angeles High School he entered Pomona College in Claremont, California, but soon dropped out to travel abroad. In Paris Cage worked with an architect. Then he began to paint and compose in response to painters and composers he met in France. Two piano lessons introduced him to Bach. He was then twenty years old. "I was completely stunned by it," he recalls. "It was just plain beautiful."

During 1930 and '31, Cage traveled extensively: to Capri, Majorca, Madrid, and Berlin. During these years he devised a mathematical system of composition he hoped would endow his works with a precision comparable to that of Bach's. None of these early pieces survives.

After eighteen months Cage returned to the United States and wrote, painted, and composed. To support himself he gave lectures on modern music and modern painting to a women's club in Santa Monica. It was there he met the Arensbergs, who possessed a large collection of Marcel Duchamp's paintings and introduced Cage to this archetypal antipainter of the time. In his "ten lessons for $2.50" at the women's club, Cage devoted much attention to Duchamp. For his sessions on Arnold Schoenberg he needed help too, and sought the advice of Richard Buhlig, who gave the first performance of Schoenberg's *Opus 11 Piano Pieces* in Berlin. Cage reports that "Buhlig paid me more generous compliments about my music than Arensberg did about my art, so I decided to study music."

"I am the son of an inventor," Cage says. "I had read Henry Cowell's *New Musical Resources* and copied by hand *The Theory of Rhythm*. I had also read Chavez's *Toward a New Music*. Both works gave me the feeling that everything that was possible in music had already happened. So I thought I could never compose socially important music. Only if I could *invent* something new, then would I be useful to society. But that seemed unlikely then."

In 1933 Cage sent some inventions and sonatas to Henry Cowell, who suggested he study composition with Schoenberg. But Cowell advised that he first take lessons with Adolph Weiss, a member of Schoenberg's circle, and follow those with lessons from Cowell himself.

56

Cowell had invented "tone clusters" on the piano. By pressing down a number of keys with his palm or forearm, he could exploit the percussive qualities of the piano in a way that had not been imagined before. In addition to this, Cowell put his hands *inside* the piano, using the finger or the nail or a specific number of fingers to elicit the particular sounds he had in mind. Once he even slipped a darning egg between the strings to alter the sound.

In 1934, Schoenberg, then teaching at UCLA, accepted Cage as a private student despite his inability to pay. Schoenberg did this frequently. All he asked in return was that the student consecrate his life to music. Cage readily agreed to do that and studied harmony, counterpoint, and analysis for two years. He found Schoenberg "inspiring but discouraging. Schoenberg very quickly discovered that I had no feeling for harmony, and that it would be useless to try to cultivate it. Once, when I wrote a three-and-a-half-measure subject for a fugue, he told me to save it for my first symphony."

During his two years as student of Schoenberg, Cage met and married the daughter of an Alaskan priest, Xenia Kashevaroff. About the same time he began to work—without pay—for Oscar Fischinger, an abstract film maker in Hollywood. Fischinger used squares, circles, and triangles in his films. "Fischinger told me," Cage recalls, "that everything in the world has a spirit that can be released through its sound. I was not inclined towards spiritualism but I began to tap everything I saw. I explored everything through its sound. This led to my first percussion orchestra."

In 1937 Cage accepted the post of composer/pianist to a dance class in Seattle, Washington. He raised enough money to buy three hundred percussion instruments and invited American composers to contribute to the then painfully thin percussion repertoire. Varèse's *Ionisation*, scored exclusively for percussion, had been performed in New York and California by then—Cage attended the Los Angeles performance—and that work clearly inspired many compositions. Over one hundred pieces were submitted to Cage, who presented concerts of percussion music each year. His press clippings began to accumulate. "My father," Cage says, "who wanted me to follow in his footsteps and become an electrical engineer, was very pleased with my success. He would often say, 'You are my best invention, John.'"

Schoenberg had impressed Cage with the value of structure in music. "Schoenberg convinced me," Cage reports, "that music required structure to differentiate parts of a whole. At first, when I

57

worked with Fischinger, I used the serial technique in connection with musical cells which I did not vary at all. Then I began to work with rhythm. Each piece was based on a number of measures having a square root so that the large lengths have the same relation within the whole that the small lengths have within a unit of it. One could then emphasize the structure at the beginning and move into far-reaching variations."

In 1938, to accompany a dance, Cage wrote his first piece for prepared piano, which he describes as foolish today. The dance, he says, was "almost barbaric in quality. There wasn't enough room on the small stage to accommodate a percussion orchestra so I followed Cowell's example with the darning egg and put nuts and screws in between the strings." In that way he transformed the instrument into a one-man percussion orchestra and obtained a whole new set of sounds.

Cage followed his first prepared piano piece with a number of others: *Root of an Unfocus, Meditation,* and *Perilous Night.* They were played in a small Manhattan studio and reviewed by composer Lou Harrison, who compared *Perilous Night* to the music of Webern. Like most Americans in 1944, Cage had never heard any Webern. But because of Harrison's review he made a special effort to track him down. And he loved what he heard.

"I used to go with my hair on end and sit on the edge of my seat. It was so completely different from anything I'd ever heard. Of course he cannot compare to Schoenberg. Schoenberg is so clearly magnificent. Boulez is responsible for the shift to Webern and I think I understand why. Schoenberg's music is traditional. It continues the past magnificently. Whereas Webern *seems* to break with the past. He gives one the feeling he *could* break with the past. For he shook the foundation of sound as discourse in favor of sound as sound itself. But in Webern the supremacy of pitch relations remains. And so he was really tied to an earlier time."

For Cage it was Satie who effectively broke with the past. "In Satie," he says, "the structures have to do with time, not pitch. Virgil Thomson introduced me to Satie just at the time I first heard Webern. I connected the two composers in my mind."

But Webern and Satie are worlds apart. Satie was a Dadaist, in a sense a Duchamp. In *Parade,* written for the Diaghilev ballet, he called for a typewriter, a steam whistle, and a rattle in the instrumentation. A full-fledged inventor who looked at music irreverently, Satie was out to destroy art, not preserve it. With his antisentimental stance, his verbal and musical attacks on culture, and his violent assaults on high art, he soon dominated Webern in Cage's head and heart. In 1948 Cage presented twenty-five Satie concerts at Black Mountain College and hungered for all he could learn about the man. Cage remains tied to Satie to this day.

During the winter of 1940–41, Cage made his first extended trip to New York. He became friendly with painter Max Ernst and his wife, Peggy Guggenheim, who invited him to stay with them. It was through the Ernsts that he finally met Duchamp. "But I admired him so much," Cage says, "that I didn't make the friendship close. In other words I maintained a respecting distance which continued until the last five years of his life when I realized I should be as close to him as possible." It was also through the Ernsts that Cage met the dancer Jean Erdman, who introduced him to Merce Cunningham. In 1942 Cage dedicated *Credo in Us* to Cunningham; Cage and Cunningham remain together today. In 1945 Cage and his wife were divorced.

It was then that Cage encountered the works of Ananda K. Coomaraswamy, the Anglo-Indian curator of the Indian Collection at the Boston Museum of Fine Arts. Coomaraswamy lectured at the Brooklyn Academy of Music and Cage listened to everything he said. Coomaraswamy also wrote a number of books in which he repeatedly suggested the idea that the proper function of art was to "imitate nature in her manner of operation." This idea attracted Cage right away. "That is very different," he says today, "from believing that one must have something to say—feelings and ideas that should be given form and content. In traditional music everything depends on your having something to say and on saying it in a perfectly fused way, with form and content balancing one another. It seemed to me there was no sense in doing that unless you were being understood. Yet no one was being understood at that time. Each composer worked in a different way and no two composers understood what each other said. Sometimes, when I wrote a sad piece, half the audience would laugh. So I moved away from the concept of understanding to the concept of direct experience."

In 1946 Cage enrolled in D. T. Suzuki's class in Zen Buddhism at Columbia University and wrote *Sonatas and Interludes*, a seventy-minute work for prepared piano that reflected his absorption with the East. The piece deals, in Cage's words, with the "nine permanent emotions of the Indian tradition. Coomaraswamy insisted that certain ideas were true and that these ideas were to be found in both the Occident and the Orient. My first reaction was to express this idea as far as I could in discourse. So I wrote *Sonatas and Interludes*. In

59

it there are some pieces with bell-like sounds that suggest Europe, and others with a drumlike resonance that suggest the East. The last piece is clearly European. It was the signature of a composer from the West."

Sonatas and Interludes was first performed at Carnegie Recital Hall in New York and was well received by both the press and private foundations. The National Institute of Arts and Letters presented Cage with an award, and the Guggenheim Foundation gave him a grant to work abroad. In 1949 Cage went to Paris and stayed for six months. He planned to do research on Satie and to look into the European scene. Virgil Thomson, who had been instrumental in securing the Guggenheim for him, suggested he look up Pierre Boulez.

Immediately after moving into his hotel on the Ile St. Louis, Cage walked the short distance to 4 Rue Beautreillis and left scores, records, and a note for Boulez. Quickly and enthusiastically, Boulez showed up at his door with the material in his hand. They became friends. Cage found Boulez "stimulating and exciting, always surrounded by interesting people." Boulez found Cage "refreshing, genuine in his search for new material." They saw each other often during the next few months.

Cage enjoyed the Boulez entourage: poet Armand Gatti, a renegade Catholic now known as a left-wing dramatist; mathematician-painter Bernard Saby, probably the closest of Boulez's friends, whom Boulez describes as an "expert in Chinese culture, butterflies, and moss"; journalist Pierre Joffroy who later wrote a book about a Christian S.S. man; and Pierre Souvchinsky, one generation older than the rest. Walking along the Seine, Boulez and Cage exchanged ideas. In each other's rooms they ate and drank. But Boulez never offered any confidences; his friendships were at best tenuous. He explains that he finally broke with Saby "because I found his work uninteresting. There's no reason to continue a friendship after that. To be faithful is just nonsense. I didn't say anything. I just disappeared."

Still, in 1949, Boulez found Cage's work interesting, and Cage did a great deal for Boulez. Thirteen years older and better connected than he, Cage promoted Boulez to Phillippe Heugel and Amphion, the two most important music publishers in France. He told them he had an invitation from Henry Cowell, then publisher of *New Music Editions* in New York, to publish Boulez's scores. Hervé Dugardin of Amphion replied that he had had Boulez's *Flute Sonatina* and *First Piano Sonata* on his desk for some time but had not yet made a decision about them. However, he said, this was a "French problem." The next morning Cage brought Boulez to Heugel and Amphion and a deal was made to publish everything Boulez wanted published then. Heugel would publish *Le Visage Nuptial*, *Le Soleil des Eaux*, *Livre pour Quatuor*, and the *Second Sonata*; Amphion, the *Sonatina for Flute and Piano* and the *First Sonata*. That evening there was a great celebration; it was the night before Cage was to return to the United States. Souvchinsky brought all his friends together at Gatti's; Cage and Cunningham were there and everyone rejoiced in Boulez's triumph.

On his part Boulez did what he could for Cage. He introduced him to Messiaen who invited him to the Paris Conservatoire to demonstrate the prepared piano in class. He also brought him to Suzanne Tezenas. Mme Tezenas, Souvchinsky, and Boulez prepared a guest list of one hundred artists and made plans to present Cage's *Sonatas and Interludes*. The afternoon of the performance, Cage spent three hours carefully inserting objects into the piano that he had chosen for the work. Something was not in order with the *una corda* pedal and Suzanne Tezenas watched with apprehension as Cage poured cognac into her Bechstein to weaken the glue between the strings so he could move the hammers in a way that would secure the effect he had in mind. Cage worked with cardboard underneath his materials in order not to damage the soundboard. He says he always leaves a piano in better condition than he finds it.

The evening of the performance the living room was jammed. Chairs were set up close together and Cunningham lay stretched out on the floor between the foyer and the living room. Boulez introduced Cage with a careful lecture in which he emphasized that Cage was a Schoenberg pupil and analyzed the rhythmic structure of the work at hand. Whatever innovations Cage brought with him that night, chance operation was not one of them. Cage had not been away from Schoenberg long enough to have lost his ties to structure in art.

Still, there were enough innovations. *Sonatas and Interludes* was probably the first Western work to have been nourished so lavishly by the East. It was also probably the first Western work in which the printed score didn't begin to tell the story. (Because of the alteration in sound brought about by the different objects in the instrument, even the Conservatoire-trained musician who reads scores the way Americans read novels could not anticipate the sounds of the *Sonatas*.) Thirdly, it was probably the first serious work that transformed the generally sacrosanct piano. Over and above everything else, the celebrated *invention*, the prepared piano, challenged accepted ideas of acoustics and pinpointed the technological impoverishment—in contrast to ideological advance—that characterized music up to mid-century.

The work was also an eloquent reminder of how, in the West, harmony had been cultivated at the expense of rhythm. The *Sonata's* highly structured metrical scheme plus its highly structured distribution of sounds and pauses made Boulez and Cage aesthetic comrades. That Boulez took his cues from Webern while Cage took his cues from Satie should have served as sufficient notice to both that their paths would diverge radically. But neither composer foresaw how radically at that time.

5

What Boulez set out to do was "to strip music of its accumulated dirt and give it the structure it had lacked since the Renaissance." He went into it, he said, "with exaltation and fear. It was like Descartes' 'Cogito, ergo sum.' I momentarily suppressed inheritance. I started from the fact that I was thinking and went on to construct a musical language from scratch."

As Boulez constructed serialism "from scratch," Cage constructed chance operation from scratch. The letters they exchanged between 1949 and 1952 reveal the development of their thoughts as each formulated the *idée fixe* of his life. Neither one has changed his fundamental concept about music since then.

In 1950 Boulez left for South America with the Barrault troop; it was his first trip outside France. Just after he left Paris, a young woman played his *Second Piano Sonata* at the Salle de l'Ecole Normale de Musique. One of Boulez's friends described the event in a letter to Cage that includes not only his judgment of her performance but an elaborate picture of Parisian musical life and of the hostility that greeted the new language:

The interpretation, while quite decent, was pitiful. I heard at least 25 times the main passage of this sonata played by Pierre. I assure you it was very different in the hands of this pianist. "Lento," "dolce," "soave," "addormentato," from the beginning to the end. Not a single forte. Not a single sustained note. A river (like the tranquil Seine) from the beginning to the end. According to Souvchinsky she took seven minutes longer to play the entire piece than it normally requires. But all this did not warrant in any way the reactions of the audience. From the very first bars, three quarters of the audience smiled with already prepared smiles and shrugging of shoulders. Already in the first movement I felt compelled to call two women utter fools and to threaten another with knocking her block off. That was nothing. The rest of the audience only increased by tenfold the hostility already rampant. The women—low breed which should be exterminated by using red hot pokers on their stomachs—were exultant. Sighs of boredom, invitation cards that they were passing along to each other on which they had put next to Boulez's name the number ZERO. At one point a few respectable musicians (and they do exist here and there in the world) felt the need to shout vehemently and indignantly, "Have you quite finished your stupid antics?" (The music being performed then was that of Boulez.) I felt compelled to intervene with invective of my own. Fortunately for the performance Max Deutsch demanded silence in imperative tones and obtained it. The scene ended with some exaggeratedly heavy applause (provided by a few of Boulez's friends) and a general lethargy on the part of a slightly amused audience. I went out without hearing the rest of the concert, shouting all the coarsest language I could muster. "It would be necessary to put a bomb in your vagina before you could ever understand that! You should all have your balls smashed in! Bunch of bastards etc. etc." A short while later Joffroy met me, accompanied by Saby and Souvchinsky. We spent the night going from one bistro to the next to get rid of some of the bitterness we felt. We tippled until we were completely drunk. Joffroy rid himself of his hostilities by breaking a considerable number of glasses. Not a single music critic in any one of the daily papers thought it wise to discuss the work. The few who bothered into it at all were to a one surprised that the public did not boo. Quite the contrary, they were full of encomiums—as was the public, moreover, for this poor ass Martinet whose sorry "fugue" sounded like a song by Edith Piaf. The whole affair made me ill for two days. Now things have fallen into perspective and I view it all with more equanimity. Unfortunately this poor lady must play the *Second Sonata* again at the Sorbonne around the end of the month. (If in the meantime we could at least graft a pair of testicles to her.) The only felicitous aspect of this story is that Pierre, having left the day before for South America (with Barrault and company) did not attend the circus that accompanied the performance of his piece and the irremediable mess that was made of his work.

64

On learning that Boulez was in South America, Cage contacted the International Institute in Middlebury, Vermont, to arrange for Boulez to give two lectures there. Cage hoped that such an engagement would help Boulez obtain a United States visa. Boulez responded with delight. From Montevideo he wrote that he was pleased with the subjects Cage suggested for him. For the first lecture: Ravel, Schoenberg, and Stravinsky; for the second: Webern, Rhythm in Dodecaphony, and his own *Second Piano Sonata* accompanied by his ideas on composition in general. Boulez wrote that he had only $85 then and expected to have $120 in a short time. But he could not obtain a visa in Buenos Aires, so he did not see Cage for another two years.

From South America Boulez wrote Cage that he was orchestrating *Le Visage Nuptial*. "It is easier to reorchestrate an old work while one is constantly changing one's environment than it is to create an entirely new work." But he also began to compose something new. He referred to it to Cage as a "work-in-progress"; otherwise he was guarded about it. "It would be premature for me to talk about it at length. Silence is more prudent and I shall break it only later. I can tell you at any rate that it will not be easily accessible."

On his return to France, Boulez plunged into *Polyphonie X* which he scored for eighteen solo instruments. Based on the organization of rhythmic cells to which all other elements remain subservient, it displays serial organization of the most relentless kind. Boulez says that the X in the title is neither a letter of the alphabet nor an algebraic symbol. "It is rather a graphic symbol. I called the work *Polyphonie X* because it is based on certain structures which intersect each other in the sense of augmentation and diminution. It is in the series of the rhythmic cells that the main point of the work can be found."

One day while at work on this piece Boulez received a visit from Heinrich Strobel, director of the Southwest German Radio, who had been told to look up the composer on Rue Beautreillis in Paris by Marcel Mihalovici, a conservative composer of operas but a man who, Strobel later said, at least understood the merit of Boulez. Like Souvchinsky, Strobel had a nose for talent and had spent his life in the arts. A student of Paul Klee's at the Bauhaus, he moved into music in his early adulthood and contributed to the music journal *Melos*. In Berlin, before the war, Strobel had held radio interviews with Schoenberg, and had published books on Stravinsky, Hindemith, and Debussy, fighting for Hindemith and the neoclassical Stravinsky. He hated Webern and Berg at that time; according to Boulez, he could "not stand the hysterical post-Wagnerian sound."

65

Strobel was forced to leave Germany because he was married to a Jew. He spent the war years in France and afterwards resettled in Germany, in Baden-Baden. There he became editor of *Melos* and director of the regional radio system as well. The radio station had been run for French troops established there during the war. When Strobel took it over in 1945 he combined it with the city's orchestra as the Sudwestfunk and engaged Hans Rosbaud as its conductor. In the winter of 1950, when Strobel made his first postwar trip to Paris, he was open to the discovery of a great talent and was certain he had found him when he met Boulez.

Seated at his composition table, Boulez was wrapped in a blanket (the small stove gave little warmth) and surrounded by a number of serial charts. "I was fascinated," Strobel later wrote, "by this young man with his sharp stare, his very progressive ideas, and a charm that did not fit at all the description I'd been given of this *enfant terrible* of the avant-garde.

"P.B. was at work on a score. The notes were so tiny, as tiny as the feet of a fly. About him were pieces of charts that would seem to have more properly belonged to a mathematician. The composition he was writing was *Polyphonie X*. I decided immediately to do it for the first performance of the festival I planned for Donaueschingen, near Baden-Baden, scheduled for October 1951." Strobel's festival became an annual attraction, providing what was probably the most important marketplace for new music in Europe. All the heads of German radio stations came, composition students came, and, at the close of the two-day event, Prince Egon von Fürstenberg hosted a dinner for the luminaries at his castle. Recalling the first performance Strobel wrote, "*Polyphonie X* was the greatest scandal I went through after the war. Unfortunately, the press, in writing about the work today, still uses some of the pejorative phrases it used at the premiere. But those who knew anything at all knew that this was a very special work, one that in both structure and color opened completely new paths."

Rosbaud reportedly hated the piece, but it is difficult to determine whether that alone made for what was generally deemed an inadequate performance. Most likely it was simply unplayable, particularly at a time when its syntax was completely unfamilar, even to the most skilled German musicians. Boulez was in London with Barrault, so he was spared the disastrous reception of the work. The audience responded with whistles, hisses, and boos. Still, the specialists celebrated it. Strobel told Souvchinsky, "Boulez is a genius." Souvchinsky replied, "He is a Mozart."

On his return from London, Boulez heard a tape of the Donaueschingen performance and must have concluded that even the most disciplined, professional musicians could not have executed the work with any degree of fidelity. Possibly prompted by the distance between the intention and execution of both his *Second Piano Sonata* and *Polyphonie X*, (Roger Desormière proved an exception to the rule of bad Boulez performances during the early years with a splendid one of *Soleil des Eaux* in 1950), Boulez turned to electronics. Theory held that the electronic instrument could do what the performer and conventional instrument could not. Joining the Groupe Recherche de la Radiodiffusion Française, recently founded by Pierre Schaeffer, Boulez produced *Deux Etudes* for magnetic tape. But his liaison with the center was a stormy one. In a letter to Cage, Boulez wrote that the shouting match between Schaeffer and himself would provide "enough material for a thick portfolio. Schaeffer," he added, "is a bastard."

In 1949, before Boulez began *Polyphonie X*, Messiaen had published his *Quatre Etudes de Rythme* of which the second, entitled *Mode de Valeurs et d'Intensités*, was probably the first European composition which extended the serial principle beyond pitch to the other musical elements. The work was organized in this way: a melodic series of thirty-six notes, a rhythmic series of twenty-four durations, a dynamic series of seven attacks, and an additional series of seven intensities. (The work is for piano, therefore timbre does not undergo permutation.) This fourfold determination is then set into three-part canon. Despite the imposition of such mathematical formulas, the *Mode de Valeurs et d'Intensités* is full, expressive, extroverted music. Messiaen used his formulas in a free and romantic way. After the completion of this work he chose not to pursue the path of total organization.

It was left to Boulez to remove the trimmings, to make music "from scratch," to go, in a sense, bone dry. "This was the zero point of writing," he says. "What I was after was the most impersonal material. Personality had to be involved, of course, in bringing the mechanism into action, but then it could disappear after that. To have the personality not at all involved was a necessity for a while."

Boulez did not merely adopt Messiaen's technique; he complicated it considerably. In place of a rather straightforward method, Boulez developed a most intricate mechanism which appears to have been designed to transmute his private anguish and joy into something distant, universal, and cold. In *Structures* even the smallest aspect of each

STRUCTURES

Pierre BOULEZ

I a

Page 1 of *Structures Book I* with a straightforward presentation of the series, both pitch and duration. The duration series ranges from one to twelve thirty-seconds.

musical event undergoes a perpetual transformation. Thus each pitch never recurs with the same duration, the same intensity, or the same attack. A staggering multiplicity of combinations occurs. Recently, Boulez has said, "Messiaen dealt with modes which were static. Everything was held together from beginning to end. When I took his material, I untied the various characteristics and made them work independently."

Going one step further than the H C A B of the *Second Sonata*, Boulez planned the work to be an *Art of the Fugue* for the serial language. It was to consist, Boulez says, of three large books covering all aspects of the grammar. Book I, written in 1952, includes three pieces numbered *1 a, 1 b* and *1 c. 1 a* exposes the basic material which is stated in the opening bars by inversion between the two pianos. The four basic constituents remain clearly defined throughout the piece. *1 a* concentrates on pitch and duration; *1 b* on differences in attack; *1 c* superimposes contrasts of dynamics on the other elements. To reduce rehearsal problems Boulez scored the work for two pianos, but he more than compensated for this instrumental limitation by pushing the piano to incredible lengths.

The excitement of the instrumental writing saves the work from being suffocated by its pedagogy. Indeed, Boulez says he sensed the dead end implied in his relentless application of the Idea and therefore inscribed on the first page of Book I a provisional title he took from a painting by Paul Klee: "A là limite du fertile pays." (At the limit of fertile ground.)

Perhaps to effect a reconciliation with Messiaen, with whom he had broken in 1948 (Boulez ascribes the break to "the inevitable disenchantment that comes after one has made a tour of someone"), and possibly to compensate Messiaen for having exploited his idea, the younger composer borrowed the row the older one had used for the *Mode de Valeurs et d'Intensités*—a deferential act. "It was a test," he says, "with borrowed material. The piece is based on choice at very important moments; then the structures are generated by the automatism of the numerical relations." In 1952 Boulez and Messiaen collaborated in a performance of *Structures* in Paris. Just before they went on stage Boulez whispered to a friend, "I hope it goes well. I believe in it." The work became a milestone in postwar music.

While in pursuit of total serialism, Boulez wrote intermittently to Cage, alternating trenchant comments about "neoclassic" composers with enthusiastic comments about the Viennese: "In Paris Horenstein will soon perform *Wozzeck* by Berg, a piece which I find more and more remarkable by its complexity, at times undecipherable, resembling the Labyrinth without Ariadne's thread. He will have fifteen orchestra rehearsals and I shall do my best not to miss one. It should be quite an event and I am exultant beyond belief."

But the most important aspect of the correspondence was Boulez's definition of serialism. In 1952 the critical letter arrived. (Because Boulez never dated letters, it is impossible to be more precise as to when.) His minuscule writing covers every millimeter of six sides of tissue-thin pages, articulating the details of the technique, listing the parameters in the following order: frequency, timbre, intensity, and duration. Almost immediately he published an expanded treatment of the letter in an article entiled "Eventuellement" published in *La Revue Musicale*. Tables, graphs, algebraic symbols abound. Boulez writes:

We must expand the means of a technique already discovered: that technique having been, up to now, a destructive object linked, for that very reason, to what it has wanted to destroy [tonality]. Our first determination will be to give it autonomy, and, furthermore, to link rhythmic structures to serial structures by common organizations, which will also include the other characteristics of sound: intensity, mode of attack, timbre. Then to enlarge that morphology into a coalescent rhetoric.

Manuscript copies of this aesthetic treatise were circulated around Paris as though it were a call to arms. This was the basic message: "Anyone who has not felt—I do not say understand—but felt the necessity of the dodecaphonic language is USELESS. For everything he writes will fall short of the imperatives of his time."

What Boulez shared with Cage was the need to destroy the tonal language. But he says that by 1952 he knew serialism would not be Cage's means. Cage's personality and correspondence left no doubt about that.

After returning from Paris to New York in 1949, Cage wrote *Sixteen Dances for a Small Orchestra* and *Concerto for Prepared Piano and Orchestra*. He composed them both, he says, "as a bridge between the earlier pieces and chance. It was then I began to work with the Magic Square, a square with an uneven number of squares. Boulez had been working with a similar diagram at the time, but he put numbers into the squares whereas I put in aggregates of sounds. They had no relation to harmony. They had no necessary direction. Each was a musical fact, without any implication at all. If one moves in this way one produces a continuity of sound that has nothing to do

70

with harmony and is freed, at the same time, from the imposition of one's own taste."

Shortly after he had developed the Magic Square, Cage learned of an Oriental idea that insured, he thought, the removal of himself from the creative process. One evening in 1950 he attended a performance of Webern's *Opus 21* and met composer Morton Feldman and pianist David Tudor. A sort of club formed: Cage, Feldman, Tudor, and a young high school student, Christian Wolff. Just after they met, Wolff brought Cage the two volumes of *I Ching*, the *Book of Changes*, a collection of ancient Chinese oracles translated into English by Richard Wilhelm.

Fascinated by the similarities of the tools in *I Ching* and those of his own work, Cage began to compose the *Music of Changes*. To determine each of his musical moves he would toss a coin. This is how he made the piece: Cage drew twenty-six large charts. To plot a single note, he tossed three coins six times. The results, noted down on paper, would direct him to a particular number in *I Ching* which, in turn, would correspond to a numbered position on the chart. That position would determine only the pitch of the note. The entire procedure would be repeated over and over again to determine the note's duration, timbre, and other elements. Because the piece lasted forty-three minutes, the number of tossings was astronomical. Cage applied the principle of the Magic Square to "all," he emphasizes, "the parameters of sound." The *Music of Changes* was to be Cage's *Structures.*

Only in retrospect do *Music of Changes* and *Structures* seem far apart. Indeed, until 1952 each man graciously acknowledged the other. In "Eventuellement" Boulez declared that "Cage's direction is too similar to my own for me not to take note of it." And in *Transformations*, a short-lived art journal emanating from New York, in which articles by Boulez and Cage stood side by side, Boulez articulated a philosophy which implied compatibility between serialism and chance: "We may conceive of musical structure from a dual viewpoint: on the one hand the activities of serial combinations where the structures are generated by the automatism of the numerical relations; on the other, directed and interchangeable combinations where the arbitrary plays a much larger role. The two ways of viewing musical structure can clearly furnish a dialectic and extremely efficacious means of musical development."

71

6

In June 1951 Boulez attended a two-week festival of the arts that was being held at the Abbaye de Royaumont just outside Paris. Musicians came from all over Europe. It was there he met Henri Pousseur, the first composer to join his quest for a new and pervasive order in art.

Pousseur was born in 1929 in Malmédy, a small town on the Belgian-German border. He says that as a child he was "fanatic" about Mozart. He heard his first Schoenberg piece when he was ten. It struck him as "something better, something sour." But as he had no opportunity to be in touch with such music anyway, the twelve-tone influence disappeared from his life.

In 1947 Pousseur moved to Liège to attend the Liège Conservatoire. When he first arrived, he and his young musical friends clustered around a young teacher, Pierre Froidebise, a specialist in fifteenth- and sixteenth-century organ practice who was interested in contemporary music as well. Pousseur describes his teacher as an "unquiet man, not convinced enough in a single direction to have made a mark for himself, but a person immensely useful to the young." For his students, Froidebise bought Leibowitz's recently published books on Schoenberg and the twelve-tone school.

Pousseur says, "I was thrown by this group when I first came to Liège. I was seduced by the intellectual aspect of new music. I had

72

always been interested in the constructive aspect of music, and when I heard Froidebise speak as he did about dodecaphony, it opened my mind and ears."

Pousseur reports that in 1949 several of his friends went to Paris and met French composers Serge Nigg, Casanova, Phillipot, and Boulez. "Boulez was not absolutely central then, not like Froidebise was to us. At that time he had written an article for *La Revue Musicale* on the rhythm and athematicism in his *Sonatina for Flute and Piano* and the article was discussed a good deal. And, because it was the two hundredth anniversary of Bach's death, he was writing an essay for *Contrepoint* in which he defined the role of Webern clearly; his point was that the parallel was not between Bach and Schoenberg—as so often had been claimed by Leibowitz—but that it was between Bach and Webern.

"Just after I read that essay I heard Webern for the first time. The occasion was the International Society for Contemporary Music—the year was 1950—and the work was Webern's *Second Cantata*, the one Boulez discussed in his essay on Bach. It was done divinely. Those intervals were sung with such facility. There was such purity of sound. It was then that I made the distinction in my mind that Schoenberg was expressionistic and Webern was not."

In 1950 Leibowitz came to Liège to teach. "I had composed my *First Piano Sonata*," Pousseur reports, "and Leibowitz looked at it with contempt. He told me I had not worked the material out, that I would first have to learn all the techniques before I could begin to compose. I was repelled by Leibowitz and his approach to the twelve-tone technique but I had not yet grasped the full spirit of Webern. I had the impression that tonality was so strong that one could avoid it only in thin, economical pieces—such as the ones that Webern wrote —and that anything on a large scale would have to fall into natural, tonal relations. So I composed a resolutely tonal piece, a *Mass*, in the winter of 1950–51."

The following June, Froidebise paid Pousseur's expenses for the trip to Paris so that he could attend the festival at the Abbaye. Pousseur showed Boulez his tonal *Mass* and an earlier twelve-tone work, *The Seven Verses of the Pentecost Psalms*, which he had dedicated to Froidebise. "Boulez put the *Mass* aside right away," Pousseur recalls, "and carefully looked at the other work. We played it together at the piano, four hands. Boulez showed me the technique of intervals. He showed me what to do so it could be correct in the Webernian sense. There were several techniques, easy enough to describe: (1) Don't use leading intervals, use a major seventh instead of a leading tone;

(2) if you have a note return in another octave, place a chromatic note between, not only in time but in register—so you can rub out the initial note; (3) do not repeat the same interval or the same group of notes in the same way: C, C sharp, E. Have the group reversed."

Boulez's objective was to move Pousseur away from the treatment of intervals in a melodic context towards the treatment of intervals in a more structural way. Schoenberg often used minor seconds and sevenths which would supersede everything else he did and reinforce a tonal base. And even when Schoenberg did not do that—as in the last movement of his *Woodwind Quintet* when he was self-consciously proclaiming the new language—his traditional treatment of rhythm often gave the notes the sound of a baroque score just a little bit out of tune.

To illustrate his lesson, Boulez lent Pousseur the tape of Desormière's performance of *Le Soleil des Eaux* along with the score. He also showed him the score of his *Second Piano Sonata* and *Polyphonie X*. "I was absolutely fascinated," Pousseur says, "for Boulez helped me to understand that Webern was not an end but a real beginning. By meeting him, all the elements had been put in place. Boulez provided the real center."

Immediately after their meeting in 1951, Pousseur composed the *Trois Chants Sacrées*. "The three songs were purely Webernian in harmony," he says. "They were very close to *Soleil des Eaux*. I didn't consciously use the Boulez work, but later, when I analyzed it, I found the rows very close indeed."

During the weeks at the Abbaye de Royaumont, Boulez spoke to Pousseur not only about his pieces for conventional instruments but also about Pierre Schaeffer's studio and how he had made his *Deux Etudes* for magnetic tape. He explained how he had produced permutations of tape. "In criticizing Schaeffer's methods," Pousseur says, "Boulez showed me exactly what he wanted to do. He wanted to restructure the material so he could have complete control. He wanted to unify the germ, to unify the seed, to have everything grow from one idea, and to apply a very precise, a very structured type of elaboration. The first piece of *Structures* is an example of that, without electronic means, of course. There is one series of numbers in a very automatic scheme. In duration it is very clear. In other words, the scheme of duration is not newly created but derived from the initial pitch row. Everything is based on the principle of permutation. There are no perceptible relations, only statistically derived relations."

Thus Boulez's music at this moment was based on the quantification of pitch and rhythm. It was, in other words, totally abstract. Boulez's need for an anchor for his imagination was shared by his young colleagues and the compass they chose was that of a large square, filled with boxes numbered from one through twelve, that charted their way through a musical work. But no logical perceptual law, no physical acoustical law connects Duration No. 2 with Pitch or Timbre No. 2, nor Dynamic No. 4 with Pitch or Timbre No. 4. Although the box could allow the composer to permute absolutely anything, the method by which choices were made had virtually nothing to do with the way listeners would perceive a work. The system was totally arithmetical; it seemed, in 1950–51, to be a logical outgrowth of Webern's *Opus 21 Symphony*.

On July 13, 1951, one month after Boulez's meeting with Pousseur, Arnold Schoenberg died. Reflecting on the death Boulez says: "Of course I was not especially touched. Schoenberg was to me part of the mystic adoration of Leibowitz. The Leibowitz cult was repulsive to me, as repulsive as the Stravinsky cult. And Leibowitz was a joke. I never forgave his dishonesty. He was serviceable at the beginning, but I began to resent him when I saw how narrow and stupid he was. His analyses of Schoenberg are an arithmetical countdown. His book is a compilation of Adorno and Willi Reich.

"Cult always kills the man at the center. Look how repulsive Schoenberg became: 'I have discovered a method to save German music.' He opened the field but he closed a lot too. The last third of his life was terribly academic. With Opus 25, his work is not attractive anymore. Opus 31 is a lesson in counterpoint and variation. In it he pursues the aesthetic of Brahms. I don't find it very interesting to go back to Brahms."

During the winter of 1951–52, Boulez wrote Cage that it was necessary to demolish the Schoenberg cult. He said that in Schoenberg the series is only the lowest common denominator and that the real reason for Schoenberg's failure lay in his lack of understanding of the structural, not the thematic, function of the series. He told Cage of an essay that he had written which was to be published in an English journal, *The Score*. In it he killed Schoenberg and crowned Webern. The title of the piece: "Schoenberg is DEAD!"

It is easy to forget that a certain Webern also labored; to be sure, one never hears this discussed anymore. . . . Perhaps we can see that the series is a logically historical consequence, or, depending on what one wishes, a historically logical one. Perhaps, like a certain Webern, one could pursue the sound EVIDENCE by trying to derive the structure from the material. . . .

Perhaps one could generalize the serial principle to the four sound constituents: pitch, duration, intensity and attack, timbre. Perhaps... perhaps... one could demand from a composer some imagination, a certain dose of asceticism, even a little intelligence, and finally a sensibility that will not be toppled by the smallest breeze.

It has become indispensable to demolish a misunderstanding that is full of ambiguity and contradiction; it is time to neutralize the setback. That correction will not be accomplished by gratuitous bragging, much less by sanctimonious fatuity, but by rigor free of weakness and compromise. Therefore I do not hesitate to write, not out of any desire to provoke a stupid scandal, but equally without hypocrisy and pointless melancholy: SCHOENBERG IS DEAD.

It is not altogether surprising that a young Frenchman, passionate in his hatred of his personal past and raised in the tradition of annihilating the historic past—Leibowitz's attack on Stravinsky provided an eloquent model for that—should embark on as strong an effort to liquidate Schoenberg as this. What is surprising is his success in recruiting disciples both in and out of France and in maintaining his leadership as long as he did. When he finally was dethroned, it was at the hands of his own "favorite son," the tall, slender German Karlheinz Stockhausen, three years younger than he and a very green composer when the two first met. What Boulez had done to Leibowitz and Schoenberg, Stockhausen would finally do to Boulez.

In January 1952, seven months after Boulez enlisted Pousseur, he met and made a strong impression on Stockhausen, who had come to Paris to study at the Conservatoire. Stockhausen also made a strong impression on Boulez. "I recall the first meeting very well," Boulez says. "I knew no German. Stockhausen knew no French. A friend, Louis Sauger, translated. We gesticulated wildly. I knew immediately that here was someone exceptional. I was right. I came to trust his music more than anything else. We talked about music all the time—in a way I've never talked about it with anyone else."

Stockhausen was born on August 22, 1928, the first child of poor people from a rural background. His father was an elementary school teacher; his mother had three children in the first three years of her marriage. Soon after the last she began to suffer an extreme depression and was committed to a mental hospital in 1933. She died there eight years later, when Karlheinz was thirteen years old; "officially killed," he claims. Karlheinz's father was killed in battle in Hungary when Karlheinz was only seventeen.

Stockhausen spent much of his early life in a Catholic monastery. He graduated from a *gymnasium* in 1947 and then attended the State Academy in Cologne. There he studied piano and music education, all the while earning his living playing piano in Cologne bars, serving as accompanist to an amateur operetta theater, and providing background music for a magician's act.

At the Cologne Academy Stockhausen studied with Frank Martin, the Swiss composer who concentrated on analyses of Bartók scores. Stockhausen's theoretical work for his civil service teaching examination was Bartók's *Sonata for Two Pianos and Percussion*. At that time he was familiar, he writes, with almost every work by Schoenberg, Stravinsky, and Bartók but knew only one piece by Anton Webern— the *Five Movements for String Quartet Opus 5*. Stockhausen composed two pieces in 1950–51: *Three Songs for Alto and Chamber Orchestra* and a *Sonata for Violin and Piano*. The strongest influence on both was Schoenberg.

During the summer of 1951, when dodecaphony was the prevailing aesthetic at Darmstadt, Stockhausen attended the summer school there and met the composer Karel Goeyvaerts who had just completed his studies with Milhaud and begun to study under Messiaen. Goeyvaerts had seen the score of Messiaen's *Mode de Valeurs et d'Intensités* and had taken off from it in much the manner that Boulez had: by writing a rigid, totally serial piece. Indeed Stockhausen subsequently claimed, when he was trying to undermine Boulez, that Goeyvaerts's piece, a *Sonata for Two Pianos*, which he and Goeyvaerts played in Adorno's composition seminar at Darmstadt, predates Boulez's far more famous *Structures*. But Boulez disclaims any importance to priority in this instance. "Goeyvaerts," Boulez says, "is an invention of Stockhausen's. He was to me what Hauer was to Schoenberg." (Joseph Matthias Hauer, a Viennese composer, formulated a twelve-tone system at almost the moment that Schoenberg did. But unlike Hauer, Schoenberg never promoted his *technique*. It was never more than a means for making music. For Hauer it was an end in itself.)

Boulez's depreciation of Goeyvaerts's talent is echoed by other specialists in the field. Still, Stockhausen was young and awed by Goeyvaerts—he named him godfather to his first child—and he followed Goeyvaerts's example by going to Paris in the late winter of 1952 in order to study under Messiaen. That is when he met Boulez.

Immediately, under the influence of the slightly older and immensely powerful man, Stockhausen made the shift from Schoenberg to Webern and to an extension of the serial principle to areas other than pitch relations. Within a year Stockhausen returned to Cologne and the post-Webern movement took roots in Germany.

And so, for one long intense moment in the early 1950s, Boulez, Pousseur, and Stockhausen were at one in their efforts to establish serialism as a common language and to seduce all those they could to the celebration of Webern.

7

When John Cage returned to the United States after his 1949 visit to Paris he did everything he could to promote Boulez in America. But by 1952, after Boulez spent several months in New York, the break between them was irreparable. Starting with the schism in thinking between them and exacerbated by criticism in the press, that break unleashed antagonisms between Europe and the United States that permeate the musical atmosphere even today.

When Boulez was traveling with Barrault in South America in 1950 and working on *Polyphonie X* and *Structures* in Paris, Cage was writing articles about him for American music journals and expounding eloquently about his work to private foundations. First he persuaded the League of Composers to program Boulez's *Second Sonata* with David Tudor as pianist for a concert in December 1950. The *Times* critic was more open-minded than the French critics had been: "The music was scattered all over the keyboard in rapid, surrealist patterns that could hardly be apprehended. Composed in the twelve-tone technique, the work was consistently arhythmic, athematic (in the usual sense), and its sonorities were acerbic."

The audience reacted hostilely; still Cage continued to promote Boulez. In August 1952 he arranged for Tudor to play the *Second Sonata* at Black Mountain College in a program that included works by Feldman, Cowell, Stefan Wolpe, and himself.

Thus, in the fall of 1952, when Boulez made his first trip to the United States to conduct and play *ondes martenot* for the Renaud-Barrault theater, he came also as an artist in his own right. The way had been paved for him by Cage. Lillian Keisler, widow of the architect and sculptor Frederick Keisler, recalls that "Boulez was the White Knight of the time. I remember a performance of his work at Carl Fischer Hall. All the abstract expressionists came. His name was legendary even among painters. We knew that conventional music had been carried to its limits and that here was a genius, a genius who brought a tidal wave of the new."

The "new" that Boulez brought was still hysterical and passionate; the *Second Sonata* was played a great deal. But it hovered on the brink of the secretive as well. Virgil Thomson has written that Boulez "loves the deeply calculated" and Boulez was not alone in this.

Perhaps to resist the increasing popularization and vulgarization of art which had flourished under neoclassicism and socialist realism and had been encouraged by radio and films, perhaps to restore a more intellectually aristocratic elite, many artists—both in Europe and the United States—began to build on the refined, inaccessible language that had its roots earlier in the century. This is not to say that it was the intent of Schoenberg, Kandinsky, or Pound to be as hermetic as they were; it is rather to point out that inaccessibility was certainly a consequence of what each of them did. But those artists who came of age after World War II elevated this secondary consequence to a primary purpose. For Boulez, James Joyce was a critical symbol. He had read *Ulysses* in French, and an exhibit in 1949 at Le Hune bookshop in Paris increased his excitement about Joyce's work. Recalling what drew him to Joyce, Boulez cites the "specificity of technique for each chapter, the fact that technique and story were one. The technique reflected exactly what Joyce *meant*; it was rich and I had never met it before in a book."

But it was *Finnegans Wake*, which cannot be understood through simple reading even by those fluent in the English language, that overwhelmed the group. In a letter to Cage written in December 1949, a young French poet wrote:

The advent of *Finnegans Wake* at Pierre's has not yet finished provoking many arguments and discussions. There were several stormy sessions on Rue Beautreillis where the tone of things reached such a high pitch that the vocabulary consisted of several forceful "merdes" which each of the participants flung at each other without any mental reservation concerning the parsimony of the words used.

If by now the heated arguments have abated somewhat, discussions are still frequent on the subject. Joffroy is still dreaming, in his idle moments, of forming a James Joyce Society and has been inhibited in the matter only by the fact that the Americans seem to have beaten him to it. I must admit, to be completely objective, that after experiencing Joyce in a very serious way my admiration for Faulkner has vanished.

It is possible that technique alone did not draw Boulez to Joyce for the similarities between the two artists transcend technique. Both Boulez and Joyce were raised devout Catholics; both became disenchanted when they were still young. Both were clearly in search of a father, a search that dominated both men's lives. (Leopold Bloom was to Stephen Dedalus what Barrault, Souvchinsky, and Strobel were to Boulez.) Both moved towards revolution in the political arena but neither liked manifestos when drawn up by others. (Boulez says he never reads the Bible because he would be anti-Semitic if he did, and that he never reads Communist papers because that would turn him into a rabid anti-Communist.) Art alone was the route for Joyce and Boulez. It gave them the stature and dignity they sought. Able to renounce the dogma they had been taught, each cast his own revolution in the most dogmatic of aesthetic terms. Thus Boulez built *Structures* on a medieval-like musical language with its secrets hidden from the public at large. Like *Finnegans Wake*, which inspired numerous "skeletons" and "guides," *Structures* still inspires musical analyses. That the traditional value of beauty played virtually no role in Boulez's conception is revealed by a passage Boulez wrote to Cage on the eve of his trip to New York:

> Soon Monroe Street will see us and hear us. Tell David Tudor, whom I am very eager to know, that he should get some aspirin ready—I am doing as much myself—for *Structures* is not easy to listen to. But since he has worked on your *Music of Changes* (here Boulez makes a diagram excerpting CAGE from CHANGES) I would say he is properly prepared.

When Boulez arrived in New York he moved into Cage's loft on Grand and Monroe Streets on the Lower East Side. Cage's studio had white walls, no "art" on display, and two windows overlooking the East River that he had carved out of the solid wall by himself. A piano dominated the room. In addition there was a studio couch but no chairs. Visitors sat on straw mats on the floor. Cage moved out so that Boulez could move in.

81

At the first meeting of Cage, Tudor, and Boulez, Tudor played parts of Cage's *Music of Changes* in the Grand Street loft. This was Cage's realization of the Magic Square, in which coin-tossing determined all the elements of every note played. For the first time in many years Cage used the piano without special preparation. He did not abandon, however, his interest in inventing new sounds and called for the instrument to be plucked from the inside as though it were a huge guitar. But he focused his attention on structure through rhythm. Highly controlled changes of tempo are used to establish the rhythmic structure. One starts at a given metronome mark (quarter note equals 69), then accelerates for five measures to a quarter equalling 176, then retards for five measures to a quarter at 100, and so on throughout the work. The form is thus presented in terms of a sliding scale of tempos rather than by an arrangement of a fixed number of measures to constitute phrases, sentences, and sections. "What I did," Cage explains today, "was to develop rhythmic structure from a fixed tempo to changes of tempo. I had not yet moved to a renunciation of absolutely all structure."

Tudor played the entire work for Boulez, who, Tudor recalls, appeared genuinely excited by the sounds. But from the start, Tudor adds, "he was unsympathetic to the idea of chance. He responded politely but it was clear that he was more than hostile to the loss of control." The work presented no real surprises to Boulez who had anticipated his response to Cage's method in a letter he wrote to Cage shortly before he left France. In it he declared: "By temperament I cannot toss a coin. . . . Chance must be very well controlled. *Il y a suffisamment d'inconnu.*" ("There is already enough unknown.")

Boulez's duties with the Renaud-Barrault theater allowed him to move about a good deal on his own. He dined several times at Virgil Thomson's and met important musicians there. Cage had a Model A Ford—already an antique—and he, Tudor, and Boulez visited friends in Stony Point, New York, and took a trip to Cape Cod to introduce Boulez to M. C. Richards, who had translated Antonin Artaud in the United States. Boulez also wrote an article of homage to Webern which was published in the *New York Herald Tribune*:

> We are only beginning now to perceive the novelty of the horizons that Webern has opened to us . . . and when we consider the limited number of his works, we are astonished at the importance of his contribution. His work has become *the* threshold to the music of the future, and its role as such is unfortunately obscured when we think of it in terms of what has been too hastily labeled: "Schoenberg and his disciple."

Boulez gave performances of his own work at Carl Fischer Hall, at the Peabody Conservatory in Baltimore, at a lecture in a course by Henry Cowell, Cage's early teacher, entitled "Musical Iconoclasts: 2700 B.C. through 1952 A.D." at the New School in Greenwich Village, and at a Composer's Forum concert at Columbia University's McMillin Theater. Boulez moderated the Columbia event—although his knowledge of English was slight—which was devoted to electronic music from the Schaeffer studio in Paris. Works by Messiaen, Pierre Henry, André Hodeir, and Boulez (the *Deux Etudes*) were played. For a bonus, he and Tudor played *Structures* (parts 1 a and 1 c). In discussing the work with the audience, Boulez said that his fundamental purpose was to eliminate from his vocabulary all trace of his musical inheritance in an effort to start from scratch and reconquer, little by little, the various states of composition and arrive at a wholly new synthesis. Despite what he said, there were ghosts in Boulez's world, for he aimed to emulate Webern, who drew on Schoenberg, who drew on Wagner and Brahms.

The *New York Times* reviewer, Arthur Berger, was unmoved. An American neoclassic composer, stemming from Stravinsky via Aaron Copland, he hit Boulez where it hurt most: "Shifts of register occur indiscriminately, without any nuance and textural variety that we find in Anton Webern, of whom Boulez considers himself a disciple." Neoclassicism still had the upper hand in the United States; the avantgarde had made little progress as of 1952, so Berger's comments should be viewed in the context of the establishment's efforts to crush the revolutionaries, as was the case in France. But in his statement, Berger touches on something valid: although Boulez repeatedly claimed he was tied to Webern, his more audible ties in the early years were to Debussy and Messiaen. To say this is not to deny the fact that Boulez's technique was infinitely more complex, even at that stage, than that of either Debussy or Messiaen. It is rather to emphasize that Boulez's attachment to Webern was more ideational than musical at that moment in his career, for Webern was never drawn to the dense texture or large form that characterize Boulez's early work.

Shortly before Boulez returned to Paris an important concert took place at the Cherry Lane Theater in Greenwich Village. It included Boulez's *Second Sonata*, Cage's *Music of Changes*, Feldman's *Intersection III*, and *Four Pieces for Prepared Piano* by Christian Wolff. The tiny playhouse was jammed, with people overflowing onto the stage, into the pit, and lining the back and sides of the house. Ross Parmenter, in the *New York Times*, emphasized the radical nature of Cage's work and the traditional aspects of Boulez: "The *Second So-*

83

nata was the most conventional piece of the evening . . . at least it did not depart from customary notions about the sort of instrument a piano is."

The review in the *Herald Tribune* was written by Peggy Glanville-Hicks, a neoclassic composer in the tradition of Thomson, her superior on the *Tribune* staff. Although she was in the conservative vein and therefore not partial to Cage, she celebrated him over the European avant-garde:

In Cage's piece . . . the arrangement of the fragmentary arabesques, the choice of infinitely varied tonal and sound-patch sequences, the contrasted pedal and staccato levels, all went to create the real impression of the real poetry that Cage's scores create.

The Boulez Sonata—to this reviewer—is chaos, organized, stabilized chaos. American composers—be they ever so dissonant and ever so arbitrary—somehow impart an *élan*, a *joie de vivre*, that transcends the unrelenting sounds used. But the European "dissonant-ers" are deadly deliberate as though maximum acidity was their only aim. To the eye and intellect, the printed page of Boulez presents logic and design, but to the ear, its true arbiter, these are not apparent.

Thus the New York press heralded the split between the music of Boulez and Cage, between the Serialists and the Dadaists, between those who, in spite of polemics, are still moved by tradition and those who will not acknowledge any debt to the past. By the time Boulez returned to Paris the lines were drawn. Boulez and Cage have had virtually no contact since then.

Discussing Boulez today, Cage recalls what attracted him at the start: "The smile, the energy, the brilliance of the eyes, all of it was electrifying to me. But in New York I saw another side. Once, on our way back from Cape Cod, we ran out of gas. Pierre thought that was inelegant. I also remember a diner in Providence. Pierre was indignant over the service and the food, and I believe that he required us to leave. I was always frightened by his superior taste. He was always uncompromising. Things had to be exactly where they should be. I was still terribly poor. I wanted to make poverty elegant but Pierre was not interested in that. What he wanted was an excellent richness. Everything had to be exactly right, aesthetically right. Once I dropped into my studio unannounced and he was wearing an elegant silk robe.

"With Pierre music has to do with ideas. His is a literary point of view. He even speaks of parentheses. All of it has nothing to do with sound. Pierre has the mind of an expert. With that kind of mind you can only deal with the past. You can't be an expert in the unknown. His work is understandable only in relation to the past. He has never said he would annihilate Webern!

"Now when I think of the face, I no longer see the electricity. What I find is a look around the eyes, nose, and mouth that is the look of a bad animal, an animal waiting for the kill."

Discussing Cage today, Boulez recalls that what attracted him at the start was Cage's search for new materials. "He was refreshing but not very bright. His freshness came from an absence of knowledge.

"There was a progressive divergence between us. Our original ground had nothing to do with technique. It was interesting to find new sounds—those of the *Sonatas and Interludes*—but finally that was not terribly exciting because the same sound always returns in the same way. One needs neutral material 'A' to become different in a different context. 'A' cannot remain the same through different structures. Cage was interested in pure material. Material was the only thing on which he worked. It was a practical exercise. Today repetition is impossible. There is no escape!"

After the New York visit Boulez stopped corresponding with Cage. Cage was devastated by the turn of events. He says he is a simple, sentimental American and cannot understand how a difference in ideas could destroy a friendship as close as theirs. But serialism was Boulez's oxygen and anyone who threatened its success was, in effect, trying to suffocate him.

As a symbolic blow to Boulez, Cage wrote a paragraph about the French being "cold in spirit and lacking in freedom of the mind" which he published years later in his book *Silence* and proudly displays today as evidence of his resolution of the entire affair. But Boulez had struck Cage in a more devastating way even before he made his trip to New York. Writing a few paragraphs for *La Revue Musicale*, which he entitled "Erik Satie: Chien Flasque," ("Erik Satie: Spineless Dog"), he decimated Satie thoroughly. If Webern begat Boulez and Satie begat Cage, then Boulez's aggressive attack on Satie was tantamount to an aggressive attack on Cage.

The bitter feelings between Boulez and Cage produced considerable reverberations. In February 1953 Virgil Thomson wrote in the *Tribune*: "Cage and his associates, through their recent concerts at the Cherry Lane Theater, have got the town quarreling again."

At its heart the quarrel was between the Old and New Worlds, between Europe and the United States, between a serially derived language and virtually no language at all. Thomson describes the manner in which this particular war was waged: "When Europeans organize they produce a real Mafia; when Americans organize they form a club." As soon as Boulez went back to Europe he and Stockhausen became very close. They were in power as the avant-garde and they developed branches in every country. That was the basis for the European organization that turned its back so violently on Cage.

Boulez with his father, mother, and sister in front of the building where he was born

Pierre with his mother

Pierre with his mother and sister

Pierre and Jeanne

Pierre and Jeanne

First row, far left: Pierre on his graduation from the Institut in Montbrison

Boulez with Messiaen at Odeon Theater in Paris (1966)

René Leibowitz (Courtesy of *The New York Times*)

Messiaen with Suzanne Tezenas (1966)

John Cage and Daisetz Suzuki (1962)

Heinrich Strobel

5/ [...] :

1	8	+1	+1
1	6	3	4

$8 - 1 = 7$
$1 + 12 = 13 - 7 = 6$

$11 - 1 = 10$
$1 + 12 = 13 - 10 = 3$

3	4	7	2
4	5	(1)	3
7	(1)	(4)	6

3	4	7	2
4	5	(8)	3
7	8	11	6

$$\frac{7-6}{15-14}$$

$$\frac{|e-b|}{|e-a|}$$

$$\frac{|b-a|}{|e-a|} \quad \frac{|b-c|}{|e-a|}$$

Last page of Boulez's letter to Cage in which he articulated for the first time the basis of his serial theory

8

The existence of the Boulez-Stockhausen "Mafia" versus the Cage-Feldman "club" reflected a long-standing suspicion—on all sides—that Europeans were superior to Americans in the production of serious music. Music was not singled out for this depreciatory treatment. On the contrary, it was part of what Henry James called the "complex fate" of the American imagination struggling against a powerful tendency to hold its historical precursor, Europe, in awe. From the other side, Europeans have often accused American artists of having no technique, soul, or mystery in their work. As early as the 1920s and '30s, European fans of George Gershwin and Charles Ives are reported to have qualified their admiration by acknowledging that Gershwin and Ives were not "real composers, of course." Gershwin's widespread use of jazz and Ives's unprejudiced approach to all sounds disqualified them from admission to the European community of intellectualized musical and aesthetic ideas.

Many Americans felt that they did indeed occupy this position and were inferior. When Nazism forced the exodus to the United States of the major European figures, some Americans privately expressed the hope that the balance of power would shift somewhat. They thought that if they were to study with Schoenberg, dine with Stravinsky, and converse with Bartók, some of the prestige of these great artists would rub off onto them. But nothing of the sort occurred.

Even Schoenberg's friendship with Gershwin (Schoenberg used Gershwin's tennis courts regularly) did not make for any such dramatic change. Americans of the 1930s and 1940s seemed particularly unsuited to the "genius" role.

This is not to say that American composers failed to prosper during the Depression and Second World War. The rise of Hitler and the start of the war generated an intense distaste for all things German which brought about a sharp decline in the performance of Austro-German works. There was a consequent increase in the performance of American works, not only by the New York Philharmonic, but by smaller organizations as well. The Pro Musica of the Middle and Far West, the New Music Society of San Francisco, and the Pan-American Association of Composers were a few that concentrated on indigenous works. Most famous of all was the League of Composers which had begun before the War and had spawned the Philadelphia Music Society and the Copland-Sessions Modern Music Concerts. In addition to the many chamber groups, two famous conductors leading great orchestras—Serge Koussevitzky, the Boston Symphony and Leopold Stokowski, the Philadelphia Orchestra—systematically championed American art.

But one fact stood out above the rest: American music, for the most part, was "derived" music, music that came over a bridge from the Old World. What is commonly referred to as the "first" or 1930 generation of American composers, the one that included Virgil Thomson, William Schuman, Marc Blitzstein, and David Diamond, took its musical cues from Stravinsky, and that tied them all to the French idiom. Roger Sessions, an important neoclassicist as well, separated himself from the French by his cerebral approach and his affection for the work of Alban Berg. Still, throughout the 1930s and '40s, Sessions rejected the twelve-tone idea and was thus a member in good standing of the American group. But such rugged individualists as Charles Ives, Charles Ruggles, and Henry Cowell stood alone throughout their lives. They never enjoyed successful musical careers.

David Diamond was a prolific composer of the 1930s. One of the youngest composers ever to receive a Guggenheim fellowship, his career was in a class by itself. To chart it is to chart the growth and death of neoclassicism in the United States. Diamond's career grew in the 1930s and reached its peak in the '40s when his works received premieres under Mitropoulos, Rodzinski, Stokowski, and Szell. By the mid-'50s the tide had turned. Looking back today Diamond says, "How did the new group of composers get famous so fast? Not through recognition by the musical public but by foundation grants and university positions. It was a mutual aid society. That in itself would have been all right but the pieces made no sense. There was no strong personality, no individuality."

By the mid-1950s neoclassicism was as dead in the universities of the United States as it was on the German radio systems. And the universities were the sole support of American composers in the post–World War II years. Serious composers had begun to create small, refined worlds of their own that called for the use of the sharpest intellect and closed out those who could not meet these demands. Serialism took hold step by step, not through a revolution such as the one ordered by Boulez, but through a more gradual evolution; for Schoenberg, the original serialist, was living and working here.

As the American serialists increased in power during the 1950s and '60s, those of their colleagues tied to the tonal syntax found themselves under the oppressive power of the new main-line modernism. Many tonal composers received prestigious positions on prize committees, in philanthropic organizations, and as executives in conservatories. William Schuman, for example, became president of the Juilliard School, then president of Lincoln Center. But institutions invariably trail creative life, and by the late 1950s serialism had displaced tonality as the musical grammar of the young artist.

Personal tragedies in this period abound. Marc Blitzstein suffered as Diamond did. Unable to reconcile his affection for tonality with his desire to be in the vanguard, Blitzstein became increasingly depressed and appears virtually to have precipitated his own murder in Martinique. Others made accommodations: Thomson cultivated a career in music journalism as critic for the New York *Herald Tribune*. Still others attached to the old grammar slowly moved into the new. Roger Sessions composed his first twelve-tone work, the *Sonata for Solo Violin*, in 1953. And Stravinsky's shift to the grammar succeeded in sweeping the rest along. After his *Canticum Sacrum* of 1957, in which he used the entire chromatic scale for the first time, Irving Fine, Arthur Berger, even Copland followed suit. But Stravinsky did not regard with affection those who shifted from the old to the new. No longer interested in disenchanted neoclassicists, he wanted to develop a new set of friends. One man whom he sought was Milton Babbitt, father of serialism in the United States, whom Boulez met at a party in Cage's loft when he was visiting New York in the fall of 1952.

Babbitt and Cage were America's major postwar avant-gardists; yet each inhabits a separate universe.

Milton Babbitt was the first son of upper-middle-class, well educated Jews. His mother grew up in Philadelphia and met her husband while touring in Russia. He was a mathematician and planned an academic career in the United States. But a short stint at the University of Illinois moved him to quit the academic life and he settled in Jackson, Mississippi, where he became vice-president of an insurance firm.

Milton began to play the violin at eight, learned classical Latin in his early years, and played with his neighbor, writer Eudora Welty. The young boy appeared to be nurtured in the best of all possible worlds. He was spared an education like Cage's, in which Bach and Mozart were unknown, and spared also what Boulez's sister has described as the "atrophying Catholic system" imposed on her brother and herself.

In 1932 Milton's uncle, a film critic, went abroad and returned with some recently published scores. One was a work by Honegger; the other was Schoenberg's *Opus 11 Piano Pieces*. The Schoenberg attracted the twenty-year-old student and precipitated his decision to make composing his life's work.

During the worst years of the Depression, when most musicians were dependent on the Works Progress Administration, a Federally-funded project to give artists work, Milton's father was prosperous enough to put his son not only through college but through graduate study as well. After leaving New York University in 1935, Babbitt selected Sessions as his composition teacher. Although Sessions still opposed the twelve-tone technique—Babbitt says Schoenberg was considered a musical freak at this time—Sessions's rigorous and intellectual approach drew the younger man to him.

A clue to Sessions's approach to music can be found in his emphasis on the Schenker system of musical analysis. Heinrich Schenker, who died in 1935, had attempted to reveal the organic structure of music by demonstrating that every composition is the elaboration of a simple, harmonic progression that makes for its continuity and coherence. Europeans paid little attention to his work; it was never, for instance, adopted at the Paris Conservatoire. But in the United States the Schenker method was widespread, with even children in some primary schools using this approach. Babbitt interprets this situation as one that reveals true "intellectual rigor here" and "basic intellectual naiveté abroad." Boulez, on the other hand, depreciates Schenker. "It's analysis for the sake of analysis," he says. "I have no interest in that."

In 1947–48, Babbitt wrote his first important work, *Composition for Four Instruments*. It was first performed in 1948 and published by New Music Editions in 1949. It was a thoroughgoing serial piece,

90

composed not only three years before Boulez's *Structures* but before Messiaen's *Mode de Valeurs et d'Intensités*. But Babbitt disparages concern about being first and adds that he and his French colleagues are so far apart on fundamentals that the fact that it is all "serial" is of no consequence to him.

Neither the Babbitt nor the Messiaen work created the attention that Boulez's piece did. There is something about Boulez's presentation that creates a strong effect, that fixes the notice of serious men upon him. When he is on the way up, attacking those who represent "the law," Boulez generates electricity. The music reflects the man. Thus Boulez's *Structures*, perhaps because of its stridency, turned out to be far more trailblazing than Babbitt's more intellectual and academic work. Still, Babbitt can claim priority for a "serial" work.

Rivalries about priorities are not uncommon. Newton said Leibnitz stole calculus from him and there followed a bitter fight that degraded both Newton and Leibnitz. Such quarrels do not imply that the thinkers are thieves; rather do they support the multicentricity of important ideas. Like natural selection, arrived at simultaneously and independently by Darwin and Wallace, like dodecaphony, arrived at simultaneously and independently by Schoenberg and Hauer, serialism was an idea whose time had come.

Babbitt's *Composition for Four Instruments* attracted the attention of "new" musicians, of course, and it particularly attracted John Cage. Cage, working on *Sonatas and Interludes*, was delighted to find another maverick, so he analyzed Babbitt's work in *Musical America*. According to Babbitt, what fascinated Cage was the numerology in the piece as well as the hidden nature of the tone row. "It is difficult," Babbitt says, "to find the twelve-note set, which was partially derived from the opening tritone chord, because the clarinet opens with twelve different pitches leading one to expect that these twelve pitches would constitute the row. Cage was also intrigued by the fact that triads appear in the score, for triads had supposedly been legislated out of classical twelve-tone writing."

But Cage's attention to this early Babbitt work was the last manifestation of genuine interest in what his colleague composed. Soon after, Cage embraced Chance and that separated him from the American serialists as much as it separated him from Boulez.

Fortunately for Cage, by 1950 he was enjoying considerable support from composers who were more attuned to him than either Boulez or Babbitt. The year after his Paris visit, when Cage became friendly with Morton Feldman, he delivered a lecture on Feldman's music in Greenwich Village, and began to build his gentle but very firm little club, a club in which Babbitt played no role at all. Babbitt says, "Cage has always referred to me—half-jokingly—as 'America's best academic composer.' The fact is we are really not interested in each other. Cage is totally honest, totally direct, but finally a very naive man. We are mostly embarrassed by each other. I knew we had nothing in common when he published the analysis of my early work."

But while Babbitt knew in the late '40s that he and Cage lived in separate worlds, he thought he was inhabiting the same universe as Boulez. For one thing, a small publishing house, Boelke-Bomart, which had printed Babbitt's earliest work, had also shown interest in the music of Boulez.

Walter Boelke, an Austrian-Jewish engraver for Schirmer, began his publishing firm in the late 1940s—not to make money, but to contribute to the cultural life of the United States in gratitude for the hospitality he had been shown as a refugee. For musical advice he turned to Kurt List, editor of the music journal *Listen,* who was a composer and a friend of Leibowitz. Because Schirmer had dropped Schoenberg in the early 1940s, List suggested that Boelke publish Schoenberg's current works as well as compositions by Schoenberg's disciples. He asked Leibowitz to submit suitable scores. Leibowitz sent pieces from his composition class: works by Casanova and Nigg and the *First Piano Sonata* by Boulez. Although List preferred the Boulez score, he found it too long and turned it down. This was one of the pieces Cage persuaded Amphion to publish in France.

Indeed the Cage-Boulez friendship of 1949 was symbolic of the interaction and good feeling that prevailed between Europeans and Americans in the musical avant-garde. Leibowitz, who had spent most of his life in France, was collaborating with the New Music Quartet in New York and was at the same time living in Paris with Ellen Adler, daughter of Stella Adler, director of the Actors Studio in New York. In 1947 Leibowitz and Miss Adler visited the United States, and Stella Adler gave a party for them. Her apartment was crowded with Europeans and Americans. Leibowitz and Babbitt played four-hand jazz. There appeared to be no rift between composers at that time.

But by 1952 the good feeling had disappeared. In the summer of that year Babbitt made a trip to Paris. List asked him to get in touch with Boulez to see if Boulez had any more works for him. But Babbitt claims that he could not get hold of Boulez. "By then," he reports, "the lines were so firmly drawn that those who remained loyal to

Leibowitz would do absolutely nothing to help Boulez in his career." Babbitt left Europe without seeing Boulez.

Later that year, when Boulez was in New York with the Barrault troop, Babbitt and Boulez met at a party in Cage's loft. Babbitt recalls the circumstances: "We went into the bedroom and sat on the bed. I showed Boulez my *Composition for Four Instruments*. Boulez was surprised at its ties to Schoenberg. He said: 'I thought you were interested in Webern.' I replied that I was interested in some aspects of Webern and some aspects of Schoenberg but that I really looked to Schoenberg. After all," Babbitt says, "there are so many more levels to Schoenberg, so much more complexity in Schoenberg. I started to talk about combinatoriality and derivation, subjects about which I knew we disagreed but which I thought could have led to an interesting discourse. I don't know whether he did not understand or did not have any interest in what I said. But I do know we never sat down with a score again."

As Leibowitz represented the apex of the European-Schoenberg school, so Babbitt represented the apex of the American-Schoenberg school. Thus the extraordinarily cultivated Babbitt, in whom Boulez had hoped he would find an ally in carving out a language based on Webern, proved to be no ally at all. Because of what Boulez calls his "academic handling" of the serial idea, Babbitt was almost as removed from Boulez's world as Cage.

Shortly after Boulez left the United States, his essay "Schoenberg is dead!" reached New York. The effect was predictable. "George Perle, Leon Kirchner and I were furious," Babbitt says. "That essay was dead wrong. That was what finally separated us from Boulez. We could never forgive him for that." Nor did they. More than twenty years later, when a Boulez retrospective at the Whitney Museum fell on the same date as the Schoenberg centenary concert at Alice Tully Hall, people accused Boulez of setting that date to seduce the already small new-music audience away from Schoenberg across town to Boulez. Tully Hall was empty and the Whitney was jammed.

9

The post–World War II generation of composers had no monopoly on hostility and aggression. Indeed, they were the direct descendents of a musical generation in which the lines were firmly drawn between Schoenberg and Stravinsky and the warring camps that stemmed from each. Of the numerous bitter battles in the history of art, that one certainly illustrates Erik Erikson's claim that "when great artists go under, it is not as slaughtered lambs but as the vanquished in the struggle for power."

The war of ideas between Schoenberg and Stravinsky began precisely in 1912, two years before the outbreak of World War I. Schoenberg was thirty-eight; Stravinsky, twenty-nine. *Pierrot Lunaire*, Schoenberg's highly expressionistic, atonal work, was performed in Berlin for the first time, and Stravinsky was in the audience. The two musical giants had never met. With the exception of one other occasion—the funeral of a mutual friend thirty years later—they were never to meet again. They remained the bitterest of enemies, attacking the opponent's mode of expression in letters, essays, and public statements. A visitor to one knew better than even to mention the other one's name. Each one's consolidation of his holdings, his depreciation of the other's holdings—all that bitterness had originated with *Pierrot Lunaire*. In *Diaries and a Dialogue*, written fifty years after that formidable premiere, Stravinsky told his amanuensis, Robert Craft, "I was aware that this was the most prescient confrontation of my life."

One year later, Stravinsky created *Le Sacre du Printemps*, that propulsive, innovative ballet which was first performed in a staged version in 1913. At its premiere it was greeted with ridicule and contempt—it was Nijinsky's first attempt at choreography and was a highly sexualized treatment of the theme; but it was vindicated in 1914 in a concert version under Pierre Monteux that established it as *the* musical landmark. The intense impact of *Le Sacre du Printemps* was not due to any harmonic breakthrough, but rather to the completely unconventional treatment of rhythm that conveyed instinctual forces unimpeded by intellect.

In retrospect, the most important result of the success of *The Rite of Spring* was the triumph of tonality and diatonicism over atonality and chromaticism, which had achieved their quintessential expression one year earlier in *Pierrot Lunaire*. Stravinsky's success set the stage for the next forty years. By the '30s, neoclassicism had prevailed, virtually drowning dodecaphony. It was neoclassicism that Hindemith celebrated in Germany, that Prokofiev and Shostakovich practiced in Russia, that Milhaud, Honegger, and Poulenc followed in France, and that Copland and his disciples embraced in the United States. And it was neoclassicism that Boulez attacked with such vitriolic words at the concert of Stravinsky's American works while he was a student at the Paris Conservatoire. The attack was motivated, in part, because neoclassicism was the "old" language and in part, Boulez says today, "because Stravinsky was such an idol, such a god." Whatever the motivation, the effect was clear: Stravinsky knew that, in Europe at least, he was in disrepute among the young.

In 1948 Stravinsky met the young conductor Robert Craft, who was leading an amateur chamber group in New York. Craft did not share Boulez's intellectual bias; he was enthusiastic not only about many dodecaphonic works but about the neoclassic Stravinsky as well. Craft reports that he "adored" Stravinsky and set about performing musical chores for him. In 1948, when Stravinsky was receiving few performances anywhere, Craft conducted the *Symphony for Wind Instruments* in Town Hall. Craft invaded Stravinsky's life so successfully—in fact he lived and traveled with Stravinsky, shared conducting chores and meals with him, and played recorded music for the older man—that he was able to promote certain aesthetic ideas, most particularly the idea of the twelve-tone technique.

In July 1951, Schoenberg died. This event set into motion a chain of events which led Stravinsky to abandon neoclassicism and to embrace the serial language; just as almost half a century before, Rimsky-Korsakov's death had led him to abandon a Germanic structure and adopt the Rimsky sound for the *Firebird, Petrushka,* and *The Rite of Spring.* While the prime innovator of a technique was alive, Stravinsky was unable to make use of that man's idea; pride prevented him from doing so. But once that formidable figure was dead, Stravinsky could readily incorporate and assimilate his technique without the slightest loss of identity.

So, in October 1951, less than three months after Schoenberg's death, Stravinsky made his first postwar trip to Europe and scheduled a stop at Baden-Baden. There he listened to the tape of *Polyphonie X* made at its premiere in Donaueschingen. Craft says that it was the "nose-thumbing force of the work that impressed the composer of *The Rite of Spring,* who may have been reminded of his own 1913 premiere, for *Polyphonie X* was at times all but drowned out by the laughter, shouts, hoots, and whistling."

In January and February of 1952, Craft repeatedly played for Stravinsky a recording of Webern's *Opus 22 Quartet.* Stravinsky showed the powerful effects of that score by composing, in April, the *Cantata* for soprano, tenor, female chorus, and orchestra in which he used the serial technique for the first time. Thus, Stravinsky began to use a method that gave rise to the kind of music he had claimed to abhor all his life. He was able to do this partly because of Craft's guidance and partly because Schoenberg was, as Boulez wrote, finally "dead!"

In May 1952 Stravinsky attended the Paris concert in which Boulez and Messiaen played *Structures.* According to Craft, Stravinsky was struck by the "arrogance" of the work. Clearly Stravinsky was drawn by the aggression and toughness of the man as reflected in his rocklike, nonflabby art. Stravinsky talked with Heinrich Strobel who gave him the following picture of the then current musical scene in Europe: Neoclassicism was *out;* Boulanger, Stravinsky's ardent defender, a spent force. Serialism was *in;* Boulez, Stravinsky's strident attacker, the man on top. In the fall of 1952 Stravinsky assisted at several rehearsals of *Polyphonie X* in Hollywood and even made an analysis of the score. Then he let it generally be known that he would very much like to meet Boulez, the revolutionary who had publicly set out to do him in.

This was not the first time in his career that Stravinsky swallowed personal abuse. In 1917 the Ballets Russes was signed for an American tour and scheduled to play the Metropolitan Opera House in New York. Stravinsky wanted to conduct his own ballets there, but the management never sent him the contract. Just before the company's second American tour, which was marked by the same neglect, Stravinsky asked Diaghilev to boycott the engagement. Diaghilev refused, and, according to the account given by Nijinsky's wife, Stravinsky visited Nijinsky in a rage, crying and cursing at Diaghilev. Nevertheless, on Diaghilev's return to Europe Stravinsky traveled to Spain to greet him there. Stravinsky often overlooked indignities—whether they came from his father or mother (not very loving parents), or from Rimsky-Korsakov (a not very loving teacher), or even from the complex and ambivalent Robert Craft.

It is therefore not at all surprising that in the fall of 1952, when Boulez was in New York for the first time, he was invited as a guest along with Stravinsky to dinner at Virgil Thomson's apartment in the Chelsea Hotel. There were a number of other musicians there as well. Thomson describes the evening this way: "Everyone there expected trouble because of Boulez's repeated and violent attacks on Stravinsky. That didn't happen. The two hit like comets. They sat together. Shortly after dinner Stravinsky left. Boulez remained for three or four hours in a very excited state. Before leaving, Stravinsky invited Boulez to visit him the next day."

Boulez accepted the invitation. The personal contact between the two composers resulted in a kind of truce. Boulez stopped speaking disrespectfully of Stravinsky, and Stravinsky began to speak eloquently about Boulez. This was natural. Each deeply admired the other's talents and, as Virgil Thomson says, "Stravinsky needed the support of the young, while Boulez was pleased to have Papa's blessing."

Boulez tells the story of the Thomson party: "Everyone waited for the clash between Stravinsky and me because of my past polemics against him. It didn't occur. As it turned out, Jean Morel was at the party, and I didn't know who he was. There was a discussion of *Carmen*. That is not my favorite opera and I said so. Morel thought I was attacking him because he had conducted it so much at the Met. So he left. People saw that. They were surprised—because they didn't expect trouble with Morel. The trouble they expected was with Stravinsky.

"On the contrary, there was no trouble with Stravinsky at all. As far as polemics are concerned, we never discussed them. Polemics are tied to a year or period. To survive musically you must be in touch with your time. The meeting took place soon after Stravinsky composed *The Rake's Progress*. He picked up on Webern at about that time."

The adoption of the serial idea by the giant of the neoclassic movement has been characterized by musicologist Hans Keller as the most profound surprise in the history of music. But Stravinsky explained

97

his ways in more modest terms. "Rape," he said, "may be justified by the creation of a child." Thus, Stravinsky in 1920 "raped" Pergolesi for *Pulcinella*, later raped Tchaikovsky for *Le Baiser de la Fée*, still later raped Mozart for *The Rake's Progress*, and, after 1952, repeatedly and passionately raped Webern.

Stravinsky's ravishing of the quiet Viennese may have replaced for him the musical oxygen that had begun to run out. For, just before *The Rake's Progress*, Stravinsky had devoted himself to the reorchestration of old scores (the lack of a copyright agreement between the United States and the Soviet Union prevented him from collecting royalties on his earlier, popular pieces) as well as to a series of hack ventures. He arranged the *Firebird* as a pop song for America's juke boxes, wrote a circus polka for Barnum and Bailey elephants, and ground out a number of movie scores all of which were turned down: *Song of Bernadette*, *Jane Eyre*, and *The Moon is Down*. But in Webern he found a new way to make music that would sustain him for the rest of his life. The serial idea motivated not only the *Cantata* but also *In Memoriam Dylan Thomas*, *Three Songs from Shakespeare*, *Canticum Sacrum*, *Agon*, *Threni*, *Movements for Piano and Orchestra*, *A Sermon, a Narrative and a Prayer*, *Abraham and Isaac*, and the *Variations*. Thus, in his late sixties and throughout his seventies, Stravinsky composed as prolifically as he did when he was a young man. What aged artist would not be elated to produce such progeny as these!

Elated and grateful. In 1955 Stravinsky acknowledged his debt to the Idea. For *Die Reihe*, an abstruse German journal dedicated to serialism and edited by Stockhausen, he wrote an eloquent tribute to Webern: "The 15 of September, 1945, the day of Anton Webern's death, should be a day of mourning for any receptive musician. We must hail not only this great composer but also a real hero. Doomed to a total failure in a deaf world of ignorance and indifference, he inexorably kept cutting his diamonds, the mines of which he had such a perfect knowledge."

Like Boulez, Stravinsky was drawn to Webern for the hard, clean edges of his music, for the nonrhetorical, nonexpressionistic purity of his art. And, like Boulez, Stravinsky was prepared to deify Webern, particularly if that meant annihilating Schoenberg—for the ghost of the proud Viennese still hovered. Thus Stravinsky and Boulez shared a common purpose, motivated by taste and private need.

In addition, each found much that was agreeable in the other. Stravinsky was "captivated," Craft reports, "by Boulez with his new musical ideas, and an extraordinary intelligence, quickness, and sense of humor." Boulez, in turn, was awed by Stravinsky's life-style and told several friends he would try to emulate it. He had never, he said, seen an artist live so grandly before.

At the end of 1952 Boulez returned to Paris. Although he had not succeeded with Cage and Babbitt, he did have Pousseur and Stockhausen in his camp and was assured of Stravinsky's blessings as well. But almost as soon as he had succeeded in controlling a totally serial world—not only with *Structures* but also through the recruitment of the talented young and old—Boulez began to break away from that world. Indeed, he pinpointed the problem inside serial research from the start: it lay in its rigidity.

When Stockhausen and Boulez first met, the younger man showed the older his first serial piece, *Kontra-Punkte*, a thirteen-minute work for ten instruments, including piano, which was divided into a number of sections and written in the manner he had learned from Goeyvaerts. Boulez told him the piece was too rigid, that he should find a way to render it more baroque. He would like to see more density, more vitality to the score. Stockhausen altered the composition so as to suit Boulez and at the same time maintain his artistic independence; he retained the original treatment in alternate sections and embellished the remaining ones in different ways. Thus, the final version of *Kontra-Punkte* was not an expression of rigid serialism in the pristine sense of Boulez's *Structures*. Still, it satisfied the aesthetic requirements of the new syntax: the score contains no repetition, variation, or development, nor was there any apparent contrast in the sense of extended sections that vary in character, mood, or key.

A similar sequence of events took place between Pousseur and Boulez. The young Belgian composer showed Boulez an early piece for three pianos tuned in 1/6 tones. Boulez declared it too mechanical and suggested ways of loosening it up. Pousseur made the suggested changes. Today Pousseur says, "Boulez was ahead of Stockhausen and me at that time."

And indeed the polemics Boulez then engaged in were directed against those who followed his lead too strenuously. "Having been preceded by a generation in part illiterate are we to become a generation of technocrats?" he asked in the essay "... Auprès et au loin" published in 1954. In that article, Boulez wrote that his generation could now take leave of its predecessors and concern itself with the problems within the serial syntax. He pointed out several seemingly self-evident truths: that all the elements of music are not of equal importance—some, like pitch, can be heard more precisely than others, that because there are twelve notes in the chromatic scale it does not follow that the other parameters should be divided twelve ways, and that some instruments are louder than others. He concluded that the composer's function is to choose among possibilities. It was not only talk. He wrote to Pousseur, "After all this work, I am writing an oeuvrette." The oeuvrette turned out to be *Le Marteau sans Maître*, his third work based on poetry by René Char, the piece hailed by Stravinsky as the best work Boulez's generation had then produced. In 1955 Boulez told associates, "*Marteau sans Maître* is my *Pierrot Lunaire*."

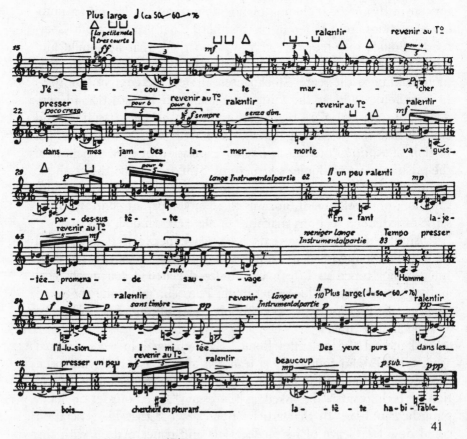

In *Le Marteau sans Maître*, the dynamics and rhythm of Boulez's music follow the accent and meter of Char's poetry.

100

In *Par Volonté et Par Hasard*, a book of interviews that appeared in 1975, Boulez expostulates about what he set out to do:

There are three cycles based on three different poems. These three poems produce different pieces. One cycle gives rise to three, the next to two, the last to four. But instead of presenting these pieces one right after the other, I distributed them in such a manner that they would actually penetrate one another. So you see that as early as *Marteau*, I was making an effort to obtain an effect of permeability, to create a dimension different from the closed musical form. The fact that there are not one but several continuities, that the cycles penetrate one another, that the last piece is a microcosm of the whole work, constitutes an important first step towards the effective breaking of traditional musical continuity.

In *Marteau* the notation does not exceed the limits of conventional notation; it is simply more complex. The changes in tempo are very striking; in some pieces the tempo is constantly fluctuating. Despite the innovations that Boulez now points to, *Marteau* is the first of his post-1948 works that appear to be haunted by elements of the past. It is almost as if Boulez had to formulate a new syntax before he could relax and draw on some of the music he loved. The length of the pieces and their sequence remind the listener of *Pierrot Lunaire*. The percussive treatment and rhythmic invention recall early Stravinsky. The tenuous balance of sound and silence, the athematicism of the plinking and plonking strings, all this owes a large debt to Webern.

The work is divided into nine sections. The purely instrumental movements function as preludes and postludes to four movements that contain the setting of Char's words. Unlike *Visage Nuptial* and *Soleil des Eaux*, Boulez chose the shortest poems, sometimes just a few lines. No two movements are scored alike, although the sixth and last make use of all the performers: flute, viola, guitar, vibraphone, xylophone, percussion, and alto voice. Boulez's "Eastern" instrumentation, which seemed so fresh at the time, has been copied by scores of composers.

Techniques used in *Polyphonie X* and *Structures* are used again here, no longer as ends in themselves but rather, as Boulez says, "to formulate thoughts." The composer's alterations of tempo, his holding back and thrusting forth of movement, his startling breaks in sound are characteristic of the piece and serve to further Char's message, which is that we are in the grip of a civilization that is marching inexorably towards its doom, independent of the individual. For Boulez the "hammer without a master" appears not only to be civiliza-

101

tion in general but an automatized musical system in particular, a "timetable of trains," he has called it, "that never move." As Boulez looked around at his own disciples and at the composers in Darmstadt, he found them being drowned in serial charts. In his essays and *Marteau* he tried to "save" them.

For in contrast to *Structures*, what Boulez was concerned with in *Marteau* was the making of music, not system. Here Boulez introduces a soft resonance which displaces his early pointillistic style. Here Boulez exhibits a complete union of word and sound and does that despite the use of a poem in which each word has a weight and meaning of its own. Here Boulez creates a work of art notable for its delicacy of feeling, for its fineness of musical thought. But the wild, free spirit of the early days is gone. Neither "violent" nor "brutal" appears in this score; there is little more aggressive than "moins lent" or "assez vite." The formidable inhibitions that gave birth to *Structures*, the annihilation of personality that that work suggests, has been transformed to far more artistic purposes in *Marteau*, but the essence of the inhibition remains intact. The personality of Webern has finally triumphed.

Because of Boulez's guarded nature, because of his refusal to reveal personal details, one cannot know what happened in his mid-twenties to move him to distrust his own imagination and invention and invest his faith in theory and system. It may be that nothing in particular occurred. If that is the case, the shift can be attributed partly to a return to his earlier ways, when system and order took precedence over everything else, and partly a result of his newly acquired deified position—articles by and about him were circulating everywhere—in which he felt it necessary not only always to be "right" but also to proclaim a set of commandments to the world, much as Schoenberg had done before him. Boulez's fame threatened to become a kind of death mask.

Whether Boulez's loss of spontaneity was due to personal or cultural factors is not of critical importance in his story. The fact remains that the prodigious invention of *Visage Nuptial*, the *Flute Sonatina*, *Le Soleil des Eaux*, and the early piano sonatas was replaced in *Polyphonie X* and *Structures* with a tight, closed, hermetic formula. Boulez himself was horrified by the result. He says *Structures* was not "Total but Totalitarian." And he tried to twist and unlock the system with *Marteau*. Here, in contrast to the transparency of *Structures Book I*, the machinery of twelve-note organization is so complex that it is impossible to trace the steps which lead from one pitch to the next.

Still, the early fire did not return. Rather than escape from his prison, Boulez successfully transformed that prison into an exquisite, secret-filled room.

10

As Pousseur said, in advocating a freer use of the serial language, Boulez was ahead of both Stockhausen and himself in 1952–53. But if "ahead" is to be interpreted as in the vanguard, then John Cage was ahead of them all.

Inspired in part by Zen teachings, Cage began self-consciously to remove his own will, to remove his own personality from his work. He says *Music of Changes* did not go far enough, for, although he did not choose the progression of sounds—that was dictated by the flipping of coins—he did choose the sounds themselves; and once those sounds were notated on the score the performer was forced into performing what was there. To go a step further than the chance operations of this piece, Cage composed the *Imaginary Landscape No. 4* for twelve radios and twenty-four players. Twelve pairs of instrumentalists sit on either side of the podium as though they were string players in a conventional orchestra. One of each pair holds the radio, the other tunes it, and a conductor presides over the action with a score. Thus Cage manipulates a dozen radios according to a precise schedule of durations and dynamics. The experiment was one of combining exactitude and chance.

The dress rehearsal for the first performance was held on a weekday afternoon when there was music on virtually all the stations. But the premiere occurred at the end of a long concert—after midnight—

when news programs dominated the air. The audience at Columbia's McMillin Theater did not like what they heard. In France the reaction would have been called a "scandale."

In reply to the criticism he received, Cage issued *4' and 33"* (four minutes and thirty-three seconds). He says he had had the piece in his mind since 1947 but did not believe it would be taken seriously then. "By 1952 it was necessary," he says.

On an evening late in August, pianist David Tudor walked onto a stage in the "art" community of Woodstock, New York and bowed, placed a score on the piano, and sat down on a stool. He remained seated, not playing for four minutes and thirty-three seconds. He did not touch the keyboard nor did he produce any other audible sound by attacking any other part of the instrument. Thus the "music" of this piece consists of the collection of unintelligible sounds that occur during the particular period of time that the pianist is seated at his instrument.

Surely this "work" represented no effort on Cage's part to revise or renew any art work of the past. Surely it represented no effort on Cage's part to transform any aspect of his artistic inheritance. Rather was it a strong theatrical gesture designed to obliterate the past, to obliterate everything from Machaut through Boulez. Implicit in this now famous work is the assumption that individual personality should be dissolved, that artistic form should be destroyed, that the formerly self-confident bourgeois listener should distrust all values of beauty and truth. Over and above everything else, *4' and 33"* loudly proclaims to its listeners that "uneventful" time is the best of all possible time and that individual talent is nothing more than a fiction, a fraud that has been perpetrated on the western world.

On his return from Woodstock to New York, Cage resumed the work he had begun the year before in the electronic music studio of Louis and Bebe Barron on Eighth Street in Greenwich Village. There, with David Tudor, Earle Brown, Christian Wolff, and Morton Feldman, he worked on building up a laboratory of sounds. Cage applied to the Rockefeller Foundation for aid but was turned down. Then Paul Williams, a student of architecture at Black Mountain College and a wealthy man, stepped into the financial void. Cage's first bona fide electronic piece, *Williams Mix*, on which he worked for nine months, consisted of a series of collages made up of over six hundred tapes and assembled through *I Ching* principles.

Strobel invited Cage and Tudor to the Donaueschingen Festival, October 1954, the festival at which *Marteau sans Maître* was scheduled for its premiere. (Boulez says that because a guitarist could not be found at that time, the first performance was delayed until June of the following year.) Strobel commissioned a piece for two prepared pianos, and Cage, delighted to be part of this serious enterprise, accepted and planned the following program: *Williams Mix*, Earle Brown's *Octet*, Christian Wolff's *Suite*, Morton Feldman's *Intersections*, and the new work, *31' 57.9864"* or *34' 46.776"*. Cage and Tudor arranged for as many performances as they could, playing much of the same material in Paris, Brussels, Stockholm, Milan, Zurich, and London.

For *31' 57.9864"* or *34' 46.776"* Cage prepared two piano scores, neither of which had any relation to the other. All the rhythms were indicated in space—an inch is equal to a certain amount of time— not in conventional durational symbols. Thus, the title indicates the passing of minutes and seconds as well as the passing of feet and inches. In addition to this innovative idea, Cage added a stroke of theater: he and Tudor would rise from their instruments and walk around and climb underneath them from time to time. This was Cage's first major effort to promote the performer at what, from the outside, most assuredly appears to be the expense of the creator. But Tudor was not an ordinary performer. In fact, his performances were probably as responsible for the success of the "new" art as were Cage's scores or lecture demonstrations.

Plans were made to make the trip by ship. Merce Cunningham, M. C. Richards, and Earle and Carolyn Brown came down to the dock to see them off. The first night out their ship rammed another. Tudor reports that Cage went "into a tizzy, screaming 'Save the scores!' "—they had manuscripts aboard of Boulez, Stockhausen, and several American colleagues. The scores as well as the passengers were saved, and they flew to Europe instead. Thus Cage and Tudor arrived ahead of schedule.

Cage spent the additional time in Donaueschingen going over the program with Strobel. Unfortunately, according to Cage, Strobel demanded an audition and hated everything he heard. "Strobel insisted that we cut the entire program down to only thirty minutes," Cage recalls. "Finally I agreed to do that, providing we could invite those in the audience to remain who wanted to hear the rest of what we had brought."

While Cage was in Donaueschingen, Tudor traveled to Cologne where he met Stockhausen for the first time. Stockhausen and Cage had never met. All that Stockhausen knew about Cage was Boulez's abhorrence of his music. Boulez demanded of composition that it be "rigorous" and "consequent"; Cage's pieces did not fulfill these criteria.

At their first meeting Tudor played Stockhausen Part I and Part IV of Cage's *Music of Changes*, Christian Wolff's *Piece for Prepared Piano*, and Feldman's *Intersection III*. Tudor says Stockhausen "was fascinated by the newness of the sounds and by the variety of keyboard attacks, particularly by the clusters Feldman used. Stockhausen's interest and excitement was obvious. For years he continued with the desire to know the music coming from John Cage and his group."

But other Europeans were not so hospitable. Everywhere Cage and Tudor went they were treated like a couple of clowns. At Donaueschingen the audience was angry and the press outraged. Complaints focused on the "noise." In describing the Cage-Tudor event to Boulez, Strobel characterized it as "poor Dada."

By the time Cage and Tudor arrived in Cologne, Stockhausen had had over a year's experience building up an electronic studio there. After his studies at the Paris Conservatoire, which had begun in January 1952, he had returned home in May 1953 to work at the West German Radio's electronic studio under the direction of Herbert Eimert, critic for the *Kölnisches Rundschau*. The studio, which had opened unofficially two years before, was begun under the aegis of Dr. Werner Meyer-Eppler of the Institute of Communication Theory of the University of Bonn. Dr. Meyer-Eppler, together with Herbert Eimert and Robert Beyer gave the first demonstration of electronic music in Germany. Beyer introduced the word "parameter" into music, borrowing it from mathematics apparently to give weight and dignity to what otherwise would be called an element or dimension. The parameters of a musical tone are its pitch, rhythm, dynamics, articulation, texture, and register, each of which was to be subjected to permutation.

At Cologne the sine tone was the raw material, produced by an electronic generator and then manipulated on tape. In contrast to the tape studios in Paris and New York (the Columbia music faculty had set up a laboratory on its campus), the one in Cologne concentrated on generating sound electronically. The production of electronically generated sound was discussed in Cologne as early as 1949 by Robert Beyer, who had engaged in such speculation since the 1920s.

Thus, when Stockhausen arrived in Cologne in the spring of 1953, he found a large and impressive body of electronic theory that could be allied to the serial principle. With the sine tone one could achieve the precision mandatory in the most complex serial works. "Work and material have the same structure" became the teaching motto at Cologne, distinguishing it from the *musique concrète* of the Paris and New York studios where the emphasis was on sound and texture. In *Studie I*, Stockhausen's first work at Cologne (he discounts his earlier work done at Schaeffer's studio), technique and material are one and the same. The piece is bone-dry, without any flesh at all. Stockhausen produced it shortly after Boulez had directed him, in connection with *Kontra-Punkte*, to try for a less rigid approach to art.

In December 1953, seven months after he had left Paris and one year before he was to meet Cage, Stockhausen invited Boulez and Pousseur to a festival of new music at Cologne in which works were to be played that had been made by Eimert, Beyer, and himself. En route Boulez told Pousseur that he did not expect to like what he was going to hear. He said he thought one heard sine tones as single pitches, not as whole sound entities. What he heard confirmed his expectations. He told Stockhausen that "to produce what you have done I would have preferred an orchestra of sine tones that was, at least, manipulated by people. I would even prefer the use of a ring modulator for that would have added considerable richness to the sound." An intense discussion ensued. Boulez dates the beginning of his break with Stockhausen from the end of 1953, just a little more than a year after they had met. "There was always the root of a split," he says. "Stockhausen had a strong ego from the start."

But Stockhausen's initial refusal to loosen the reins of his electronic work did not mean he was generically opposed to loose reins. The impetus to let them fly wide was provided, one year after Boulez's visit, by the arrival of Tudor and Cage in Cologne. Here was an ironic turn of events. By its call for precision, serial music had accelerated the development of electronically generated sound. But almost at the very moment when the electronic medium made that precision a reality, instrumental music became the suitable arm for freeing just about everything.

As egos go, Boulez's, of course, was not weak. But the arrogance he had displayed in the early years of his career became less apparent when he began to receive recognition. And he received it in turn from the Barraults, Souvchinsky, Strobel, and Suzanne Tezenas, then from the thoroughgoing professional, Roger Desormière, the first conductor to perform Boulez's work and perhaps the finest French conductor of his generation.

By the early 1950s, therefore, Boulez was well known in avant-garde circles throughout Europe. His polemics made him famous among intellectuals outside the arena of modern music. Within it, pianists grappled with his *Second Sonata*, and composers paid attention to his most recent verbal utterance. The serial language, which he identifies as his own, was on the road to becoming *the* musical language of the post-Einsteinian age.

Late in 1953, Boulez proclaimed that it was time for his generation "to prove itself with a series of chamber concerts that would serve as a means of communication between the composers of our time and the public that is interested in its time." This was the first occasion on which he indicated any concern about bringing the listener closer to his own musical world.

Boulez persuaded the Barraults to launch a modest series of chamber concerts at the Petit-Marigny, a tiny, airless theater with wooden seats. The series soon expanded; it became known as the Domaine Musical. Boulez did virtually everything. He invited the people, determined the repertoire, handled the library, collected the patrons' checks, put up the chairs and stands, selected the performers, edited the program notes, handed the musicians the cash himself, and put out one issue of a journal, *The Domaine Musical*, which included essays by Stockhausen, Pousseur, Nono, and himself. His contribution, "Incipit," was an unqualified tribute to Webern. Boulez dropped the journal after the first issue because his work with Barrault, the Domaine, and his own composition did not leave time for such a taxing enterprise. The next year, Universal Edition began to publish *Die Reihe*, a revival of its *Anbruch* of the 1920s; the journal did not appear regularly, only when there was enough material.

During the early years of the Domaine, Boulez did very little conducting, delegating this responsibility to Hermann Scherchen. He says he found very few conductors who were competent in the contemporary repertoire and willing to take on the risks involved. Apart from Scherchen there was Hans Rosbaud, whom Boulez invited along with the Sudwestfunk orchestra. According to Boulez, these two men were practically the only ones capable, and he adds that what was even more striking was the fact that both were then around sixty years old. "There were no younger men who could assist them besides myself."

In his initial statement of aims, Boulez wrote that he would offer . works that played a vital role in the evolution of music, particularly those rarely performed pieces by Stravinsky, Bartók, Varèse, Debussy, the Viennese school ("especially Webern so little known in France where he is practically ignored"), as well as the motets of Machaut and Dufay, the madrigals of Gesualdo, Bach's *Musical Offering,* and pieces by Messiaen, Stockhausen, Nono, Pousseur, Fano, Maderna (Boulez had not yet met Luciano Berio whose work would be often performed at the Domaine), and Cage, Brown, Wolff, Barraqué, and Phillipot. Even then Boulez presented pieces he did not like, offering them as "documents."

But he concentrated on those compositions he loved. Between 1954 and 1964 the Domaine Musical presented almost sixty percent of the combined works of Schoenberg, Webern, and Berg. Often these works were being played in Paris for the first time. In 1957 Hans Rosbaud conducted the Sudwestfunk in the first Paris performance of Berg's *Three Pieces for Orchestra Opus 6,* almost fifty years after it was composed. Boulez says that, before the Domaine, when Schoenberg and Berg were played in Paris they were performed so badly that there was no relation between the scores and what the listeners heard.

The first program of the Domaine Musical took place on January 13, 1954, and presented Stravinsky's *Renard* (not only because it was composed during Boulez's favorite "pre-neoclassic" period of Stravinsky but also because Barrault could provide the mimes), pieces by Stockhausen and Nono, and Webern's *Opus 24 Concerto.* Boulez invariably offered very long programs. American pianist Paul Jacobs recalls the following incident. In 1954, in response to a request from William Glock, then editor of the English music journal *The Score,* to prepare an interview with Boulez, Jacobs visited the composer on Rue Beautreillis. Boulez had heard Jacobs play the year before but had assumed then that Jacobs was touring Europe. When the pianist told him he had settled in Paris, Boulez handed him a pile of scores and said they were to be played in ten days. "In other words," Jacobs notes, "the program had been listed and scheduled but there was no one to play the pieces. It was an immense program—almost five hours —which included Berg's *Lyric Suite,* pieces by Webern and Bartok, several by the French, e.g. Phillipot and a number of other compositions as well. There was too much on one program but Boulez often made that mistake." The fact is that Boulez demands of others as much as he demands of himself. He appears either not to care what the "other" thinks and feels or he assumes that everyone else should be as indefatigable as he is.

In this case the people took what he dished out. The series became fashionable very quickly, attracting both the far-out and the chic. But the cost proved to be prohibitive for the Barraults, who bore the deficit for the first season but could not do it again, offering only their theater rent-free. There was no question of state support; in the early years, the French Radio would not broadcast a single program. Private funds finally came from Suzanne Tezenas, who made Boulez and the Domaine the primary concern of her life.

Because of the shift in patronage in 1955, the series' name was changed from Les Concerts du Petit-Marigny to the Domaine Musical. Mme Tezenas not only gave her own money but worked very hard to get contributions. After each concert she gave a lavish reception attended not only by the very wealthy but by painters and men of letters as well. In a short time she succeeded in inducing members of the *haute bourgeoisie*—including Mme Robert Germaine who owned property in Algeria, and the Baron and Baroness Philippe de Rothschild—to become members of the Board. Even Nadia Boulanger, Mme Tezenas reports, "was a little member, right from the beginning. At that time we had so many people against us. Like Sauguet and Marie Blanche de Polignac, whose aunt had presided over the Stravinsky-Boulanger salon before the war. Yet Mme Boulanger came regularly to the concerts. She would say, 'You are occupying yourself with scientific music' but she came, nevertheless.

"Almost everyone was against us in those days. Modern music was for Austria, not for France. There is something about French nationalism that makes this so. When we gave *Pierrot Lunaire*, Poulenc and Auric told me that they had heard the premiere in Berlin. Still they would not expose that composition here. Auric was the only one, the only French composer, who helped us at the beginning. He was one of the first members of the Domaine Musical."

The antagonism of the Establishment in France only heightened the success of the Domaine, for, as Sir William Glock explains, "There is a snobbish support among the French for contemporary art." Pousseur recalls the atmosphere of the concerts: "The climate was immensely favorable. There was incredible fervor. Soon Boulez had to do the same program twice. The house sat only 200 people, so he did it Saturday night and Sunday afternoon. On Sunday morning he would moderate a round table discussion and those involved in that particular concert would talk about the pieces in that program. In those early years we thought we had found a common language and were together in trying to strengthen it.

"If I were to pinpoint the decision that I think was fatal to Boulez," Pousseur, a Marxist, went on, "it was the involvement of the *haute bourgeoisie*. This seems to have changed his attitude towards musical

111

life. To get money for his cause he started this particular business. Then he found himself very well in the world, very comfortable in the *grand monde*."

Thus, by the mid-1950s, Boulez, enemy of the status quo, was king of the musical avant-garde. Writing about him a few years later, Souvchinsky claimed, "There are not many who, between the ages of twenty-two and twenty-six, succeeded not only in making a mark on their art, but in changing its face and even its essence."

11

Boulez's sister says, "Pierre has no trouble with women because women are not important to him. He has no trouble with cats and dogs either."

Confronted with information about the early affair that precipitated *Visage Nuptial*, Boulez acknowledges that it took place and that it culminated in a double suicide pact. But he refuses to identify the object of his passion or to say anything more than that the person was "neither intellectual nor intelligent." He adds that in such matters "only one can be strong; the other weak." Boulez's demand for inequality in bed does not preclude extremely decent behavior with women out of bed. And in fact he maintains such friendships with a few women, friendships that are remarkably free of the intensity and the breaks that generally characterize his relations with men.

To say that Boulez's emotional life has nothing to do with women is not to deny him an emotional life. It is rather to assign his feeling for ideas its due and heroic place. And because ideas have generally been embodied in men, here Boulez is out to conquer and destroy. Between 1945 and 1952 Webern displaced Schoenberg, Leibowitz displaced Messiaen, and Strobel displaced Souvchinsky in his life. Robert Craft, who through his ties to Stravinsky knew Pierre Souvchinsky well, says Souvchinsky was bitterly jealous at this turn of events. But Craft is quick to add that "Souvchinsky himself was typically French:

bright, faddish, quick to pick up a new talent and to exploit the new at the expense of the old." Souvchinsky's shift from Stravinsky to Boulez provides the prototypical example of what Craft has in mind.

In fact such intellectual jousting, playing people as though they were pawns in a chess game, appears to be a popular French sport. There is something unique about the lycée discipline which encourages a curious kind of self-denying rigidity coupled with an imaginative rationalization that leaves little room for intimacy and accounts for a good deal in Boulez's temperament and behavior. In any case, if one wants to get anywhere in France—or, for that matter, in most countries—it helps to have a steel-tempered soul: how better to test the quality of the steel than to engage in combat with the powerful father, be he composer, teacher, or conseiller of the arts. To carry the question one step further: how better to test one's ultimate strength than to insult, attack, and repudiate one's country and then move on to bigger and better nations?

Boulez's move to Germany took place in cautious, somewhat tentative steps. The summer courses at Darmstadt—held in a local school where the guests could be housed and fed—began to function under the aegis of Wolfgang Steinecke in 1946. Although Boulez was by then immersed in Schoenberg and Webern, the German program still clung to neoclassicism: Stravinsky, Hindemith, and Prokofiev. Leibowitz arrived in Darmstadt in 1948 and singlehandedly changed all that.

By 1949 dodecaphony was the prevailing aesthetic there. But Boulez did not make the trip until 1952 when he had already premiered Structures in Paris and knew the serial language was under control in his hands.

That same year, 1952, Boulez left his French publishers, Heugel and Amphion, and moved to Universal Edition, the Viennese house of Schoenberg, Webern, and Berg. Stockhausen introduced him to Alfred Schlee, director of Universal Edition, when Schlee was on a visit to Paris. Significantly, Structures was the first Boulez work Universal Edition printed. It may be that "à la limite du fertile pays," which the composer inscribed on the score, did not imply the end of fertile ground—as Boulez now claims—but rather the beginning of a new and fruitful grammar that he then felt would be as life-sustaining as tonality had once been. And so it was only right and proper that, on the eve of what he anticipated would be a lengthy voyage, Boulez should establish roots in an Austro-German world.

Although Darmstadt was not physically glamorous—the school took over a tent and a few buildings that were evacuated by the

Seventh Day Adventists—it was bursting with vitality in the mid-'50s. Richard Bennett, a British student of Boulez, says that until he went to Darmstadt in 1955 he had heard only one piece by Webern in London. "To hear Berio, Stockhausen, the *Flute Sonatina* by Boulez—you cannot imagine how fantastic that was! Either you were at *the* performance in Darmstadt or you knew you wouldn't hear that masterpiece for a very long time."

Still, Boulez says he had reservations about Darmstadt. Although his works were played there a good deal, and although he appeared sporadically to conduct and lecture (in 1956, '59, '60, '61, and '65), he says he was not often physically present and that he never identified with Darmstadt's activities. The Germans devoured Boulez's serialism as thoroughly as they had devoured Leibowitz's dodecaphony and Boulez was critical from the start of the obsessive way composers were handling the serial language. According to Pousseur, he was also critical of Steinecke. "As early as 1954 and 1955," Pousseur says, "Boulez spoke of Darmstadt with disgust. He said it was boring, there were always the same heads, that Steinecke was a fat bear who was never talking, always smiling, that he was nothing more than an organizer who profited from what Boulez, Stockhausen, and I did."

If Boulez complained privately about Darmstadt, he was no more sanguine about France. "The French Establishment," he says, "was exactly like it had been before the war. It loved the neoclassical Stravinsky and hated the Viennese school. Only Max Deutsch, a third-rate musician, and Leibowitz, a hanger-on to the Merleau-Ponty group, were promoting the Viennese. I wanted to show you had to promote the Viennese not because you were a 'left-over' but for the right reasons. It was a kind of guerrilla warfare."

Thus, while Stockhausen was working in Cologne absorbing the effects of his encounter with Tudor and Cage, Boulez was engaged in guerrilla warfare in Paris fighting the tradition that pervaded Parisian musical life. His fight against authority did not interfere with his creative work. On the contrary, it appeared to nourish him. It was, after all, in the early years of his career, when he was virtually the only rebel, that Boulez appears to have been sustained by a prolonged ecstasy of creation.

In the mid-'50s, Boulez worked obsessively. He not only did everything for the Domaine Musical, but he continued to publish articles in journals and to serve as music director for Barrault, going on a second (1954) and third (1956) South American tour with him. Still, composition took precedence over everything else. In 1955 Boulez

115

wrote the score for Barrault's *Orestes*, and between October 1954 and April 1955 he completed *Marteau sans Maître*, doubling the note values, which he says were much too small, and adding the ninth and final movement. The first performance of *Marteau* took place in June 1955 at the International Society for Contemporary Music Festival in Baden-Baden, with Hans Rosbaud conducting the Südwestfunk. Boulez conducted a second performance at the Domaine in April 1956; the work was then on the second half of a program that included Webern's *Opus 21 Symphony*, Nono's *Incontri*, Stockhausen's *Kontra-Punkte*, and the *Opus 8* and *Opus 13* songs by Webern, all important, "rigorous" works.

Throughout this period Boulez remained faithful to the Barraults, although the elitism of French artistic circles decreed that they, being performers, were not in the same league as Souvchinsky, Strobel, and most of Boulez's newer friends. Boulez also remained loyal to Roger Desormière. In 1952 Desormière suffered a stroke that left him paralyzed. During that time Boulez sent scripts to the French Radio in Desormière's name in order that the conductor could collect the fees. He also escorted Desormière to musical events and social evenings— lifting him in and out of cars—to make life as bearable as he could for the stricken man. This side of Boulez—and the Desormière situation is not exceptional—did not then, as it does not now, reach the public eye. The public sees only the aggressive fighter. Mme Tezenas describes Boulez in the 1950s: "He was terribly trenchant then. He attacked everyone who did not see music in the purist way that he did."

Boulez was insulting not only to critics—he attacked them with obscenities to the press—but also to performing musicians. His treatment of some in *Orestes*—his beating the rhythms on their backs —has been referred to before. But he took out his wrath at imprecision on no less a figure than Hans Rosbaud, whom he met for the first time when Rosbaud was preparing the premiere of *Marteau* for the 1955 ISCM Festival. Boulez went to Baden-Baden to supervise the last eight days of rehearsal—Strobel had arranged for more than fifty sessions!—and stood above and behind Rosbaud in the broadcasting box shouting out every major and minor mistake. William Glock, who by then was intensely interested in Boulez (his publishing Boulez's "Schoenberg is dead!" cost him many friends in Europe and the United States) went to Baden-Baden at Strobel's invitation and reports that Boulez's comments were "so precise, so very tough." And it was not as though Rosbaud was delighted to be there. Hired by

Strobel for the Südwestfunk, he had conducted the premiere of *Polyphonie X* and, according to several reports, genuinely hated the work. Strobel's widow reports: "My husband fought Rosbaud every step of the way. He told Rosbaud that Boulez was a genius, that he would be the new Stravinsky. And he worked on Boulez as well. Strobel told Boulez that to set things right, he should dedicate *Marteau* to Rosbaud." Such an action was not out of character for Boulez, who generally dedicated each of his works to the person who commissioned or conducted it.

Strobel's strategy worked. From then until Rosbaud's death, Rosbaud and Boulez cooperated. In any case, Rosbaud was the first conductor after Desormière to perform any of Boulez's music, so the composer was very much in his debt. But Boulez's primary tie was to Strobel, the eclectic scholar with the sarcastic tone, who could shift his allegiance from Hindemith to Webern. Boulez describes Strobel as "rough-edged and peasantlike, not intellectually articulate like Rosbaud, but a man with extraordinary flair. He had an earthy instinct for things that I liked very much. Rosbaud, on the contrary, was a clever man, like a character out of E. T. A. Hoffmann. It was hard to know what he thought. He was very closed within himself."

It is also hard to know what Boulez thinks, but there is no doubt that he thinks a great deal. In response to which men influenced him, Boulez, without pausing, spills the following names, all of which belong to artists who have rejected tradition in favor of moving into unexplored worlds: "Klee, Kandinsky, Mondrian, Joyce, Char, Michaux, Artaud, Genet, Becket, Messiaen, Webern—of course you know that—Schoenberg, and Stockhausen. Stockhausen had a very strong influence on me."

Curiously Boulez left out the name of Stephane Mallarmé, the Symbolist poet who died in 1898. In 1952, on a train from New York to Baltimore where he was to play at the Peabody Conservatory, Boulez told David Tudor that he would write his masterpiece by the time he was thirty and that it would be based on Mallarmé. Boulez hit the target late; he was thirty-four when *Pli Selon Pli* was completed. But it turned out that Mallarmé moved his art a good deal more than by just providing him with words he chose to set.

Boulez says he was drawn to Mallarmé because of the "density of his texture, because of the obscurity of his language. I like work that resists easy comprehension." He was also drawn to the open form described in Mallarmé's *Livre*. It provided a model for his own formulation of controlled chance which calls for a freedom for the performer limited, to a greater or lesser degree, by instructions from the composer. Boulez considers this formulation one of his most striking contributions. Even Mallarmé's topography influenced Boulez. Perhaps Boulez left Mallarmé off his list because his debt to him was so great.

Boulez was first attracted to Mallarmé because of the analogy he found between his own solutions to compositional problems and Mallarmé's solutions to poetic problems. Rejecting poetry as a decorative exercise, Mallarmé searched for the deeper structure behind the words, for the essence, the music, behind the poetry. Thus Boulez found parallels between Mallarmé and Webern, both lyric artists, who rejected rhetoric and expressionism; what the phonemes in the French phonological system were to Mallarmé, the intervals derived from the twelve-note scale were to Webern. In "Recherches Maintenant," published in La Nouvelle Revue Française in November 1954, Boulez compared Mallarmé's efforts with his own in relation to carving out an ars poetica for music:

These reflections on the composition of the musical work make me hope for a new poetics, a different way of listening. Perhaps it is precisely at this point that music manifests its greatest lag in relation, for example, to poetry. Neither the Mallarmé of the Coup de dés nor Joyce was paralleled by anything in the music of his own time. Is it sensible or absurd to use these points of comparison in this way? (If one thinks of what they loved: the one Wagner; the other Italian opera and Irish songs. . . .)

Although I do not want to refer too closely to their investigations, they having dealt with language, to see them as having been marked by a search for a new musical poetics is not illusory.

Even when the most essential contemporary works reject formal classical schemes, they do not really abandon at all a general idea of form which has not varied since the development of tonality. A musical work is made up of a series of separate movements; each of them is homogeneous in both structure and tempo; it is a closed circuit (a characteristic of Occidental musical thought); balance among its different movements is established by a dynamic distribution of tempos. . . .

For the moment I want to suggest a musical work in which this separation into homogeneous movements will be abandoned in favor of nonhomogeneous distribution of developments. I demand for music the right to parentheses and italics; a notion of discontinuous time, thanks to structures that will be bound together rather than remain divided and airtight; finally a sort of development in which the closed circuit will not be the only solution envisaged.

118

I want the musical work not to be that series of compartments which one must inevitably visit one after the other. I try to think of it as a domain in which, in some manner, one can choose one's own direction.

That essay was published in November 1954, one month before Stockhausen met David Tudor and John Cage. Thus, at this specific juncture, Boulez was ahead of his European colleagues in advocating a break from a strict serial syntax locked into otherwise traditional forms. That to which he addressed himself was the recapturing of the deep meaning that he felt had been lost under a mass of serial charts. Against the overrationalization that shackles man's mind, he sought a more mysterious, more ambiguous way. In his searchings he found an ally in Mallarmé, who had been dead for more than fifty years. Boulez shared with Mallarmé not only a profound respect for structure but, more important, the deep intuition that knowledge, however useful, must be secondary in art.

In 1954 and 1955 Boulez met Stockhausen from time to time in Paris and Cologne. In between they corresponded sporadically, tackling the pulverizing of classical meter, the other face of the pulverizing of classical tonality. Boulez and Stockhausen shared ideas on "discontinuous time," on tempos controlled by the limits of a player's breath or by the player's ability to articulate rapidly. But along with the exchange of aesthetic ideas, the friendship began to show strain. Pousseur recalls a Domaine concert that took place on April 27, 1955. The program was drawn up in the following way:

I. Ionisation (1930)...............Edgar Varèse
   pour instruments de percussion
   Pièces pour Piano...............Karlheinz Stockhausen
                          (1 re audit.) Paris
              Marcelle Mercenier, pianiste
   Symphonies...............Henri Pousseur (creation)

II. Musique electronique
    avec le concours du studio électronique de la N.W.D.R.
                                        Cologne
    (Director: Herbert Eimert)
    Etudes de: Henri Pousseur, Karlheinz Stockhausen
    suivies d'une presentation des moyens de travail
    employés au studio electronique

119

Pousseur reports: "Stockhausen and I were like brothers at that time. Both of us were there with our young wives. Boulez, as always, was quite alone. Stockhausen was furious at the printed program. He was furious that we had been lumped together. He expected to be singled out."

Stockhausen didn't express his anger directly to Boulez. But there is no question that his anger grew. And it took shape in an increasingly opposing aesthetic commitment, a commitment derived from the chance procedures of Cage that moved much farther than anything Boulez had in mind when he proselytized for some opening up of form. The medium Stockhausen used to effect this shift was the pianist David Tudor, whose every gesture symbolizes the aesthetic of "uneventful time." Commenting on Stockhausen's appropriation of Tudor as his pianist in the late 1950s, Boulez says, "Tudor was an exceptional interpreter, and Stockhausen—like Wagner—had an acute sense for knowing the people who could serve him."

In retrospect, it appears that the bond that tied the early serialists together was not merely love of an aesthetic idea but included—to a greater or lesser degree—aggressive energy against the power structure. At first Stockhausen identified with Boulez's goal, the overthrow of traditional authority: tonality. But when Boulez, or the serial language, became a new authority, when the goal of musical revolution had been in good measure achieved, then Stockhausen redirected his hostile energies against Boulez and the idea for which he stood. "In 1953 and '54," Boulez says, "I put these composers on the map. Then, very quickly, they turned against me."

Thus Boulez's position shifted radically. Rather than continue to fight primal fathers, he became engaged in an effort to hold his own against sons. And so new allies, new enemies were born; "avant-garde," one must remember, was a military term. The organization that Thomson defined, Boulez and Stockhausen against John Cage, was displaced by another less advertised one: Stockhausen and Tudor against Boulez. At the close of their 1954 meeting in Cologne, Stockhausen gave Tudor his *Piano Pieces I* through *V, VII* and *VIII* (he planned to revise No. *VI*) for Tudor to perform in New York. And indeed, as quickly as the following month, Tudor programmed them along with Cage's *31' 57"* in a recital at Carl Fischer Hall. Stockhausen and Tudor were corresponding then; Stockhausen had virtually perfected his English and the exchange between them grew. During the winter of 1955–56, at a time when Stockhausen was telling colleagues that Boulez was "overrated," that his music was "too homogeneous," that everything Boulez did was "much less interesting than people in general thought," he also chose a more active course to undermine Boulez—and that was to undermine the idea in which he believed. Stockhausen got in touch with Steinecke and persuaded him to invite Tudor to Darmstadt in order to give three seminars there on the music of Cage and his friends.

In May 1956, David Tudor played parts I and IV of the *Music of Changes*, the very work that had precipitated Boulez's break from Cage, in a seminar at Darmstadt attended by such formidable figures as Bruno Maderna, Luigi Nono, Stockhausen, and Boulez. After the performance, Stockhausen and Boulez engaged in a fight that, by all counts, lasted at least one hour. Stockhausen fought passionately for the ideas of the work; Boulez fought against them passionately. Tudor says, "Boulez cared enough about Stockhausen to do everything he could to get Stockhausen to change his mind." But his efforts were unsuccessful. Stockhausen gave Boulez a kick in the shins. Still, the kick did not produce blood, and the composers persisted in their professional relationship.

In fact, before this event Stockhausen had sent Boulez his most recent work, a wind quintet called *Zeitmasse*. In *Zeitmasse* (tempo) Stockhausen applied the new theories of relative rhythm that he and Boulez had so often discussed. Boulez found the piece impressive; today he says it is Stockhausen's best. And so, despite the bitter fight at Darmstadt, and the world premier there of *Zeitmasse* in July 1956, Boulez programmed Stockhausen's new work for the Domaine Musical. First he prepared an analysis of the piece; then he delivered a meticulous performance on December 15, 1956, and finally he made a noncommercial recording that virtually put *Zeitmasse* on the map.

12

In *Zeitmasse* Stockhausen works with the serial syntax that Boulez first articulated in *Structures*. But he breaks ground radically in regard to meter. Boulez had been thinking about "unlocking meter and form" as early as 1954, but, as Virgil Thomson says, "Pierre is a hen that hatches slowly," and as he was exploring these ideas, Stockhausen began not to leak but pour.

Zeitmasse was the first shock Stockhausen delivered to Boulez. Here the composer alternates strict metrical passages with passages in which he directs the player to execute a phrase in one breath but leaves the playing time of that phrase up to the player himself.

The effort to involve a performer in the creation of a work came in reaction to the almost servile position the composer of serial music had reserved for him. Within a few years of its birth, post–World War II music had gained the reputation of not only despising the listener but of working at odds with the performer as well. Paul Jacobs has never played Boulez's *Second Sonata*; he says that he has never had the six months he feels the piece requires. Tudor, on the other hand, moved all the way to Boulez. Not only did he gain control over the notes but he felt he had to conquer the spirit as well. And so he went to the trouble of learning French in order to be able to read Char and Artaud, for he knew Boulez was reading them when he composed the work.

While Boulez was unwilling to move toward the performer—even insofar as arranging performances of his work—Stockhausen began to move strongly in that direction. He not only consulted with Tudor on the aesthetics of performer involvement; he also was "responsible," Tudor says, "for my going to Darmstadt and bringing the American composers with me. All the invitations I received from Steinecke, beginning in 1956, were arranged through Stockhausen."

During the period between 1954 and 1958, Tudor played Stockhausen wherever he could, not only in Europe but in the United States. And as Tudor spread Stockhausen he dropped Boulez. "After 1954," Tudor says, "I refused to play Boulez anywhere in Europe because his music was so successful there and my mission was to promote newer things. If I were to have played Boulez—at Darmstadt or anywhere else in Europe—that would have been all the audience wanted and would have interfered with the reception of newer work."

In 1956 Tudor made two exceptions in regard to Boulez performances; he played the *Second Sonata* at the Domaine and gave the first public performance, with Severino Gazzelloni, of the *Flute Sonatina* on a program at Darmstadt that included Webern's *Six Bagatelles*, Schoenberg's *Opus 26 Woodwind Quintet*, and the world premiere of Stockhausen's *Zeitmasse*. The concert, on July 15, 1956, was one of two concerts given that day. The weeks at Darmstadt were filled with music, but Tudor notes that this was a particularly "high-class" program. He adds that the *Flute Sonatina* was so successful that he and Gazzelloni had to play it twice. Tudor says, "Many composers were very jealous of Boulez on that day."

During that particular session at Darmstadt, Italian composer Luciano Berio was in attendance for the second time; he first came in 1955 with his wife, singer Cathy Berberian and his friend Bruno Maderna. He recalls the July 1956 concert: "I was attracted to the *Flute Sonatina* right away. It took me longer to feel close to *Zeitmasse*. As a work, *Zeitmasse* belongs to the typical Germanic tradition, an idea pushed to its very limits. Immediate contact with the piece can be difficult. I had the impression at that first concert that it was a tight, coercive piece. The elasticity in meter was absolutely not apparent. In fact *Zeitmasse* had very little impact on me until Boulez conducted it at the Domaine about six months later.

"The problems between Stockhausen and Boulez," Berio recalls, "always had to do with ideas. I recall very strong discussions. Usually they had to do with Webern. In fact, Stockhausen wrote an analysis of Webern's *Opus 24 Concerto* that proved to be an incredibly important moment in modern music."

In this essay, published in *Melos* in 1953, Stockhausen attempted to reveal to composers how Webern had used the serial principle in areas other than pitch relations. Today Boulez says: "Stockhausen found a symmetry of parameters in Webern. All that I discovered in 1946 and 1947. There's a piece by Stockhausen in *Die Reihe* that goes to absurdities in this domain. It deals with the Webern *Quartet*. Here Stockhausen takes the consequence for the cause. He did it to help him formulate his own ideas."

The tension between Stockhausen and Boulez grew and crystallized into a race between the two men, into a need for setting precedents, for being first. Paul Jacobs, who played piano for the early Domaine concerts and was in close contact with Boulez in the mid-1950s, describes what went on between them at that time: "Stockhausen and Boulez developed a lot of ideas together: tempos controlled by the limits of a player's breath or by his ability to articulate rapidly. But each time Stockhausen got there first. Perhaps the most important idea was that of 'controlled chance.' But even here Stockhausen beat him to it. Boulez began his *Third Piano Sonata* before Stockhausen began *Klavierstücke XI* (the outstanding models of the new principle). Yet Stockhausen's piece was played at Darmstadt first."

Stockhausen wrote *Klavierstücke XI* for David Tudor, to whom he dedicated it. Tudor gave the world premiere at Carl Fischer Hall in April 1957 and was scheduled to give the European premiere in Darmstadt a few months later. Tudor speaks of the genesis of that work: "When I was in Darmstadt in 1956, Stockhausen asked me how I would react if I were given a piece in which I could choose what I would play next. My immediate reaction was to say that I would accept it as a matter of course, that Morton Feldman had written such a piece. Stockhausen replied, 'Then I shall not write it.' Of course I beat a hasty retreat and said that the Feldman piece had not been performed or published. The fact is that the idea may have been in the air in New York but if there was a specific antecedent to *Klavierstücke XI*, I am certain Stockhausen was not aware of it."

If the external form was not inspired by American music, its aggregate of piano sounds certainly was, ranging as it does from single pitches to clusters made by pressing the palm of the hand, forearm, or elbow on the keyboard. As for the external form, Stockhausen's score consists of one large sheet of paper. The pianist sees the whole work without having to turn a page. On this sheet there are sixteen unnumbered groups of music. The performer starts with the one he sees first and plays it exactly as he wants to: loud, soft, staccato, et cetera. Then he reads the dynamics at the end of the section and applies it to the next group on which his eye lights. If his eye moves to a group he has already played, then he plays it again, for the possibilities of varying the material are so great that it should be virtually impossible to play the same group in the same way. If, when he feels he has finished the piece, he discovers that he has left a group out, he knows he can still play it. On the back of the score—in German, English, and French—Stockhausen instructs the performer to play the piece at least twice in any single concert.

Tudor played *Klavierstücke XI* at the scheduled concert in New York. But when it was time for him to go to Darmstadt, he experienced a "tightening of the hand and arm muscles" in addition to a kidney infection and canceled his trip less than two weeks in advance. Tudor admits deep disenchantment with the work. "I had the impression," Tudor reports, "when Stockhausen was talking to me about the piece that it would be much freer than it turned out to be. I remember my shock when I found the rhythmic values notated. How frantically I tried to get out of the four walls that the piece represented to me."

So Tudor said no to his colleague abroad, and as soon as Stockhausen received that message he sent the score by mail to Jacobs in Paris. Stockhausen had met Jacobs only once, in 1955, when Jacobs and Boulez had visited him in Cologne. On that occasion Jacobs played Debussy and Webern and came armed with the reputation of playing the most difficult contemporary music at sight.

As soon as Jacobs received the score he brought it to Boulez. At the moment of Jacobs' visit, the Boulez-Jacobs friendship had just suffered a traumatic shake-up. A trip to the south of France with Bernard Saby, who had become a close friend of Jacobs', ended in a fight and in Boulez's immediate departure for Paris.

"But the rupture was not so great," Jacobs says, "that we ceased entirely to speak to each other, so I went to Boulez and showed him the Stockhausen score. He was very interested in it. If he felt any anger that Stockhausen had anticipated him with 'controlled chance' or any sense of betrayal that Stockhausen had called upon me, Boulez did not indicate it. But then, one never knows what Boulez thinks or feels. Still, he suggested I go immediately to Darmstadt to have as much time as possible to work with Stockhausen on the score."

Thus Jacobs went to Germany and gave the first European performance of *Klavierstücke XI* in the summer of 1957. No aesthetic commitment interfered here; the muscles did exactly what they were told to do. And the piece created its intended effect; everyone talked about the new performer freedom. But not everyone was equally impressed by it. Berio says: "I knew right away that there was something superficial, some sheer exhibitionism in this work. I had the sense that Stockhausen had made a philosophical mistake, for whatever connects the various sections is purely arbitrary. There is not enough musical thinking on the inside to justify the openness of form."

When he began to plan *Klavierstücke XI*, Stockhausen had shared his ideas with Boulez. Pousseur reports: "Boulez replied he was against the conception. He had already begun his *Third Piano Sonata*. He thought of composing several "formants" (or sections) in which the sections would have a certain kind of character and would be divided into various parts. He had in mind a fixed sequence; he referred to the Beethoven *Ninth* as a model. But when he finished the work he had it flexible. Mallarmé's *Le Livre* had been published in the interim. It describes a book in which pages could be taken out and read in every possible order. Clearly it affected Boulez very much."

Indeed, Jacques Sherer's *Sketches of Mallarmé's Le Livre* reveal in great detail Mallarmé's plan for a constantly variable work of art. And that was Boulez's purpose with the *Third Sonata*. "I have often compared this work with the plan of a city," he said recently. "One does not change its design, one perceives exactly what it is, and there are different ways of going through it. One can choose one's own way through it, but there are certain traffic regulations."

Here is how Boulez's *Third Sonata* was made: the first section, *Antiphonie*, consists of pairs of lines that are interchangeable. It is four minutes long but it is not included in the published score. The next part Boulez composed was *Tropes*, a title he borrowed from the medieval "trope" in which there were melodic interpolations in the cantus firmus. But in Boulez's work the "tropes" are not of melodies but of whole complex structures. There are four sections within this "formant" (another word for movement). The sections are *Texte*, *Parenthèse*, *Glose*, and *Commentaire*—titles borrowed from literary scholarship. The performer may start with any of these sections and *Commentaire* must be played before or after *Glose*; otherwise the order is fixed as stated above. *Texte* contrasts subsections in strict rhythm with subsections where the rhythm is left to the performer —in much the same manner as Stockhausen's *Zeitmasse*. But with Boulez, each of these sections never lasts more than five seconds. In *Parenthèse*, the strict sections are very slow and the free ones, now longer, have a continuously changing beat.

After *Tropes*, Boulez wrote *Constellation-Miroir*, the longest formant, which lasts twelve and a half minutes. *Constellation-Miroir*

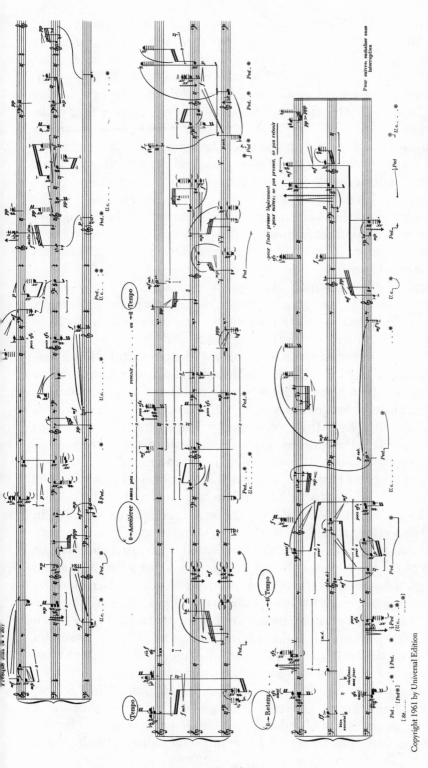

First page of the formant *Texte* of the *Third Piano Sonata* in which "strict" rhythmic sections alternate with "free" rhythmic sections. Note that "retenu II," a "free" section, really consists of only three chords. Another composer, unconcerned with making an innovative gesture, might just have used the marking "retard."

127

can be played either forward or backward and was planned as the middle piece. Groups of notes are strewn together on long sheets of thick paper—to withstand the performers' handling—producing what Boulez calls "constellations." There are particular rules of play for the succession of these groups. Taking off from the special typography that Mallarmé used in the *Coup de dés*, which Boulez considers "one of the most important poems in French literature" (Mallarmé's typography changes on each page with the white background being transformed into a kind of stage), Boulez uses green and red ink for staves and musical notes carefully placed on the long, thick, unfolding pages, reminiscent of the form of Mallarmé's *Le Livre*. The order of the fragments is not fixed but is very carefully controlled. Each fragment is followed by another from which the performer can choose between one and four possibilities. The composer indicates the various choices by means of arrows.

After *Constellation-Miroir*, Boulez composed two one-minute formants but, like *Antiphonie*, has not released them for publication. He says he is revising all three sections, increasing each in length to secure a better balance with the long middle part.

Paul Jacobs comments on the *Sonata*: "The piece works only in one particular order, that is the one published and played. No omission or repetition is permissible. It is nonflowing and frenetic. Boulez does not allow himself either to love or relax with a sound. What he does concern himself with is the exploitation of harmonics, with scrupulous instructions for the pedaling: one-half pedal for sixteenth notes, a full pedal for eighth notes. It's subtlety carried to absurdity."

Jacobs' lack of enthusiasm is shared by Tudor. If Tudor's muscles tightened at *Klavierstücke XI*, they became paralyzed at the sight of the *Third Sonata*: "With Boulez the form is completely external. In the big section, there's a breathtaking sound that is just like glass. With one of us younger cats the sound itself would have dictated the form of the whole work, whereas that section is just a minor insertion in a great big dialectical piece." Tudor adds that in *Klavierstücke XI* the segments are short so the performer is offered choices which involve a small amount of time. "In Boulez the sections are much larger; the performer is really not involved at all." Tudor also notes that musical considerations were not what moved Boulez to chance: "When he finally took the leap, it was because of Mallarmé."

Contrary to the recollection of Pousseur, Tudor, and Alfred Schlee, Boulez's publisher at Universal Edition—that Mallarmé's *Le Livre* was the particular stimulus that moved him to make his *Sonata* flexible —Boulez maintains he saw *Le Livre* only after he had completed the work. He reports that he was delighted to find that Mallarmé had moved, over fifty years before, in a direction that he, on his own, was moving then. He adds that he and Mallarmé even used the same words; "constellation" was the most striking one. To support his shift toward interchangeable structures, Boulez wrote an essay he entitled "Alea" for the *Nouvelle Revue Française*. It appeared in November 1957. In the first two paragraphs he attacked free-floating chance in his most violent, polemical way. Then he sailed into a lengthy and complex discussion of "how to reconcile composition and chance," or, in simpler words, he gave his recipe for "controlled chance." Finally he concluded with a mock prayer for those who would not temper chance with discipline: "Peace to these angelic creatures; we can be sure they run absolutely no risk of stealing our thunder, since they wouldn't know what to do with it."

Cage was enraged. He says, "After having repeatedly claimed that one could not do what I set out to do, Boulez discovered the Mallarmé *Livre*. It was a chance operation down to the last detail. With me the principle had to be rejected outright; with Mallarmé it suddenly became acceptable to him. Now Boulez was promoting chance, only it had to be *his* kind of chance."

Cage still feels a sense of rage today. For, from the time of Boulez's famous essay, chance music has been widely known as "aleatory music." Cage still rejects this title. The most intolerable insult of all was that it was Boulez's erudite word with its esoteric roots (alea are dice) that gave Cage's fresh invention its quasi-official new name.

13

Several years after Stravinsky's death, Robert Craft wrote in the *New York Review of Books* that "the creative eruption that started with *Firebird* and that seemed to come entirely from within . . . had run its course" with *Pulcinella*, written when the composer was only thirty-six years old. Craft says that Stravinsky's acceptance of Diaghilev's commission to rearrange Pergolesi's music for his ballet company "may imply an awareness that he could no longer subsist on his own inner resources."

Virgil Thomson suggests that Boulez followed a similar course which, he says, is not an uncommon one in France. "The strategy to create before thirty," Thomson writes, "through talent, brains, determination and hard labor a handful of unforgettable works, then to retire into private or public life and wait for an immortality which, when all production is complete, arrives on schedule" is also characteristic, he says, of such figures as Duchamp and Rimbaud.

It is true that in his early twenties Boulez produced powerful and original music. Yet after his early affair and these violent expressive works, Boulez shifted considerably. In *Polyphonie X* and *Structures* one no longer feels the violent expression alone. And, by the time of *Marteau*, the violence and energy of the artist lie hidden behind a hard and closed shell.

The radical inhibition in Boulez's creative life was accompanied by an increasing withdrawal from personal relationships that recalls the isolation of his childhood days. In the 1950s there was no longer a group of friends comparable to that of Bernard Saby, Armand Gatti, and Pierre Joffroy with whom he spent time in the mid- and late-'40s. Paul Jacobs reports that when he met Boulez, early in 1954, the composer addressed him with the formal "vous." Jacobs asked Boulez how long one had to know him before being addressed by the familiar "tu." Boulez replied he gave no thought to such things and continued to address Jacobs with "vous."

Other composers note the same shift. Tudor says that after 1952 Boulez refused to discuss ideas, saying that he was saving them for publication. And Babbitt claims he never had a serious conversation with Boulez after the one in Cage's apartment that same year. Boulez's form and facade had become that of the isolated hero, in need of no one and nothing.

That such withdrawal indicated internal trouble and an awareness of his own blockage is suggested by Boulez's statement to Tudor, when he was twenty-seven, that he expected to write his "master work" at thirty. But to say that Boulez anticipated the height of his creative power to be that of a mathematician is not to say he would have preferred it that way. At a concert in the Whitney Museum during the spring of 1974 which was devoted exclusively to his work, he told the New York audience that it was good to get away from his duties as music director and return, for one evening, "to what is really myself." Repeatedly Boulez reveals what he wants most: to be the best and most advanced composer of his time; to be in power, of course, but with the power emanating from his centrality to the spirit of his age.

In 1955 Boulez's production began to taper off as Stockhausen's began to soar. Boulez worked on *Marteau* for two and a half years, completing it in the spring of '55. He did not finish his next work, the *Third Piano Sonata*, until the fall of '57. Between these dates, Stockhausen knocked off pieces with incredible rapidity, each of which introduced some new structural concept. As though *Zeitmasse* and the *Klavierstücke XI* were not enough, he produced *Gesang der Jünglinge*, the first striking European electronic composition, which proceeded from the idea of bringing sung notes and electronically produced notes together in a single sound. The piece was played on Cologne Radio in May 1956; Boulez repeated it later that year at a Domaine concert, where he told his listeners to fasten their seat belts, that they would be hearing sounds they had never heard before.

Able to work on several pieces at one time, Stockhausen began, in 1955, to develop ideas and materials for Gruppen, that aggressive, large-scale work which, according to his own published notes, "initiated the spatial deployment of instrumental music." (The "spatial deployment of instrumental music" was, in fact, initiated by Giovanni Gabrieli and Berlioz a good while before, and used again more recently by the American composer Henry Brant. Indeed, composers who visited Stockhausen while he was at work on Gruppen report that an American Composer's Alliance Bulletin (1955: volume 4, no. 3) containing Brant's article "The Uses of Antiphonal Distribution and Polyphony of Tempi in Composing" was invariably open on Stockhausen's desk; Brant's own first "music-in-space" work was then two years old. In Gruppen three orchestras surround the listener. Each is under its own conductor. Each plays independently and in different tempos, from time to time meeting in a common rhythm. Gruppen was an immediate success.

The new music world was aware of the difference in production between Stockhausen and Boulez. Earle Brown deprecates Stockhausen's "lustful race" to pick up new concepts and rush into print. But others note only that Stockhausen "won." Jacobs says: "Stockhausen showed an intense energy in regard to composition. It started in 1955 to affect Boulez who was terribly shaken by it." Thomson reports: "Boulez was threatened with sterility early on. Stockhausen, on the contrary, is a faucet; all you have to do is turn him on." Tudor adds: "Stockhausen's pieces kept coming all the time, each of them strong, each of them striking. There was Boulez slaving over his desk to complete works that had been in the process for years. Why the slowness? Because his compositional plans are so elaborate, because there is so much concern for system. In 1956 Boulez was confronted with many things happening. He knew he couldn't move fast enough. But Boulez is a person capable of assessing himself absolutely accurately. He knew he couldn't succeed through composition anymore."

Of course, it is impossible to know what Boulez knew. Prisoner of his own idea—that being most advanced is being best—he appears to have consciously pulled back. "In Stockhausen's good period," he says, "I came to trust his music more than anything else. I felt he could solve all the problems, that it was no longer necessary for me to address myself to them."

Thus Boulez shifted his career, turning from composition to conducting. The shift made it possible for Boulez—and interested listeners everywhere—to hear new scores played with vitality and accuracy.

And, as he confessed to Mmes Tezenas and Strobel, the act of conducting "intoxicated" him.

Boulez had begun to conduct with the Barrault company as early as 1946. But precision was all that was required here, precision applied to works that did not interest him at all. Boulez's primary duty was to coordinate sounds from the pit very precisely with what was happening on stage.

It was in 1955 that Boulez began to conduct chamber music at the Domaine. First he tried a *Quintet* by Pousseur, then the Schoenberg *Serenade*, and in 1956 *Marteau sans Maître*. It was also in 1956 that he had his first opportunity to conduct a full orchestra. On his third South American tour with Barrault, Alejo Carpentier, a Cuban novelist and friend of Barrault, invited Boulez to conduct the Venezuelan Symphony. Boulez says he thought to himself, "To conduct so far from home is not dangerous." The program was scheduled to be Debussy's *Jeux* and *Ibéria*, Stravinsky's *Symphonies of Wind Instruments*, and Bartók's *Music for Strings, Percussion, and Celesta*. But the parts for the Bartók did not arrive, and Boulez conducted Prokofiev's *Classical Symphony* instead. He says that he promised himself then that he would never conduct the work again, and that he has fulfilled that promise. But the fact that he did conduct—even once—what surely must be the epitome of neoclassic music indicates that Boulez could compromise.

But then, he was not in a position to dictate events. Boulez says of the year 1957: "It was a shaky one financially. I did lectures and two piano concerts with Yvonne Loriod at radio stations in Germany. We performed my own works and pieces by Debussy. I made some recordings, too, but there were not many financial gains. I was aware that I would have to leave Barrault."

In the fall of 1957 Barrault left the Théâtre Marigny, with which he had no contract, and moved to the Palais-Royal. "That meant," Boulez goes on, "that Barrault was no longer connected with the Domaine. At that, all he had done for the previous three years was to give us the theater rent-free. The Domaine then moved to the Salle Gaveau. I thought this change in arrangement made it a good moment for me to make a change in my life. So I left Barrault. My interest in him was fading at the time. It had been a good relationship, but you can't stay in one place forever. You can't conduct incidental music for the rest of your life." And so Boulez left the company, returning only to help with an occasional premiere and to accompany it to New York that winter.

In 1957 Boulez had a few composition pupils, Richard Bennett and Susan Bradshaw among them. Bennett, who was the first to play *Structures* and the *First Piano Sonata* in London, says that they "worked hard on Webern. His lessons were designed to get to the roots of music. He never flattered or complimented. I only went when I had some music written. He would not accept a fee and refused to 'ritualize' the relationship by regular sessions. Boulez was working on a flute piece at the time in which the flutist moves around the other instruments."

The flute piece remains unfinished in Boulez's portfolio. But the fact that he began to think in such "stagy" terms then indicates how much he tried to follow Stockhausen's lead, which had its roots in Tudor and Cage.

Just before Easter of 1957, Boulez had an opportunity to conduct his own work at Cologne, the first such opportunity outside the Domaine. "Hermann Scherchen was preparing *Visage Nuptial*," Boulez explains, "and he simply did not know the score. He was more or less floundering. There was a crisis between the orchestra and him. I was asked, 'Are you strong enough to do it?'

"It is a very difficult work, for chorus and orchestra. But everything went well. I had no feeling then of embarking on a conducting career. The career took on great proportions without my making any effort. At that time I had a good deal to learn. I had no connection with the performing side of music. I had no idea of how to cope with large forces. It was interesting for me to see the realization from the inside of big instrumental forces. The professional consequences I never foresaw. I made no effort to make a career. I did it only to benefit my composition."

Boulez took over again unexpectedly, eight months later, when he was in the United States with Barrault. He flew to California, he says, to visit industrialist Hans Popper, a generous patron of the Domaine. While there he attended a rehearsal of the Monday Evening Concerts at which Robert Craft was preparing *Marteau*. The Monday Evening Concerts, then in their eighteenth consecutive year (now its 37th), were under the direction of Lawrence Morton, a good friend of Stravinsky's and Craft's. The series was not the only one in the United States devoted to the presentation of contemporary chamber music, but it probably reflected more accurately Boulez's particular view of twentieth-century music than any other group. The concerts presented the complete chamber works of Schoenberg, Webern, Berg, Stravinsky, Bartók, Ives, and Varèse. Among its world premieres are two by Webern, and *Eclat* (1965) of Boulez. Among its American premieres are pieces by Stockhausen, Berio, Nono, and Boulez, as well as works by Boulez's students, Heinz Holliger and Jean-Paul Eloy.

Morton, introduced to Boulez's work by Stravinsky, who had brought the score of *Polyphonie X* back from his 1951 trip to Europe, began programming Boulez in 1952. In 1957 Morton scheduled *Marteau* with Craft at the helm. For some reason Boulez took over from Craft. The stories differ. Boulez reports that Craft was having trouble with Piece No. 4—"with all those fermatas"—and that the musicians had a meeting and voted to invite him to conduct his own work. Morton recalls that Craft simply deferred to Boulez as the composer and, on his own, suggested that Boulez take over the podium. In a published essay in the *Saturday Review*, Craft writes that Boulez came to Los Angeles precisely to conduct *Marteau*. In any event, Boulez did conduct the piece, and although the musicians responded warmly to him, presenting him with a pair of cuff links—a gesture Morton characterizes as exceptional—*Marteau* earned harsh criticism from the musical press.

In Manhattan, Boulez was conducting Barrault performances at the Winter Garden theater, and those who visited him backstage report that he appeared quiet and depressed. There was no friend in New York to arrange for concerts and lectures as Cage had once done. Then too, Boulez had little to say at that time, no new system to promulgate. After a performance, Babbitt dined with him. They talked about Schoenberg's *Variations for Orchestra*, Babbitt reports. "Boulez said he was thinking more as a conductor these days and that he found the hard parts of the work unplayable. I told him why I thought there were minor third doublings but either he didn't understand or wasn't interested."

On his return to Europe in the spring of 1958, Boulez appeared in Cologne as one of the three conductors of Stockhausen's *Gruppen*. Along with Stockhausen and Maderna, he conducted one of the three orchestras for the premiere. The piece contained enormous difficulties and there were moments when Maderna threatened to leave. But finally the three artists conquered the work. Tudor says Stockhausen was immensely pleased with the results. *Gruppen* was played twice. In between, Boulez gave a performance of his *Third Piano Sonata*, a third performance for that work. The piano piece must have suffered in its spectacular surroundings, for it sounds more like an analysis of what piano music should be than a genuine composition for the keyboard. As ungratifying as it is to the ear, the *Third Sonata* is beautiful to the eye. In fact, I have the thick sheets of *Constellation-Miroir* framed and hanging in my library.

Being an interpreter of Stockhausen's big work at a moment when he himself was not making news must have been very painful to Boulez. Even John Cage, who professes to be unconcerned about matters of prestige, concedes that he was enraged when in his sixtieth year Feldman manipulated him into a position where *he* was the pianist for Feldman's work in Germany. Boulez repeated his conducting assignment with *Gruppen* in a second performance at Donaueschingen the following fall. But by 1965, when a third performance was scheduled for Paris, Boulez sent regrets and Michael Gielen in his place. Speaking of *Gruppen* recently Boulez says, "It was good, but there were already some compromises, an abstracted jazz that I found very vulgar. Sometimes Stockhausen would blast his way. There was a cheap side showing that I did not like very much. I could see it in *Gesang der Jünglinge* as well. Stockhausen was covering abstract categories with splashy gowns."

That the relations between Stockhausen and Boulez were then tense is accepted by those who knew both men well. Pousseur says that in 1957, in an effort to restore good feelings between them, Stockhausen named Boulez godfather to his third child. The gesture seems to have made professional relations easier, but it cannot have gone very far in abating Boulez's fury against the younger man who displaced him in the new music world as he himself had displaced Leibowitz a decade before. Surely there are many men who resent their students' climb to their own status level. But it is possible that Boulez's particular and intense reaction, which resulted not only in more withdrawal but also in deeper, more mysterious musical systems, was exacerbated by his own psychology. Psychoanalyst Jacob Arlow writes that a boy born after the death of an earlier son fantasizes that he murdered his predecessor in the womb. Such a man, Arlow says, is destined to fear retaliation from a younger man and to react in an exaggerated way if it should seem to come.

Whether or not this was true of Boulez, the rage against Stockhausen became increasingly difficult to suppress. Less than a month after the *Gruppen* premiere, Boulez began to work on a commission from Strobel. Following Stockhausen's lead in *Gesang der Jünglinge* (for voice, conventional and electronic instruments) and *Gruppen* (for three orchestras), he composed a piece for voice, two orchestras, and tape. For his poem he chose one by Henri Michaux, *Poésies pour Pouvoir* (Poems for Power), a title that must have held much mean-

136

ing for Boulez at a moment when he found himself drawing on Stockhausen's ideas. The poem is one man's curse on another, and is as murderous a set of verses as I have ever read. (See Appendix.)

Poésies pour Pouvoir received its first and only performance at the Donaueschingen Festival in October 1958. Otto Tomek, then a music director at Cologne Radio, attended and says the piece was exciting. "There were soft, dark sounds, very low, then building up. It was music that took you not only by the ears and mind but by the entire body. But it required technical facilities that were not available at the time. There was a loudspeaker turning slowly in the room. The result was highly unsatisfactory. At that, it was fortunate the words could not be understood."

Freud, in his book on dreams, quotes Socrates: "The good man does in his dreams what the wicked one does in actual life." Socrates might have said, "in his dreams and his art." Boulez uses poetry to this effect.

Cage attempts to prove that Boulez's interest really is in literature rather than music by citing Boulez's essay of 1954 in which he demands "italics and parentheses in music." Stockhausen, in an article in Die Reihe, illustrates with musical examples how the instruments in Marteau serve only to "intensify the comprehension of the words" and adds that under these conditions "the phonetic properties of speech" cannot be sufficiently exploited for composition. Boulez freely admits his passion for poetry and says Stockhausen is uncultivated in this realm: "Otherwise he would know better than to write his own texts."

But Boulez's sister provides the ultimate clue: "My brother is completely closed. The only way to know what he has thought is to read very carefully all the poetry he has set."

Recently Boulez said that a period in music ended in 1958. "I know it sounds egocentric," he added, "but that period began in 1944." Thus Boulez identifies the birth and apparent death of the serial language with his own endeavors to establish and nourish it. Once he was displaced by Stockhausen, who introduced to Europe a new "idea," the sense of loss must have been unbearable.

In 1959 Boulez left France and moved to Germany.

14

In June 1958 Boulez went to Baden-Baden. He took a room in a hotel next to the Southwest German Radio station and across a lawn from the apartment building in which the Strobels lived. Twice a day, at noon and in the evening, Hilda Strobel called out her window to Boulez's balcony to announce that dinner was about to be served.

Mrs. Strobel describes Boulez: "He was a young man with enormous charm who had something spiritual about him. One could speak on any theme, on literature, the fine arts, anything at all. There was always much joking, many obscenities. He could be as nice as he was aggressive. He thought of us as his parents, perhaps even as his best friends. His parents gave him nothing. At the beginning Pierre hated his father and Pierre had a cruel temperament. He could get as furious at an orchestra as he could get against his father."

Boulez spent two weeks in Baden-Baden that June working on *Poésies pour Pouvoir*. Because he had to complete it for the Donaueschingen Festival in October, he canceled his plans to teach at Darmstadt.

"It was in 1958," Tudor says, "that Stockhausen surpassed Boulez as a power in Europe." Stockhausen, as Boulez describes him in those days, was "very sure, very strong." And he used that certainty, strength, and power to move the musical world into an altogether new realm.

When Stockhausen learned of Boulez's cancellation, he persuaded Steinecke to hire Cage in Boulez's place. Steinecke wired Cage in New London, Connecticut, where Cage was at work with Merce Cunningham. Elated at the invitation, Cage decided to leave the dance company right away. "In 1954," Cage explains, "Europeans had taken me as some kind of clown. I thought that my presence at Darmstadt would mean that now I'd be taken seriously."

Cage proved to be right. "If the truth were known," Tudor says, "it was Stockhausen who turned the tide. If ever a question of negation came up, Stockhausen came to our aid."

In Darmstadt, Cage delivered a series of lecture-demonstrations in English that were translated into German by composers Hans Helms, Wolf Rosenberg, and Herbert Bruhn. "The lectures," Cage says, "were on composition as process." Steinecke had requested that he give particular attention to the *Music of Changes*. Cage decided to do that in the following way: he planned the talk exactly the length of the piece so that whenever he would stop talking, *Music of Changes* would be played. "Each line of the text," Cage explains, "whether speech or silence, would require one second for its performance. The music was never superimposed on the speech but heard only in the interruptions of the speech which, like the lengths of the paragraphs themselves, were the result of chance operations."

So many people jammed the event that Cage's second and third lectures were held in a large concert hall. Not to be intimidated by his benefactor, Cage spent the second lecture attacking Stockhausen, most particularly *Klavierstücke XI*. Cage said that Stockhausen had not gone nearly far enough in regard to chance principles. "The indeterminate aspects of the work," he said, "do not remove *Klavierstücke XI* from the body of European musical conventions. . . . The work might as well have been written in all its aspects determinately. It would lose, in this case, its single unconventional aspect: that of being printed on an unusually large sheet of paper which, together with an attachment that may be snapped on at several points enabling one to stretch it flat and place it on the music rack of a piano, is put in a cardboard tube suitable for safekeeping and distribution through the mails."

The third lecture was made up of questions and quotations, the quotations, in large part, from Cage's own writings. The quantity and order of the quotations were determined by *I Ching* principles. Here, for instance, is one of the questions: "Which is more communicative? A truck passing a factory or a truck passing a music school?" Cage never offered any answers.

139

In addition to dispensing his curious brand of pedagogy, Cage collected mushrooms from the vicinity of the town and prepared many mushroom dishes. Cage reports that at the end of his stay, Steinecke told him that if he had not done a service to music at Darmstadt, he had at least performed a service to food.

Cage was not invited to return. He attributes that to the fact that "I was too upsetting."

It is certainly true that Cage turned things around. Richard Bennett describes the change this way: "Until then the school was serially oriented. Serial plans and charts were everywhere. Cage preached a different doctrine. It was so striking. He shook people awfully. Everyone started to think his way. His became *the* forthcoming style. Stockhausen went absolutely overboard. And almost everyone went along with Stockhausen."

Berio recalls the *Music of Changes* event: "I was bored to death. But it was the best moment for Cage to come. With his simplicity he accomplished a great deal. He proved to be a strong catalyst."

Boulez agrees: "In Darmstadt between 1952 and 1958, the discipline of serialization was so severe that it was ridiculous. Cage represented a liberation from this. In his mind psychology and theater are more important than the structural aspects of a work. In 1958 Cage came to Europe with a bagful of tricks, of theatrical gimmicks. It was because of the tricks that I was repelled; one cannot recite jokes forever. All his invention was in the action, not in the composition. Still his performance had its good side; it cleaned out the academics."

It certainly moved Stockhausen towards "psychology and theater." In the summer of that same year, 1958, at the Brussels World's Fair, Cage gave a talk on new forms in instrumental and electronic music illustrating that the presence of electronic music had made changes in instrumental music. Cage says, "Stockhausen took the text and had it published in No. 5 of *Die Reihe*. Hans Helms made an elaborate typography for it so the piece would look intellectual."

Stockhausen, in fact, embraced Cage with such fervor that by absorption he all but annihilated him from the musical scene. Appropriating Cage's interest in Eastern mysticism as well as his notions of performer involvement and chance, Stockhausen continued to pour out work after work. *Refrain*, of 1959, is in a large circle of notation with a plastic strip that can spin. Cage says that many composers at Darmstadt asked him if he would be offended if they were to adopt the ideas on graphism, many of which were, in fact, Feldman's, that he had presented to them in 1958. "I made it clear," Cage says, "that none of these ideas belonged to me personally."

140

And in no time they hardly belonged to him at all. Hans Werner Henze, a German composer, had been at Darmstadt in the early Leibowitz days. But he left in 1954 because of the excesses he then felt in serialism. He describes how Stockhausen "embraced" Cage. Henze extends his arms in a wide circle, then brings them together as though to caress a friend, and finally crushes them tightly against his chest.

To be maintained, power must always be increased, and Stockhausen knew that very well. By the end of 1958 he refused to play a role in any program in which works by any other composer were to be included along with his own. Stockhausen demanded exclusive treatment, and generally he received exactly that, for the young German could pretty well determine conditions by then. And the propagation of the serial syntax was just about the last thing he had in his mind.

Thus Boulez saw his Idea slipping away and he attempted to move along with the tide: *Pli Selon Pli* continues the efforts he made in the *Third Sonata* to combine improvisatory with fixed elements. But as Messiaen says, "He never had his heart in aleatory work. Whatever he did was with great prudence." The grammar for which Boulez had had such high hopes was being displaced, in his lexicon, by theatrical gimmickry, by anarchic and nihilistic philosophies. Boulez, in 1974, summed it up in one sentence: "Stockhausen, with his hippie, hormonal cure, pedantically revived what was genuine in Cage."

The higher the hopes, the more bitter the disillusionment. Death and despair are evident in the hour-long work, *Pli Selon Pli*, all of which was mapped out in 1958–59. The dates of the realizations of specific movements follow: *Don*: 1961; *Improvisation I*: 1958–60; *Improvisation II*: 1958; *Improvisation III*: 1960; *Tombeau*: 1959. (See Appendix.)

The first movement begins with the opening line of the Mallarmé poem *Don du Poème*: "Je t'apporte l'enfant d'une nuit d'Idumée." ("I bring you the child of an Idumaean night.") Wallace Fowlie, a Mallarmé scholar, writes that "from the title we know the gift is a poem but the image signifies it is a dismal birth. The poem is inadequate and the birth is covered with blood. The poem is disinherited as soon as it is created and is thus compared to the child of Edom, which was the country of Esau, the brother disinherited in favor of Jacob." What more accurate paraphrase could there be of the way Boulez viewed the birth and savage assault on his Idea?

The end of the last movement declaims the last line of Mallarmé's poem *Tombeau*: "Un peu profond ruisseau calomnié la mort." ("A shallow rivulet misrepresented is death.") It was composed in re-

One page of *Une dentelle s'abolit*, Third Movement of *Pli Selon Pli*. Note the long, held notes in the voice. There is no attempt to reflect the poetic phrase here.

sponse to a commission by Strobel on the death of Prince Max Egon von Fürstenberg, whose castle in Donaueschingen had been the site of the festival. The sonnet which ends with the line above suggests that the artist does not die—as ordinary men do—but lives on in some extraordinary way after death. Written to commemorate the first anniversary of the death of Verlaine, *Tombeau* was composed shortly before Mallarmé's own death. Boulez's choice of it as the only line of text placed at the end of the last movement of a work he had long planned as his "masterwork," suggests that, just as this was the end of Mallarmé's life, so was it the end of his own creative life.

The Mallarmé poems used in their entirety for the intervening movements, *Improvisations I, II, III*, confirm the despair and sense of death the outer movements evoke.

The first, *Le vierge, le vivace et le bel aujourd'hui* ("The virginal, lively and beautiful day"), is one of Mallarmé's most popular poems. The poet paints a picture of a swan stuck in the ice and unable to fly. The second, *Une dentelle s'abolit* ("A piece of lace disappears"), is replete with tomblike images: a room without a bed, a mandolin with a hollow inside, each impotent in its effort to give birth. The third, *A la nue accablante tu* ("To the overwhelming cloud hushed"), concerns the catastrophe of a shipwreck. "The poet imagines," Fowlie writes, "the highest mast, stripped of its sail, sinking last into the water. Something has been abolished. . . . The threatening cloud, pressing low against the water, has followed a storm that has left its mark in some unaccountable way. . . .

"Some act which is just over must have been tremendous in its spectacle and meaning. Almost nothing of it remains: a low cloud and a bit of foam. The act has descended into its own secret."

Something tremendous had happened to Boulez. He had brought forth a consequent and rigorous grammar that he designed to replace the tonal grammar and to serve his art for hundreds of years. Now almost nothing of it remained.

Boulez took his title, *Pli Selon Pli* ("Fold by Fold"), from another of Mallarmé's poems in which the poet describes how the dissolving mist gradually reveals the city of Bruges. "In the same way," Boulez writes in program notes to his Columbia recording, "as the five pieces unfold, they reveal, fold by fold, a portrait of Mallarmé." One might add, "and of Boulez, as well."

Boulez has repeatedly revised the music of the five movements. The work is performed frequently in various partial and tentative versions. The still incomplete *Third Piano Sonata, Poésies pour*

143

Pouvoir, and *Pli Selon Pli* indicate Boulez's unwillingness to commit himself to print because of "improvements" he knows he will want to make. Anything he has published since then is merely a fragment of a larger whole.

The *Improvisations* are set for soprano and chamber ensemble; the ensemble varies from movement to movement but consists, primarily, of percussion instruments. The outer pieces are written for a larger ensemble and produce an orchestral sound. *Don* is scored for three orchestras.

Before 1959, Boulez had set three works by René Char and one poem by Henri Michaux. He explains his shift to Mallarmé:

> I found many sources of inspiration in Char and Michaux, but preoccupation with form was not one of them. Char's interest was in an extremely tight vocabulary; Michaux's in the creation of an original imagery. But syntax itself, the arrangement of words and their cohesion and sonority, was not the obsession of either poet.
>
> What seduced me with Mallarmé was the formal density of his work. Not only is the content extraordinary—for his poems have a very particular mythology—but the French language has never been led further, from the point of view of syntax. I wanted to find a musical equivalent and that is why I chose the strictest forms.
>
> There are various levels of convergence between poetry and music. The simplest is the conveying of the sense of the words. Thus, when Mallarmé speaks of "absence," there is a musical sonority—a sound held for a long time—that can convey this idea. Another point of convergence is the form itself. The sonnet has a very strict form which calls for a certain musical structure. My purpose was to attribute a kind of form to each verse according to the rules of the sonnet itself. There is also numerology here: one structure is based on the number 8 because it is a verse of eight syllables. Gradually these improvisations become analogous with the structure of the sonnet, but in a manner more and more detailed, more and more profound. That is why I call them Improvisations I, II, and III."

Boulez's elaborate discussion of technique in the interview quoted above, which was broadcast on Belgian Radio in 1972, serves to hide from the listener the real "meaning" of the work, which can easily be discovered in the words of the poetry.

Few listeners could pick up Boulez's devices, for the system is impenetrable. Few could even pick up the words, for they are virtually drowned in the music. What the listener *will* pick up is the dazzling instrumental color: *Pli Selon Pli* is a remarkable work for its instrumental passages of great beauty, for its technique and proportion. The first two *Improvisations*, commissioned for the concert series *Das neue Werke* in Hamburg, were performed there in 1958. The complete five-movement piece received its premiere in 1960 in Cologne under the direction of Boulez. Stravinsky was there. Craft reports that Stravinsky was disappointed, that he thought *Marteau* presaged a "stronger next work." Craft says Stravinsky thought it was "pretty, a piece with no balls." By then the Stravinsky-Boulez alliance had undergone considerable strain. Stravinsky was angry about a disastrous performance of his *Threni* at a recent Domaine concert, so his judgment may have been spiteful. Then too, the judgment may not be his but Craft's, for it is virtually impossible to distinguish the opinions of the composer from those of his amanuensis. Still, the point has validity. The lacy arabesques of *Pli Selon Pli*, the play of one resonance against another, is a world away from Boulez's early expressive works and suggests that something had muted him.

In December 1958 Boulez went to Baden-Baden for a second time. He stayed in servants' quarters just above the Strobel apartment and spent Christmas with the Strobels that year. The following month Boulez signed a contract with the Sudwestfunk which, he recalls, "lasted two or three years." So the Germans, who captured him in 1952 through a publication contract with Universal Edition, now had physical possession of him as well through a well-paying composer-in-residence arrangement: "I was to perform my works with them and also conduct some chamber concerts. It provided enough money for me to keep going."

Hilda Strobel found an apartment in the Pension Rubens on which he took a one-year lease. In 1961 he moved into the first floor of Mrs. Strobel's dentist's house, a vast four-story building banked against a hill. And so Boulez took up residence in a town of parks, patisseries, and Marienbad-like hotels, a town which still looks like a little German principality of the nineteenth century. He gave up his quarters in Paris.

A little earlier, owing to Hans Rosbaud's illness, Boulez's conducting career received an unexpected boost. Strobel asked Boulez to fill in for Rosbaud by conducting a performance at the Domaine. "When he saw I did well with that," Boulez says, "he gave me more: the big orchestra. I was again and again given opportunity to do some work. That is what happens when someone else is ill."

In July 1959 Rosbaud invited Boulez to lunch and told him he was suffering from cancer of the kidneys. Rosbaud asked Boulez to substitute for him, conducting in a festival at Aix-en-Provence. Boulez says

145

he took over Rosbaud's complete program: "*Wozzeck* excerpts, Webern, Pousseur, Hindemith—that awful *Concerto for Orchestra*."

In October 1959 Rosbaud could not conduct at the Donaueschingen Festival. Boulez again took over the podium. "I was called in on Thursday for Saturday and Sunday and there were five new scores, including Berio's *Allelujah*. Everyone was enthusiastic; I had saved the festival." Mrs. Strobel was at the Donaueschingen Festival and recalls: "There was Boulez: small, fat, a real peasant, a peasant from Auvergne. He came as a *paysan*, without making compliments to the orchestra or paying deference in any way to the audience. At the end there was a tremendous success. Boulez had conducted the *Miraculous Mandarin* and there was total disorder in the orchestra. He had only a few rehearsals and he knew nothing about conducting then. So naturally the Bartók could not have been very good. But Boulez's temperament enchanted the public. People were so taken by his personality that they didn't seem to care how bad the Bartók really was."

From that point on, conducting proliferated in Boulez's life. He says he never "studied" conductors for long periods, that he "observed" Desormière and Hermann Scherchen. Boulez adds that after 1955, when he visited Baden-Baden regularly, he had the opportunity to watch Rosbaud and pick up some details, "particularly Rosbaud's patience with the musicians when they made mistakes. If musicians make mistakes, it is not because they want to make mistakes, but because there is something they do not understand and it is up to the conductor to help them. How can I describe my development as a conductor? I always had a good ear, could catch mistakes and correct them. But it is true that I gradually became more sensitive to stylistic matters, to phrasing, tempo, balance, timbre, color, and all the rest."

In addition to the Sudwestfunk, Rosbaud had been principal conductor of the Concertgebouw Orchestra of Amsterdam. Boulez moved into his place there too. He also began to teach composition and analysis in Basel in 1961. Strobel arranged the appointment through Paul Sacher, general director of the Academy of Music there. Boulez would receive one thousand Swiss francs ($250) in exchange for one or two days' teaching a month. Sacher's wife was the widow of the pharmaceutical manufacturer, Hoffman La Roche. In her youth she had been a friend of Klee and Kandinsky and she had a great collection of abstract expressionist works. Mme Sacher asked Boulez for a sheet of his manuscript. On receiving it she pressed him to accept a

146

fee; when he refused, she gave him a Karmann Ghia instead. Once almost unaware of money, Boulez began to taste what it could bring.

Many of Boulez's most impassioned early admirers believe he had given himself up to a vulgar career. But Boulez's former student Susan Bradshaw, who was in contact with him during the 1960s, comes considerably closer to the truth in suggesting that Boulez's striking change was motivated not by choice but by need: "Stockhausen was such a strong musical personality that Boulez felt driven into a corner. It is ridiculous to feel rivalry but that is clearly what happened. Boulez was conscious of being in Stockhausen's shadow.

"Boulez's conducting career made it impossible for him to compose. And he probably prefers it this way. Conducting is just reproducing other people's work. It means you never have to reveal yourself."

Messiaen articulates the particular causes that lay behind the shift: "Immediately after World War II, serial music was everything. Since then there have been many other things: concrete, electronic, aleatory. . . . And some of these have finished already. The eighteen-year-old looks for still another way.

"Boulez is very intelligent. He understands the changes and they make him suffer. There are people who go unperturbed through change. Like Bach. Like Richard Strauss—who lived to know Debussy, Wagner, and Stravinsky. But Boulez cannot. This is extremely sad because he is a great composer."

Souvchinsky refuses to make it a question of either-or. "Boulez became a conductor," the French aesthetician declares, "because he had a great gift for this. The phenomenon of his genius is complex. He is not in a class with Ravel and Messiaen but with Beethoven, Mozart, Wagner, and Debussy. He stands among the highest categories of creators."

15

Boulez says he never "stopped" composing, that he just shifted his energies, that he "fell into" his new career. "I quickly discovered," Boulez says, "that I was able to conduct without taking any lessons. I think one can learn to conduct only by conducting. People began to offer me engagements and I accepted them. At first I had no intention of conducting 'classical music.' My aim was to make known what I call the 'classics of the modern period.' Those were very rarely played. But orchestras always have limited rehearsal time and as contemporary music needs a great deal of rehearsing, it is best to 'buy' this time by including in your programs a large proportion of standard pieces which the players already know. So I began conducting Handel and Haydn as well as Schoenberg and Webern. Then the thing began to snowball. There is such a need for conductors today that if you are just a little bit gifted you get sucked into the machinery."

Simultaneously with his initial foray into conducting, Boulez turned to pedagogy. He had begun to teach at Darmstadt in 1956, but these sessions were seminars and did not call for the articulation of an aesthetic creed. In 1960 Boulez presented a series of formal lectures there which were designed to do precisely that. They were published in German in 1963 and translated into English by Richard Bennett and Susan Bradshaw as *Boulez on Music Today*, published in 1971. Unlike Stravinsky, for whom Souvchinsky wrote the Harvard lectures twenty years before, Boulez asked for no help at all. Souvchinsky admires Boulez for his pedagogy: "What Boulez has done is to make a school, build a base. It remains intact as a kind of academicism. It is a system he follows but passes around. Still, the school stays."

In these talks Boulez made an effort to reverse through words the musical situation he found intolerable. His language was turgid, but one thing is clear: very few escaped his wrath. Several attacks follow, with interpretations following the English translation:

" 'Responsible' analyses almost managed to discredit the object chosen for exhaustive study." (Analyses in *Die Reihe* almost destroyed the music.)

"A further confusion arises between the detailing of the resultant structures—those obtained by the process of derivation and combination—and the investigation necessary for a proper study of the processes themselves." (The analyses of Babbitt and his American school were no better than those of *Die Reihe*.)

"This mania for graphics can lead to illiteracy." (The use of graphs in place of notes will lead to a situation in which no one can read scores.)

"The power of shock is quickly exhausted. The sensation is dulled, the sparkle vanishes, leaving a definite sense of having been cheated." (Theatrical gimmickry is less nourishing than musical material.)

"The summary use of stereophony borders on the delights of Cinerama." (The use or rather abuse of several orchestras playing at once is both cheap and sensationalist.)

"Musicians have always been in the rearguard of the revolutions of others. In music, Dadaism still retains the prestige and (naiveté) which it has long since lost everywhere else." (Composers were wrong to follow Stockhausen who followed Cage, for it puts them half a century behind the times.)

Boulez issued his attacks without mentioning a single name. The enemies were there but never identified. Boulez never names names, he explains, because he refuses "to make such people martyrs."

In place of all he despised, Boulez advocated a balance of control and chance, of both improvisatory and nonimprovisatory elements, of "being at once both free and disciplined." And through it all he insisted on Webern's paternity, not only for the previous decade, but for future decades as well: "It is obvious that Webern—who emerged very early as the chief landmark in defining our personalities—stands at the center of these explorations."

The lectures were dogmatic and pompous, lacking the grace of his offstage manner. Rather than "I am," he said, "We must." And the

149

musical analyses he offered were meticulous and dry. Miss Bradshaw says, "The explanations are so intricate and detailed; even when challenged he refused to explain them. I believe it was willful secrecy on his part. He showed little interest in the book. He never looked at the copy of the typescript."

Here is Boulez on the second formant, *Tropes*, of his *Third Piano Sonata*:

The series is divided into four groups, of four, one, four and three notes respectively, which I will call a, b, c, d. Groups a and b/d are joined isomorphically, the original figure a being at the same time inverted and permutated; group c consists of two isomorphic figures. Figure a is reducible to two generative intervals, the semitone and the fourth, which will create the vertical and horizontal relationships (E♮–F♮/B♮–F♯; E♮–B♮/F♮–F♯); the connecting intervals are the augmented fourth and the whole tone (F♮–B♮; F♯–E♮). In the figure b/d obtained by inversion and permutation, the vertical relationships are the augmented fourth and the whole tone (G♯–D♮/C♯–E♭); the horizontal relationships and the connecting intervals being the semitone and the fourth (G♯–C♯/D♮–E♭; D♮–C♯/E♭–G♯). Figure c is composed of two isomorphic elements, minor thirds (G♮–B♭/C♮–A♮) observing globally the transposition of a whole tone (G♮–A♮/B♭–C♮); but if the notes obtained by inversion

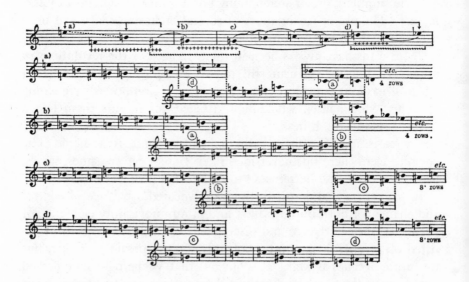

are seen in apposition to those of the original figure the relationship of the semitones and the fourth will again be found (G♮–C♮; B♭–A♮). Finally, the series is composed of two isomorphic figures: a/

150

bd, and of a group which itself includes two isomorphic figures: c; this last group—which is *divisible*—divides the second isomorphic figure bd into two unequal parts: b (one note, G♯) and d (three notes: D♮C♯E♭). Thus there is, on the one hand, manifest symmetry within c and, on the other hand, concealed symmetry between a and the two fragments b, d. In addition the intervals which relate the groups to each other are the same as the fundamental intervals of the groups: whole tone, semitone and fourth.

A single series can obey several isomorphic laws. A figure of three notes (e.g. B♮B♭D♮) may undergo an augmentation (E♭C♯A♮) in which all its intervals are doubled, and then appear in a symmetrical, retrograde form (G♯E♮F♮); finally, to complete the twelve notes, a figure is added which is irreducible to the principal figure.

What do we notice? Other isomorphic relationships result from this triple succession of three-note isomorphic figures. There are two four-note figures linked by very obvious relationships; these include a pair of intervals a, separated by another interval b, a and b being interchanged from the first to the second group. The first pair of intervals, two minor seconds (B♮–B♭/D♮–E♭), is separated by a major third; the second pair, two major thirds (C♯–A♮/G♯–E♮), is separated by a minor second (A♮–G♯). The minor seconds are inverted in relation to each other (descending and ascending seconds), whereas the major thirds are parallel (descending); moreover, one of the central intervals that act as axes of symmetry is ascending, the

151

other descending. The third four-note figure is irreducible. Once more let us take the same three-note figure; this time it will be augmented, then inverted, and to complete the twelve notes, another irreducible figure will be added to it.

What do we notice now? Two isomorphic figures, each of five notes, the second of which is the retrograde of the first; the last three notes correspond to the first three, by retrogradation (B♮B♭D♮–G♯E♮F♮); from the pivotal third note, the retrograde is combined with inversion of the intervals (D♮E♭C♯–A♮G♮G♯). The final figure of two notes (C♮F♯) is apparently irreducible to the other two. Notice, however, that the interval between the last note of the second figure and the first of these terminal notes is the same as that between the second of these two notes and the first note of the first figure (F♮–C♮/F♯–B♮); if the second note (F♯) is placed at the beginning of the series, we shall have two six-note isomorphic figures. This series will obey two different isomorphisms; the first, partial, forming three figures; the second, total, forming two.

Finally, there are totally asymmetrical series; these occur principally when a limited number of elements is used, because isomorphic elements are almost inevitable, even if only of a single interval or a given proportion, as soon as the number of basic elements increases.

In conclusion, there are three distinct types of serial structure:
—totally symmetrical
—partially symmetrical and asymmetrical
    manifest isomorphic figures
    concealed isomorphic figures
—totally asymmetrical.

Boulez notes, "If I have dwelt at length on the structure of the series itself, it is because it forms the basis of an entire organization of series derived from it."

Thus Boulez's method of making music can be seen as one in which some kind of mathematical equations have displaced man as the center of art. Purpose and intention have capitulated to structure and system. Boulez's ties to both can be traced, perhaps, to Catholicism and his early rigid life. But in subscribing to this method he was also in line with many important intellectuals in France for whom structuralism had become an overriding philosophy. Claude Lévi-Strauss has built a creed on the way in which a myth changes as it moves from one culture to another; he deemphasizes the meaning of the content of the myth. Jean Piaget concentrates on the way a person conceptualizes the world; he never really deals with what the person wants to do with that world.

Lévi-Strauss, Piaget, and their colleagues imply that structures are ultimately logico-algebraic in nature—whether they involve myths, behavior, or interval relationships. Thus the structuralist is oriented towards mathematics and away from the interpretation of life. The most complex of such formulae underlie *Tropes* and every other composition of Boulez's post-1952 career. Still, Boulez derives no satisfaction when someone else discovers the mechanisms at work. Claude Helffer, who has recorded the *Third Piano Sonata*, says: "In Boulez there is always the aspect of a sphinx. One assumes there is always structure, although he will not talk about it. Once I noted the structure of the tempos in *Constellation-Miroir*. Boulez was not pleased at all. He feels that what's important are the periods at the end of sentences, not the grammar itself. When I ask him to explain something, he says, 'I don't remember.' He has his own language. He believes: if it's good, I'll use it but it's not important to understand it."

The problem of new music is one of language. Language is a set of propositions to render the world around us concrete. But language is something we must catch on to, not something that can be contrived. As the meaning of life lies outside what can be said, so the meaning of music lies outside any syntax.

Boulez knows this only too well. And he has steadfastly addressed himself to transcending these propositions in order to see the world both freely and right. Still, the rigor of his approach, with its sparse sensuous contents, may allow him to be great, but not popular. Not popular with the public at large or popular even with the specialists, most of whom, in the early 1960s, were moving onto a suggestive, more symbolic art in which disciplined intellect played a minimal role.

Boulez never wants to expose himself, not through his handwriting, his clothes, his furnishings, or his art. Thus the structuralist approach is exactly suited to his needs. Even his most complex works are not "hidden" enough for him. Boulez says he hates Picasso "because everything is visible," and adds that he does not like to study his own

153

scores "because that is like looking at yourself in the mirror and you can't be pleased with only your own head in the mirror." So, much as Boulez would love to be advancing the advance guard, he cannot move into their seemingly uninhibited world. He is locked into a demanding and dignified language; nothing has moved him to turn his back on the serial syntax and the infinitely complex techniques that that grammar inspires in him. Souvchinsky says, "Boulez's last piece is no different from his early ones. There is nothing contradictory in his work from beginning to end." That Boulez's ideas about composition have not changed from the start of his career is supported by the fact that, in 1963, he gave permission to *Editions du Seuil* to publish a collection of his essays that had appeared in the *Encyclopédie de la Musique*, published by Fasquelle, and in various journals between 1948 and 1962.

In the early 1960s, Boulez's polemics appeared in Darmstadt through the lectures, in Paris through the published essays, and in New England besides. In the spring of 1963, Boulez was named Horatio Appleton Lamb Lecturer at Harvard University where he discoursed on the "Aesthetics of Composing." His opening statement acknowledged his awareness that there were other messages in the air than his own: "My vision is only my wager and, as Baudelaire said, I have the right to be wrong."

In class Boulez analyzed *Wozzeck*, *The Rite of Spring*, and Webern's *Opus 21 Symphony*. The sessions were open to auditors, but the number who attended decreased with every session. One student, Stephen Jablonsky, who virtually adopted Boulez in Cambridge, attributes the loss of listeners to the "brilliance" of Boulez's talks. An "outside" visitor was a journalist on assignment from a nationwide magazine. Her story never materialized, but she left the following comments on file:

Boulez lived in Adams House.... His room was devoid of personal effects. I asked him why the room was so neat. "Because I'm against disorder," he replied....

Boulez was upset by the music floating in all of the windows. "About midnight they all get to Chopin discs." He sighed and waved his hand in a gesture of complete despair....

A graduate student in philosophy showed him around Lexington and Concord. "Boulez is a real tourist type," the student told me. "He's well informed and doesn't like it when people explain things he already knows. Someone asked him today if he knew who Thoreau was. That was a mistake...."

The lectures are not coming off. In class he is very lively and technical. He is fighting his way through the translation and has no time for communicating with the audience because he is so busy with the translation. . . .

I have never worked so hard to get so little information. Or specific quotes. It is very difficult to get him to answer a question although he doesn't answer it in a most pleasant way.

16

In 1961, the year after Boulez's German lectures, Steinecke was killed in an automobile accident. Pousseur says: "Steinecke was the man behind things at Darmstadt. He rendered everything possible materially. By 1961 each composer had begun to go off in his own direction. With Steinecke alive, they were still together although their paths had long since gone astray.

"During the summer of 1961 each person felt an immense hole. Steinecke was present in his absence. We all went to the cemetery. Boulez had planned to make a speech. He began to speak to the man himself, as though Steinecke were alive and could hear everything he said. He began by saying that we were all there, that we would go on doing what we had done. But almost immediately he began to cry. Then he cried so uncontrollably he had to run away. Everyone was surprised at his reaction. Everyone was surprised at the depth of his feeling."

Everyone was surprised because Boulez's behavior was not only out of character but without apparent motive. His assessment of Steinecke was well known. But as people tend to cry for themselves, so Boulez must have been crying for himself, for what he knew was now lost. For Steinecke was a symbol of a time when unanimity of taste and homogeneity of purpose spared music the scattering influence that bewilders it today. Steinecke's reign coincided with a moment when music was concentrated in a single style that was genuinely at one with its time. Several summers before his death, it was clear that serialism was not to be *the* way. But by the summer of his death it was equally clear that serialism would not be supplanted by a single, burgeoning art—like the preclassicism that displaced the high baroque —but rather by a plethora of styles. "In Bach's time," Boulez says, "there was an accepted language, an accepted convention. It is not at all the same today. There is no longer a complete frame of expression. That is what there was at Darmstadt. That is what is needed again."

When the Darmstadt lectures were published in 1963, Boulez dedicated them to the memory of Steinecke.

Boulez never stopped composing, but, as Virgil Thomson later wrote, everything began to "come out small." There was no lowering of quality in his work. But it came out small and incomplete at the same time.

"For me," Boulez told an American interviewer in 1963, "the external shock value of music matters little. The work I find really important is the one that has a kind of metaphysical truth, a truth in harmony with its time. An artist must be able to speak for his time in language of both precision and freedom. The trouble with 'beautiful' and 'ugly' as criteria is that they are tied up with superficial pleasure. I know I'm Germanic in this respect because I find sensual pleasure only a rather limited part of music. That is quite un-French, isn't it?"

In 1958 Boulez began *Doubles for Orchestra* on commission from the Sudwestfunk. He abandoned it to work on *Pli Selon Pli* but returned to it in 1964, expanding it as *Figures, Doubles, Prisms*. Boulez revised and added to it in 1968 and still considers the work unfinished. He conducted the first performance in Brussels in 1964. The work shows the influence of his experience conducting large orchestras. The orchestra is symmetrically grouped: there is a solo ensemble in the middle of two larger groups. The woodwinds are divided into three groups, the brass in four, the strings in five. The harps, xylophone, vibraphone, celesta, timpani, and percussion are placed individually between these main groups. He says that his writing for strings in this piece was a deliberate gesture in homage to Berg's *Violin Concerto*.

Here is Boulez on the title in program notes for the Cleveland Symphony in 1966:

Figures refers to simple elements, sharply characterized by dynamics, violence, softness, slowness, and so forth. These elements can be purely harmonic, or more rhythmically oriented, or purely melodic.

157

They are not themes in the conventional way, but "states" of musical being.

Doubles has two meanings: the first is that of the eighteenth century word *doppelgänger*, which means a human double. Thus, in the process of development, each figure may have its *double*, which is related only to it and no other.

Prisms occur when the figures or their *doubles* refract themselves one through the other. And in this case, one figure becomes the *prism*, and the other is refracted through it. By this process the maximum complexity is obtained, and the effect will be comparable to that of a kaleidoscope.

This confusing description dates from 1965. Today Boulez does not tell the public even this much about the making of a work. In response to queries about a new piece, he will generally limit his answer to mentioning the instrumentation and performance time. *Figures, Doubles, Prisms* is neither published nor recorded, but a look at the manuscript reveals a dense, contrapuntal texture and a hint of the aggressive style of his earlier years. But here the explosion is under control; no "hysteria" or "spells" anywhere in the score. Otto Tomek, who heard the piece, says, "It is a dramatic work. I would call it 'controlled explosion.' Comparing it to his early pieces is like comparing Schoenberg's *Orchestral Variations* to *Erwartung*."

An effort towards drama and excitement is also evident in *Structures, Book II,* begun in 1958 and completed in 1962. With its organization into chapters and texts, it reaffirms the author's attachment to literature. *Structures, Book II* has more in common with the *Third Piano Sonata,* composed only a short time before, than it has with *Structures, Book I,* dealing, as it does, with elements of choice as well as with sonorities and continuity. The precise instructions for pedaling (exactly how high to raise the pedal) are consistent with the tiny gradations in dynamics that can be seen from the enclosed sheet of *Structures, Book II.* Tomek says, "Boulez's late works may not be as explosive as the very early ones, but they do have particularly fine structures. Not big structures, of course, but structures in the most minute details. If you're quiet enough to hear the music, if you can hear the tiny differences, you can discover a whole world of invention."

Defining his aims of the 1960s, when he was not composing as prolifically as at other times, Boulez says the period began in 1958 when he wrote *Poésies pour Pouvoir:* "I was concerned with reconciling opposing elements. I wanted to bring electronic and orchestral sounds together. I was also working with small and large groups, with improvisation and nonimprovisation." The balance between control and

pierre boulez
(1925)

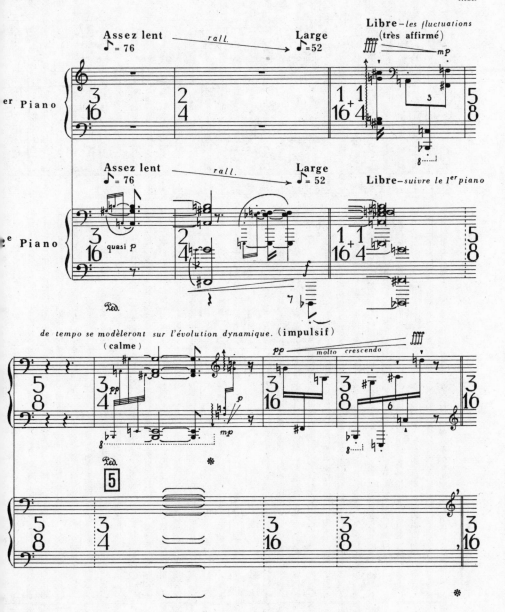

Page 1 of *Structures Book II* which begins with a "chapter," illustrating Boulez's strong tie to literature.

FIGURES , DOUBLES , PRISMES

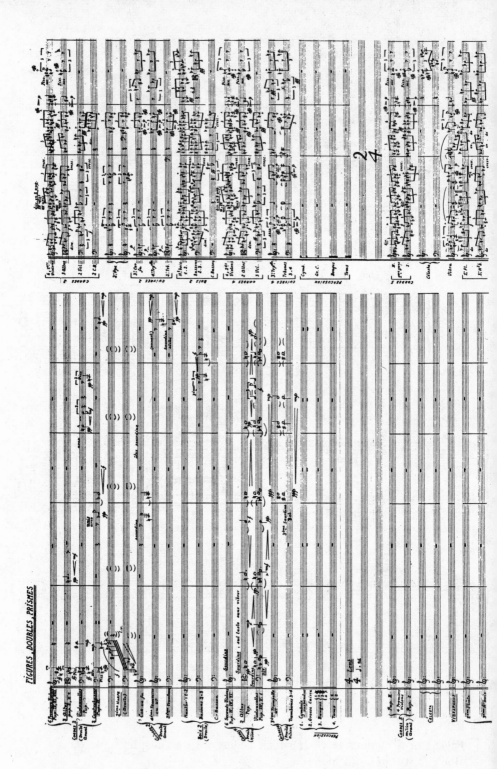

160

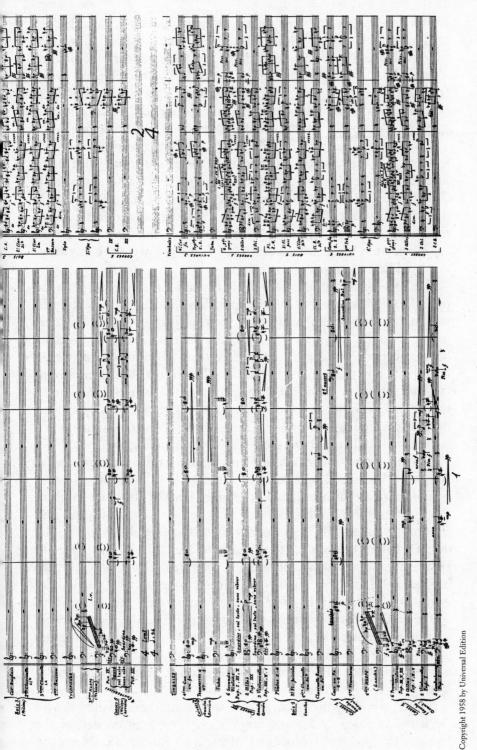

Copyright 1958 by Universal Edition

Two pages of *Figures, Doubles, Prisms,* the first piece Boulez composed after beginning to conduct large orchestras.

aleatory procedures occupied his attention in *Structures, Book II*. The sections called "texts," within rigorously defined limits, are open to various choices in the manner of the *Third Piano Sonata*. Boulez and Yvonne Loriod gave the first performance in Donaueschingen in October 1962. In a program note Boulez asked, "Is a musical work conceivable only in one precise and organized direction? Must one treat it as a kind of novel in which events move in one direction alone?"

Obviously still inspired by Mallarmé's *Le Livre*, Boulez attempted, in his own words, "to break completely the closed form." But he refused to share responsibility with the performer. In a 1964 interview in *The Times* of London, Boulez deprecated the performer's ability to participate in the creative process. "I have no confidence in the imagination of performers," he said. "The performer's head is full of formulas drawn from the music he plays. If he had the necessary invention, he would be a composer himself."

Boulez's harsh attitude towards interpreters separated him from the prevailing aesthetic and caused bitter feelings among many performers with whom he worked, particularly those playing supposedly aleatory works. Susan Bradshaw says, "The Mallarmé contains certain freedoms but no freedom. It's 'Play it as you like as long as you play it my way.' " Richard Bennett says much the same: "The second Mallarmé *Improvisation* seemed a beautiful, free piece. In the pauses I did pretty things under another conductor. That was not so when I played it under Boulez. He snaps the whip. Then you do it. The performance gets tension and vitality, but not the vitality from being happy."

In 1963, after completing his Harvard lectures, Boulez went to Los Angeles to conduct *Improvisations I and II*. This particular Monday Evening Concert also included *Structures, Book II*. In order to please Boulez, Morton not only programmed his most recent works and gave the *Improvisations* all the rehearsal time Boulez wished, but he also devoted half of the concert to a tribute to Mallarmé by including the Debussy and Ravel Mallarmé settings. An ardent Boulez fan, Morton, between 1952 and 1973, presented nineteen performances of Boulez works in his Monday Evening Concert series. Just before the 1963 performance of *Improvisations* and *Structures, Book II*, Morton wrote a letter of invitation to a music critic: "The other 'modern' music you have heard at our concerts (Ives, Serocki, Penderecki, Pousseur, et al.) is perhaps a little mild compared to the music of Boulez. Also Boulez is the master. As even Stravinsky might admit."

Boulez, who responds positively to such adoration, decided to give the world premiere of his next work, *Eclat*, at a joint concert of the Monday Evening series with the University of Southern California in

March 1965. He worked on the score until the day of its premiere. The date of the concert coincided with his fortieth birthday, and Morton gave a party for him. The Stravinskys and Craft were there. All the old wounds appeared to be healed. The early attacks on neoclassicism, the bad performance of *Threni* for the Domaine, all that belonged to the past. As with *Marteau sans Maître*, *Eclat* moved Stravinsky to pay tribute to Boulez. In *Themes and Episodes*, written when Stravinsky was still checking Craft's attributions to him, Stravinsky is quoted:

Boulez's *Eclat* for piano and chamber ensemble is another small masterpiece and one which introduces a new technique of time control. The score does not list the conductor's part along with those of the other performers, yet it is composed just as any of the instrumental parts are composed, and is, in fact, the most interesting of all, so much so that for the moment one fails to see any conductor being able to perform it half so well as Maître Boulez himself. Indeed, to watch him conduct it as I recently did, is an experience inseparable from the music itself. What a sense of timing he has! The score contains only verbal directions for tempo ("très vif," "plus modéré," "très longtemps," etc.) and is therefore at the opposite pole to mechanically geared pieces such as my *Variations*. Every event is controlled by cue, ordinal in most places but aleatory in others. The aleatoric idea is not new—each player stands by cocked and ready to play his group of notes, his turn determined by the flick of Maître Boulez's fingers—but the effect is attractive. . . . *Eclat* is not only creative music, but creative conducting as well, which is unique.

The eight-minute score, published later that year in a photocopy of Boulez's manuscript, contains more music than that played at its first performance. Boulez has been adding to the work ever since; he says it is now three times its original length. In 1974, at a Boulez retrospective in New York, the composer conducted and talked about *Eclat*: "Western music always seemed moved by gestures from here to there. It is never static. We in the Western world are always running, even in the slow movements. That is because we consider music part of our aesthetic life, not part of our ethical life. I became fascinated by the different conception of listening to music from the East.

"I had been acquainted with Eastern music since 1946. But sometimes it is a long time before an acquaintance becomes an influence inside of you. The big thing in *Eclat* is time. There is no meter. You will see I do not beat. Sometimes I leave the sound by itself. The sound never dies in the same way twice. I decide at the last minute

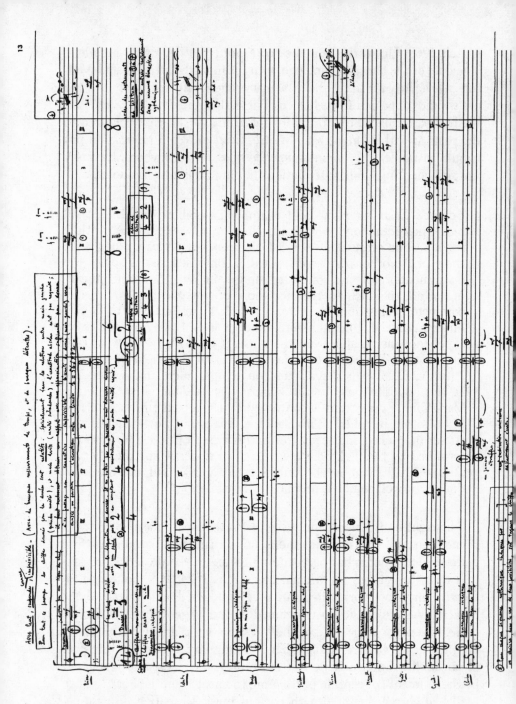

164

Quite slowly, suspended, as though unforeseeable (with sudden contractions and slackening of tempo)

At these places the figures given for durations are relative. Especially as regards the relationships between the left hand (large units) and right hand (subordinate units), absolute precision is not required; it is only necessary to achieve an approximate relationship sufficient to give this passage its "unforeseeable" character. The unit of duration (left hand) may be chosen, for reasons of acoustics, within the limits 1 = 56 ♩ ↗ 72

The conductor determines the disposition of durations. He does not "beat time", but gives each sign with a single gesture, reckoning mentally the required number of units

order of instruments ad libitum – from 1 to 7 the entrances are given irregularly and without any rhythmic direction

never dampen unless expressly prescribed

*) For each rhythmic sequence, indicated by [ ], select, in the case of two possibilities, always either the upper or the lower number

The published score of *Eclat* is a photograph of Boulez's manuscript. To the left is page 13 of the score, and above are instructions for that page that the publisher gives the performer in the event that he or she cannot read Boulez's handwriting.

what I will give as cues. The performer waits and waits. Then. Here it comes. It takes time to listen to this very complex sound that is progressively dying. In this work conducting is no longer something that has nothing to do with sound [much laughter from the audience] I mean, of course, there's always balance and all that in conducting. But here sound is part of the structure and the form. In *Eclat* the conductor controls the sound."

In *Eclat* the conductor virtually takes over the role of the composer, for he gives the cues that determine the form at each performance. The performer can play his sections in any order once the conductor gives the cue, but it is the timing that takes precedence over everything else.

Boulez says he chose the name *Eclat* for its ambiguity. "First, 'éclat' means fragment, and the first *Eclat* was a very short piece. Second it can mean éclat-explosive—a kind of burst or sudden shattering. Finally it suggests reflected light, reflections that are very fleeting. Any of these meanings can apply equally well to the poetic expression of the piece."

Boulez's need to exercise control was thwarted partly because of the accident that placed him in Baden-Baden when Stockhausen was asserting himself in Cologne. In the area which the Sudwestfunk reaches from Baden-Baden, eighty percent of the population lives in rural communities. Cologne Radio, on the other hand, reaches a highly urban group. Because taxes support the radio system, Cologne enjoyed a large subsidy.

German Radio virtually created new music in Europe, the directors competing for the biggest and the best. Strobel had initiated the reorganization of the system, taking over the Sudwestfunk after the war. The West German Radio at Cologne followed. Eimert brought the electronic studio to life when Stockhausen was still a young man. Then Hamburg, Munich, Bremen, Berlin, Stuttgart, and other cities followed suit. They sponsored concerts in their studios placing a high premium on first performances.

It should not be supposed that the German people at large looked with favor on this activity. New music was programmed after eleven o'clock at night when most were asleep. Boulez emphasizes, in fact, that "for the general audiences, neither Stockhausen nor I were the subjects of glory. Rather were we an embarrassment."

But there was no new music anywhere else in Germany. Not in public concerts, not in the universities (as was the case in the United States), not as accompaniment to plays (as was the case in France). So the focus of attention was radio, and Cologne was Number 1. At Cologne there were big performances, made possible by a big orchestra and chorus, which became the most important ensemble of modern music in Europe. It toured the big cities, dwarfing the activities in Baden-Baden (Cologne had three times the subsidy of the Sudwestfunk), and drowning out the activities of the Domaine Musical, which Boulez continued to go to Paris to conduct. Although the Domaine began to receive a government subsidy in 1959 when it moved to the Odéon, that subsidy was infinitesimal when compared to Cologne's.

Cologne had a star to match its resources. By 1957, although Eimert was still in charge, Stockhausen began to exert a strong influence, and in the late 1950s and throughout the sixties the influence was an aleatory one. Tudor characterizes his movement as one "towards freedom and opening out." Musicians began to regard Stockhausen with the fear and awe an earlier generation had reserved for Schoenberg. And Stockhausen felt he was entitled to such deference. Once a devout Catholic, Stockhausen dropped his ties to structure and God at the same time. He left his wife and their four children and married a painter and produced more progeny. Then he built a splendid house in the suburbs of Cologne and expected both women and all the children to live with him. Despite the domestic chaos, his work moved on. Pousseur says, "After 1961, after the death of Steinecke, Cologne became the mainspring of contemporary music with Stockhausen the primary animator." Boulez comments that even Strobel turned: "At

166

first Strobel thought Stockhausen was too close to kitsch. Then he became his strong defender." Hilda Strobel tells why: "What Stockhausen does is not démodé. It is true he can be very close to kitsch. That is because he is not frightened by these sentiments. He feels, 'It's in me; it must be free.' "

Stockhausen heeded Cage's admonition of 1958 to go still further in following Cage's lead. In 1960 Cage presented *Theater Piece 1960* in Greenwich Village; it consisted of a series of incoherent "happenings" and featured several performers, including David Tudor. In 1961 Stockhausen presented *Originale* in Cologne; it consisted of a series of incoherent "happenings" and featured several performers, including David Tudor. Stockhausen also went further towards indeterminacy in his purely "musical" works. In *Carré* (1959–60) scored for eighty players (four orchestras) and sixty-four singers (four choruses), the tones do not matter. What matters is the density. Thus the choice of tones is left to the performers themselves. About *Carré* Stockhausen writes, "You can confidently stop listening for a moment if you cannot or do not want to go on listening; for each moment stands on its own. . . ." His comment recalls the description of *Music of Changes* by Cage which he articulated again at Darmstadt in 1958: "The aggregates of sound have no necessary direction. Each is a musical fact, without any implication at all."

To say Stockhausen adopted Cage's philosophy is not to suggest Cage was delighted with the results. Cage says, "Stockhausen's work resembles Feldman's more than it does mine. In Feldman there is a concern with different registers. I have never had such a concern. A good deal of Karlheinz sounds like mezzo-forte Feldman. A little louder, but unsurprising."

As for Stockhausen's acknowledgment of his debt to Cage, that was never to be forthcoming. Otto Tomek, who replaced Eimert at Cologne and served Stockhausen there throughout the 1960s, says, "Cage had a tremendous influence on Stockhausen. But Stockhausen always refused to confess this. Sometimes he would say, 'One has to help Cage. He is such a big man.' Then he would turn around and be very hard: 'Let's do nothing. It's not music at all.' "

In fact, by the 1960s, when the revolution against old music appeared almost to have been won—Cologne Radio began broadcasting new music in prime evening time—the danger lay in the new composers' annihilating each other. Fratricide, not patricide, became the order of the day. Wolfgang Becker, who replaced Tomek at Cologne, characterizes the situation: "It's like the antagonism of one big company to another. Each composer wants to take the whole market."

17

Boulez did not go into conducting "to take the whole market." That aim crystallized somewhat later when he decided, he says, that he had a "missionary job to change the organizations, to change the threshold of our period," to lead, in other words, large audiences up to but not beyond the language he loves.

But at the beginning his aim was more modest. Lawrence Morton says: "Boulez told me long ago how concerned he was about the poor performances he had heard in his young professional days of the music of the Viennese, Bartók, Stravinsky, etc. How could conductors ever be expected to do his own music decently if they still didn't know how to conduct the classics of the twentieth century? And I remember my first visit to Cleveland in the late 1960s: he commented then that even at this late date he had found errors in Debussy scores that had so far escaped conductors everywhere. So his first impulse towards professional conducting was stimulated by the need for accuracy in the twentieth-century classics, and I feel he must have been encouraged in this by the two people with whom he surely must have discussed the problem: Strobel and Rosbaud."

Between 1960 and 1963 it was on-the-job training for Boulez. Many who played under him at the beginning say they would never have predicted he would go far. Several support Mrs. Strobel's description of the chaotic performance of Bartók's *Miraculous Mandarin*. Some add that in 1961 they played an *Eroica* under him that led them to believe that Boulez neither liked nor admired that work.

But why should anyone expect Boulez—who was out to "kill the musical past," out to erase repetition and contrast from his own and his colleagues' musical scores—to suddenly do an about-face and find those attributes admirable ones? In addition to problems of phrasing and drama, Boulez's early performance of the *Eroica* was sloppy. Wolfgang Becker was there and says that although it did have the clear structure for which Boulez is known today, it was "not at all note-perfect." Boulez did not then have the precision and control he sought.

In those years he concentrated on his conducting technique, avoiding the baton which he calls a "*crochet de manchot* [the one-armed man's hook] that keeps you from expressing yourself with your fingers." Boulez's use of his fingers and thumb as against his arms and body in conducting seems analogous to his use of tiny gradations in dynamics and durations as against big structure in his own music. Boulez has a marvelous ear, a remarkable sense of rhythmic exactitude. But what separates him from the other major conductors is the precision of his digital gestures, immeasurably useful in the intricate twentieth-century scores he loves. Boulez indicates time and rhythm with the forefinger and thumb of his right hand. The left is rarely used to imitate the right. It is as though the "ethics" that legislates against the repetition of a "theme" in composition also legislates against the left hand imitating the right. Instead he raises or lowers the left hand steadily with his fingers extended rigidly to indicate an increase or decrease in volume.

After moving to Germany, Boulez went to Paris to conduct four or five of the Domaine's five or six concerts a year. While there he stayed with his parents, who then lived on Boulevard Raspail. Although the family's favorite newspaper was *Le Figaro*, whose music critic at that time attacked Boulez not only for his revolutionary music but for his character and personality, the bitterness between generations had diminished: Boulez's contract with the Sudwestfunk convinced the father that his son had done well. In fact, not only he but his son-in-law, Jack Chevalier, were members of the board of directors of the Domaine Musical.

While in Germany, Boulez says, he did not miss France. "I always felt very good there, never alien in Germany. I am very adaptable, not like the French in this way. The French generally adapt poorly out of their own country. I find this attitude unbearable. There was always great anger in France when I spoke of Germany."

169

In January 1963, Boulez conducted the Orchestre National in a fiftieth anniversary performance of *The Rite of Spring*. It took place in the Théâtre des Champs-Elysées where he had staged an anti-Stravinsky revolt twenty years before. The piece was recorded; Boulez also recorded, with the same orchestra, Stravinsky's *Les Noces* and *Renard*. These were his first commercial discs.

In 1962 Georges Auric, one of the original supporters of the Domaine Musical, was appointed director of the Paris Opéra. In order to stage something of a coup d'état, Auric invited Boulez to preside over a new production of *Wozzeck*, an opera Boulez had regarded with awe from his earliest composing days. Boulez insisted on thirty rehearsals—instead of the usual three or four—and he got them. He also insisted on a performance in the original German, which appears to be an even more outrageous demand, for it had been only twenty-three years since Parisians had watched Nazis strut in their streets and sing "Deutschland, Deutschland, über alles" in the Tuileries. But the fact is that as early as 1950 a German company did Wagner at the Paris Opéra to packed houses and with no protests. So Boulez's German *Wozzeck* should not be interpreted—as has often been the case—as his personal triumph over the resistance of his countrymen.

Boulez at the helm of the Paris Opéra proved to be a tremendous success. After the first performance the musicians rose to applaud him. The man who felt himself the much-maligned son, both in relation to his family and to France, made his first impressive move towards a triumphant return home.

Having flirted with Germany, and having received a diploma from France, Boulez was ready to move on to England. The invitation was extended by William Glock who, like Auric, was an early Boulez supporter and the man who commissioned the essay that proclaimed the dogmatic "Schoenberg is dead!" In 1952 Glock was director of the Bryanston and Dartington Summer Schools, where he brought in such advanced and not then very well known figures to teach as Stephen Wolpe, Luciano Berio, Elliott Carter, and Luigi Nono. Glock had been a pupil of Artur Schnabel, the pianist in Schoenberg's early Viennese circle and the man in whose home René Leibowitz grew up. The "new music" circle in Europe was small, but it was intelligent and exerted great influence.

Boulez had begun to think about conducting even when composition seemed to fill his life. In 1954 he started to send Glock regular bulletins from the Domaine Musical, emphasizing those performances he would conduct himself. In 1956 Boulez visited London with Barrault. Glock was then director of the International Musicians Club, an association of musicians from all over the world. During that visit Glock invited the Domaine Musical with Boulez at the helm to give a concert in London the following year. Boulez agreed. He conducted *Zeitmasse*, Webern's *Opus 24 Concerto*, Nono's *Polyphonie*, and his own *Marteau sans Maître*, all works which met his standards as difficult and demanding scores.

By 1959 Glock was Controller of Music, the highest musical dignitary in the BBC, and a man deeply committed to new music. English critic Andrew Porter writes that Glock "singlehandedly changed the concert life of London by making the music of our time central to the BBC Symphony's concert series, to the Proms (that enormous 'festival' of orchestral music which for weeks fills the Albert Hall, and over the air reaches a wider audience still), to the countless concerts and chamber and solo recitals promoted by the BBC both in public halls and studios, to the broadcast relays of new works up and down the country, to recordings and relays from abroad and to the broadcast talks about music and the printed commentary and discussion appearing in the BBC's publications. . . ."

Glock invited Boulez to be guest conductor of the BBC in 1964. "Boulez brought a tiny list," Glock recalls, "not more than twenty works. We gave a whole series in Festival Hall of twentieth-century programs. I was tremendously impressed by the way Boulez rehearsed. The concerts were so fresh, so entirely new for everyone. Many people wrote and told me that. He gave the orchestra a beautiful sound, not velvety, but delicate and disciplined."

Between 1963, when he had twenty pieces in his repertoire, and 1969, Boulez rose to be music director of the BBC and the New York Philharmonic orchestras. In between he appeared throughout Europe at the head of such orchestras as the Orchestre National, the Lamoureux, the Paris Conservatoire, the Concertgebouw, the Berlin Philharmonic, the Vienna Philharmonic, the New Philharmonia, and the London Symphony. Boulez's rise as conductor was therefore as meteoric as his rise as a composer had been. Nobody who knows him seems surprised. Alfred Schlee, director of Universal Edition, says, "Boulez is a musician above all. What else is there to say?" Lawrence Morton says a little more: "Boulez is 95 percent musician. The other five percent is worrying about his diet and taking long walks." (When Boulez is in Baden-Baden, he spends his late afternoons and much of the weekends walking in the Black Forest.)

But while rising in his conducting career, composition still seemed to determine his moves. Those who have had Boulez as a guest report that the light never goes out in his room until after 3:00 A.M. Boulez's decision to record with Columbia instead of E.M.I., one of the largest companies in the world, was determined, he says, by Columbia's offer to record his own works. And his move to replace Michel de Koos, the manager he had inherited from Hans Rosbaud, with Howard Hartog of Ingpen and Williams was stimulated by Hartog's efforts to bring the Sudwestfunk to Edinburgh for a full-scale Boulez festival. Hartog's efforts did not succeed at that time. But his plan materialized in 1965 when Edinburgh mounted the largest retrospective of Boulez's work that has yet been presented, with Boulez conducting *Marteau sans Maître* and *Pli Selon Pli* in Hamburg.

An eloquent testimonial to the fact that conducting never displaced composing in Boulez's esteem is his absence of difficulties with other conductors. Like women, conductors are not important to him. On the other hand, the troubles with Stravinsky grew. Stravinsky was, after the death of Schoenberg, universally recognized as the greatest living composer. True, his serial works were rarely played, but there was a tacit acceptance of the fact that the genius who had composed *The Rite of Spring* was at work on something too difficult to understand. There was, therefore, little speculation—as there had been at one time—about the Master drying up.

So the competition, the war, broke out again. It did so with the performance of *Threni* in November 1959 at the Domaine Musical. This is Boulez's view of what went on: "Craft had prepared *Threni* and Stravinsky was to conduct. The disaster came from two directions. The singers had not been chosen by me but by an agent in charge of the Aix-en-Provence festival. They were absolutely awful. I, myself, with Stravinsky, did the piano rehearsals. I quickly knew the worth of the singers. Four or six could not manage their parts. Rehearsing at the piano, I told Stravinsky that he should be stronger with them. But Stravinsky was fatherly and supported them. He refused to be strong. And he was not a good conductor; he was a terribly lousy conductor. I was in the middle of the choir myself, giving cues. I told him, "We will have a catastrophe." We did. The admiration the singers had for him could not compensate for the minimum of clarity. And the orchestra had been ill-prepared by Craft. The reason *Agon* had gone so well two years before was that Rosbaud had prepared the Sudwestfunk thoroughly."

Craft says that Boulez had given his assurance that he would rehearse *Threni* himself and that he was unable to fulfill his promise because he was finishing a piece for Donaueschingen. "In consequence," Craft writes, "*Threni* was so badly sung and played that it was received with jeers by the audience. And when, at the end of the performance, Boulez tried to maneuver Stravinsky into taking a bow, the humiliated composer curtly refused, swearing that he would never conduct in Paris again, a promise that he kept."

Craft says Boulez added insult to injury by offering for sale in the lobby a new book by Antoine Goléa, "Stravinsky's archenemy," devoted to conversations with Boulez. "On all counts," Craft continues, "the Paris *Threni* was a disaster and the true cause of the rift between Stravinsky and Boulez."

Still, the friendship picked up again. The Stravinskys and Craft celebrated Boulez's fortieth birthday at a small dinner in Lawrence Morton's house and Stravinsky (as we saw) wrote generously about *Eclat* in *Themes and Episodes*, published in 1966. But another incident occurred in 1967 that proved to be the last. In a film directed by Richard Leacock and distributed over network television, Stravinsky is shown looking at his own *Les Noces*. Boulez is looking at the piece with him. Boulez notes that at the end there is one bar's rest too much. Stravinsky, in his eighties, appears confused. Then he concedes that the score is wrong. As the scene closes Stravinsky seems to be muttering something in Russian.

Boulez says that the actual incident occurred before the filming, that Rolf Liebermann, the director of the Hamburg Opera, was present as Leacock was following the Stravinsky entourage around in California, and that Liebermann suggested they restage the incident for the cameras. Boulez says Stravinsky was not disconcerted about that, and even added that he would sign his name to the effect that Boulez discovered this particular error.

But Craft says that the television incident coupled with an interview which followed soon after in which Boulez referred to Stravinsky as being "Webern-influenced"—Stravinsky did not want to appear influenced by anyone at that late date—convinced Stravinsky that Boulez was two-faced and made him resolve never again to have anything to do with him. Boulez thinks Craft was the instigator of the trouble, and that too is possible. In any case the bitterness persisted beyond the grave. In a "conversation" published just after Stravinsky's death in the *New York Review of Books*, Craft quotes the aged and very ill composer in an attack on Boulez. Boulez shot back in a "commemorative" article on Stravinsky for the *Saturday Review*, in which he took Stravinsky severely to task for his reliance on old music. It was not as harsh as "Schoenberg is dead!" but Boulez was older and more controlled then. "I am no longer wild on the outside," Boulez said in 1973, "because I found that useless to me. But I am still just as wild on the inside."

In the 1960s, Boulez was still somewhat wild on the outside, and his pattern of testing authority, of seeing just how far he could go in undermining or insulting Stravinsky and still retain his affection, was also the pattern he followed in regard to France. Regarding Boulez's relations with his country, his sister explains, "If my brother seems antinationalistic, it is because he was not recognized in France. He is uncompromising. The only meaningful thing to him is quality and he feels he was not recognized in France. He was truly le fils mal aimé."

The most flagrant example of Boulez's fight with France occurred in 1964 when André Malraux, Minister of Cultural Affairs and a famed novelist and art critic, established a commission to investigate the "deficiencies" in French musical life. Malraux did not know Boulez well. He had come to Domaine concerts only twice. But Gaeton Picon, director of the Department of Arts and Letters and a longtime Boulez fan, introduced the composer to E. J. Biazini, an official under Malraux. Biazini, according to Boulez's account, told Boulez that he was the only one who could help them. Boulez responded by sending Malraux a long letter full of suggestions. One suggestion was to divide all of Paris's five orchestras into two large and flexible groups, one managed by the State, the other by the city. The plan threatened many who made their living through the established system, and Boulez displayed his idea of diplomacy by becoming honorary president of the musicians' union in order to persuade them to agree to his plans.

It was all to no avail. Malraux named Marcel Landowski, a neo-Romantic composer, to the office of musical director of the ministry. Boulez protested with a vitriolic essay published in Le Nouvel Observateur which began, "André Malraux has just made a decision concerning music in France which I find unthoughtful, irresponsible, and inconsistent." Then he canceled all engagements with the Orchestre National, forbade the newly formed Orchestre de Paris to play his music, cut off his connection with the Domaine Musical, and publicly announced that he would never again live in Paris where music was in the hands of incompetent men.

Some journalists attributed Boulez's failure with Malraux to the efforts of André Jolivet and Henri Sauguet, "neoclassic" composers and long-standing enemies of Boulez. But Suzanne Tezenas offers a still more reasonable explanation: she says it was the Comtesse de Fels, Marcel Proust's niece and the powerful patroness of a Proust salon, who maneuvered Landowski into a position where he could beat Boulez for the post under Malraux.

Boulez's periodic efforts to return to France as the one in control is a contrapuntal theme—but a very important one—to the main motive of his ambitious thrust to make the big time with his ideas. After London, Cleveland seemed right; many musicians consider that orchestra to be the greatest in the world. In 1964, George Szell went through Baden-Baden and called Boulez. Szell had heard about his conducting through the Concertgebouw and engaged him as a guest for March 1965. Boulez says he learned to conduct the classics in Cleveland. Szell, whose conducting was lean and lucid, became progressively more enthusiastic about Boulez. The next year Szell heard about Boulez's troubles with Malraux. "He knew," Boulez says, "that I had given up all my French engagements and that I would be free in 1967. He thought I had a good attitude about Malraux and invited me to conduct again, this time for a four-week engagement in 1967. A four-week engagement is unusual."

Carlos Moseley, then managing director of the New York Philharmonic, had engaged Boulez for a guest appearance in the spring of 1969. Moseley notes that the Philharmonic has a tradition of hiring composer-conductors that extends from Tchaikovsky to Gustav Mahler. After Boulez's Cleveland performance, Moseley met with him to plan programs for a second guest appearance in 1971. "I think," Boulez says, "he more or less began to consider me as head of the Philharmonic then."

Moseley confirms this. But that information did not get through to Sir William Glock, who engaged Boulez for long periods as a guest conductor with the BBC orchestra. After conducting the BBC in three concerts at Carnegie Hall in 1965, Boulez took the British orchestra on tour with an exclusively twentieth-century program: Schoenberg's *Opus 16*, Webern's *Opus 6*, Debussy's *Images*, excerpts from *Wozzeck*, the Berg *Altenberg Lieder*, and his own recently composed *Doubles*, *Figures*, *Prisms*. In 1967 Boulez brought the BBC and much of that same program, adding to it his own *Eclat*, to Czechoslovakia, Poland, and Russia, countries that had not been exposed to contemporary music.

Glock recalls Boulez's early days with the orchestra: "Up to 1967," he says, "the concerts were really revelations. Boulez was still conducting a repertory every note of which meant a great deal to him. During the spring of 1968, the BBC was on the lookout for a new chief conductor; Colin Davis was preparing to leave. I told my bosses at the BBC that Boulez was the only man for the job. He was then conducting the Hague Orchestra at Scheveningen. My plan was to invite him for a three-year term beginning in 1971. I flew to Holland

and we went for a seven-mile very fast walk on the beach. He said one thing which typifies his orderly and planning mind: 'I'll do it if you stay on.' He didn't want to be a new boy with a new man. I was nearing sixty; in the BBC when you are sixty they can say 'thank you very much' and let you go."

But the BBC did not let Glock go, and the plan was made for Boulez to spend two five-month sessions a year in London. Glock says that he had a "slight unease, even then, that this was not using Boulez in the best way. I always wanted him to get on with composition."

18

Although conducting never displaced composition in Boulez's mind, it certainly began to occupy the greater part of his time. In 1969, Boulez was scheduled not only to conduct *Pelléas et Mélisande* at Covent Garden and to fulfill his guest commitment with both the BBC and New York Philharmonic orchestras, but he also engaged himself for the demanding position of principal guest conductor of the Cleveland Orchestra, where he was to concentrate on the contemporary repertoire—which, with the exception of Berg, held very little interest for Szell.

"Inevitably," Lawrence Morton says, "this kind of career earned him a good income. I think Boulez has enjoyed having money—after all, he had known intimately the lack of it. I never saw but I heard accounts of his quarters on Rue Beautreillis where he lacked a good many of the essentials of genuine comfort. But I think that with him money has been less a motivation than a reward. Surely no one has worked harder for it."

Boulez's greatly augmented income made it possible for him to take over the entire Baden-Baden house and to decorate it as he wished. He selected austere furnishings, in harmony with his favorite period of Webern and Klee, and asked the former wife of the late pianist Géza Anda (she was also an interior decorator) to arrange the pieces for him. The outside of the house, turn-of-the-century William II, successfully disguises its Bauhaus interior. Mies van der Rohe's Barcelona chairs make for an airy, antiseptic look. No memorabilia are permissible in a Bauhaus world. Not a photograph, not a newspaper is visible. Richard Bennett describes it as a house which would not allow a love letter anywhere.

In addition to chairs, couches, and tables on pale carpeting, the living room contains a television set that enables the viewer to see four programs at one time, and a leather and marble bar—not a gratuitous piece of furniture, for Boulez can drink an extraordinary amount without suffering any diminishment of his wits. An evening meal may include several cocktails, the better part of a bottle of wine, a cognac, and two or three scotches. (Recently, on orders of his physician, Boulez has reduced his drinking considerably.)

On the walls are paintings by Miro and Klee; Giacometti's drawings of Webern and Stravinsky hang in his study. His desk appears as if never used; 4 x 6 cards on which he composes stand stacked next to a container of sharply-pointed colored pencils. In a larger library are the complete works of Haydn, a gift from Universal Edition; a Steinway grand piano, a gift from the Sudwestfunk; and a framed letter from Debussy to Varèse, a gift from Varèse's widow, Louise. One has the impression that Boulez buys nothing, that he just accepts whatever is given to him. He does this not because he is frugal—he gave his nieces very costly wedding trips to Egypt, Greece, and Turkey, and he invariably picks up dinner checks no matter how expensive the party—but because it requires too much time and trouble, too much of an expenditure of taste, to make a purchase of anything at all. Impersonality oozes out of every pore of this large house; about a dozen seemingly identical dark suits hang in as orderly a fashion in his closet as the pencils stand straight-backed in their container. Boulez sleeps in an exceptionally narrow Bauhaus bed.

As a conductor, Boulez not only made enough money to live exactly as he wished, but he was now in a celebrated enough position to dispense with writing his own polemics, for journalists were delighted to interview him. The first of the news-making interviews was published in the weekly German paper Der Spiegel in September 1967. Boulez accused Liebermann, director of the Hamburg State Opera, of having hoodwinked the public into believing that he had transformed his traditional opera house into a center for genuine music drama. As is usual with his public pronouncements—a far cry from his exceptionally courteous personal manner—Boulez's tone was abusive in the extreme. He said Wozzeck and Lulu were the last operas worth mentioning (thus putting the knife deep into Stravinsky's back); that Hans Werner Henze was like de Gaulle: "Whatever rubbish he puts out he still thinks he is King" (thus insulting both socialist Henze and de Gaulle); and that Liebermann had "institutionalized his own bourgeois tastes as director for the Hamburg Opera." He also attacked the Paris Opéra as a house "full of dust and dung... a place where only tourists go, because it is part of the circuit, like the Folies-Bergère and the Invalides."

Jean Vilar, founder and director of the Théâtre National Populaire, under which the Paris Opéra is run, called on Boulez to collaborate with dancer-choreographer Maurice Béjart in a thoroughgoing reform of the Paris Opéra. The institution needed it. Although the Opéra was receiving $12 million a year in subsidy, forty-seven percent of the Culture Ministry's entire budget, its repertory had been feeble, its performances drab.

But Vilar's invitation to Boulez came in 1967, only one year after the episode with Malraux, when Boulez swore never again to work in France. Vilar's assurance that the Paris Opéra did not come under Malraux's Ministry—as far as artistic direction was concerned—was apparently enough for Boulez to go ahead on the project without any significant loss of personal dignity. By May 1968, Boulez and Béjart had their reforms ready. The Opéra-Comique, the company's second house, was to be closed for good. The Opéra would give nothing but concert performances for one year. The orchestras and choruses of both houses would be amalgamated and their standards raised. When the Opéra reopened, it would offer a more limited but more substantial repertoire. Workshops in music and drama would flourish. An entirely new theater would be built, suited to the needs of the late twentieth century. Finally, the most striking reform of all: Boulez, who writes Verdi off as "dum de dum, nothing more," would be music director of the Paris Opéra.

Boulez says of this apparent paradox: "The general object was to deal with music among other things. It was to have been called the 'Center for Music and Theater.' It would have involved exploring many possibilities concerning theater, dance, music, and the rest. It was in the making of these plans that I started to think in different terms, in terms of changing the threshold of the music of our time through rearranging the musical life of an important city."

But the month that the plan was ready for action was also the month of the tumultuous political events of 1968. De Gaulle issued a call to his supporters to resist the revolutionary situation. Vilar, a man of the Left, refused to resist it and resigned. Glock learned Boulez's most recent French project had collapsed and offered him the BBC orchestra in its place.

179

Boulez's London appointment was announced in January 1969. It would seem to have given him everything he wanted. Apart from providing a decent salary, the BBC post carried the assurance that he would be under no great time pressure and that he could try to do in London what had been aborted through the political events in Paris. "Being part of as vast an official organization as this meant no tight budget problems," Boulez says. "Of course the orchestra has a budget, but those in the administration understand that you have to lose money if you want to provide a genuine cultural life."

It was during that same month, January 1969, after reading of Boulez's tour of the United States, that I suggested an interview for the New York Times. My editor accepted the suggestion on the basis of Boulez's appearance as a conductor. As a composer he would not then have passed the Times's test: a New York performance of a news-making work. It is true that older established composers often make it on less than that. I interviewed Benjamin Britten when he came to New York to do nothing more than accompany Peter Pears at the piano, and I interviewed Elliott Carter to celebrate his sixtieth birthday. But in 1969, at the age of forty-four, Boulez's entrée into the Arts and Leisure Section of the Sunday Times was as a guest conductor who had established himself as a leading composer abroad.

Hurok Attractions had arranged a Monday lunch at Boston's Ritz-Carlton Hotel. The day before the appointment, the East Coast was blanketed under a fierce blizzard. I called Boulez in Boston to arrange another date. We settled on a day later in the week. No intermediary was involved. No member of the Hurok firm, no officer of a public relations business, no secretary, no adoring disciple or devoted friend. I was struck by the spartan simplicity of the man. Now that I have known Boulez seven years, I think that "formidable isolation" seems a more appropriate description than simplicity.

The Times headlined the interview, "A Fighter from Way Back."

In 1945, when he was 20, Pierre Boulez led a group booing a performance of Igor Stravinsky's "Four Norwegian Moods" at the Théâtre des Champs-Elysées in Paris. "I was not attacking Stravinsky," he explained recently over lunch in Boston's Ritz-Carlton, "but the Establishment, which considered him the God, the Idol, the Only Truth. I did it to draw attention to Schoenberg, whose influence was still limited to Vienna and Berlin." A few years later, when 12-tone writing was accepted by the avant-garde, Boulez attacked Schoenberg to bring attention to Webern. And sure enough, post-Webern serialism dominated the 1950's and early 60's.

Boulez played a crucial role in shifting the balance of musical power from Stravinsky and Stravinsky's American disciples, trained in Paris under Nadia Boulanger, back to the Austro-German domain, where it had prevailed from Bach through Wagner. In 1959, he even left France and moved permanently to Baden-Baden: "Germany was the most exciting country for contemporary music."

Boulez won the significant battles. Stravinsky, in a famous about-face, adopted the serial technique and hailed Boulez as the best composer of his generation. And after Boulez conducted at Bayreuth, a German critic wrote that he could teach the Germans how to handle Wagner. Today the 43-year-old composer-conductor is in demand all over the world. I spoke to him just after he served as guest conductor for the Boston Symphony Orchestra and before he left for Chicago, his last engagement before New York. Thursday Boulez starts a month-long assignment here conducting the New York Philharmonic.

Dressed with the same attention to unusual combinations of color that characterizes his musical work—a dark blue shirt under a brown tweed jacket, with a subtly hued plaid tie—Boulez was restrained for about half an hour. He ate red snapper, drank German beer, and spoke politely about his parents and his teachers. When I mentioned an American composer whose work he dislikes, Boulez suddenly came to life, launching a virtuoso attack on various facets of U.S. music.

Electronic music: "This same frenzy for technology began in Europe about 1953. By 1958 it had all died down. The idea of electronics as the big future of music is just an American trick of fashion. Next year they'll discover the viola da gamba. Playing Bach on the computer doesn't interest me at all because it's artistically irrelevant. All this indicates a simplistic way of thinking—an appallingly low level of thinking."

As for "Perspectives of New Music," an avant-garde journal published by the Princeton University Press: " 'Perspectives' is similar to 'Die Reihe,' begun in Germany about 1953. Its writers think they are great scientists. They are not. I know great scientists and *they* possess invention and imagination. Composers who publish in this journal never discuss important questions of choice and decision. They write only about putting different things together. This is not an esthetic point of view. It's what I call a 'cashier's point of view.' "

New Image of Sound, the Hunter College concert series at which Boulez appeared last week as composer, conductor and performer, is, says he, "the best series in New York. It is just like the Domaine Musical, which I began in Paris about 1953—the same kind of programming, the same six concerts a season."

But after a second beer, Boulez relaxed and described how he views the gulf that separates the American composer from his European colleague: "There should be no antagonism between the American and European composer. I am always fighting the nationalistic point of view. Americans are jealous—I'm not sure if that's the right word—thinking the Europeans are taking attention away from them. The Americans do operate under a severe handicap, of course; they have no strong personalities in the field. If they were strong enough to establish their personality on the world, they would see that no national favoritism exists.

"After World War II, Europeans were thirsty for all America's creative products—Faulkner, Cummings, Jackson Pollock. Europeans bought, almost without discrimination, anything Steinbeck or Dos Passos wrote. But for an American artist to be exported to Germany he has to be better than the German product. They have no one in America as good as Hans Werner Henze, and that is not setting your sights very high. A composer the stature of Stockhausen they have not."

Boulez diagnosed what he feels is the American malady: "European music is not connected with the university. There is no ivory castle for us. But here, university people and practical musicians ignore each other. It's a very unhealthy state of affairs.

"I do not like this pedantic approach. I do not like scholars who bring only Death to music. The university situation is incestuous. It is one big marriage in which the progeny deteriorates, like the progeny of old and noble families. The university musician is in a self-made ghetto, and what is worse, he likes it there."

I mentioned some American university composers who deny the role of self-expression in new music. Boulez said: "They do so because they are not expressive. It is a type of dialectic I find very childish. Not that I consider expressivity to be the final goal of music. The goal of music is far richer than that. But university composers have no mystery, and music must give a sense of mystery.

"This endlessly, hopelessly academic work reminds me of the Conservatoire. There is no difference between this music and an eight-part counterpoint study. Composers must start with a strong technique, but a technique is just the beginning; it is the means and not the end.

182

"I have no confidence in those who think they know their goals. You discover your goal as you come upon it. It's out there in front of you; you discover it each day."

Commenting on the unhealthy situation separating intellectual composers from practical musicians, Boulez prescribed his own specific treatment: "An intellectual must use intellectual power to change things not directly related to intellectual affairs. When I compose, I have Debussy, Stravinsky and Berg in my background. For an audience to listen to my compositions, it must have the same background as that. So I conduct early 20th-century music to prepare people to listen to more advanced pieces. The fact of conducting is not exciting to me. I'm not super-happy to conduct a large orchestra. But I feel compelled to bring new creative aspects of music to the whole of musical life everywhere. To go into the crowd without losing my integrity, that is what I want to do.

"It is useless only to complain about the 'degraded' audience. That is why I conduct. In Boston I played Debussy's 'Jeux,' which this orchestra played the last time about 10 years ago, and the infrequently heard 'Three Orchestral Pieces,' by Berg. The job of a conductor is to bring an audience to realize it's as important to hear Berg as to hear Mahler."

Boulez does not think that the United States is beyond all hope. But, he feels, salvation will be difficult. "It must lie with an American who is both intellect and practical musician. What is needed in America is a musical John Kennedy. As long as you have no Kennedy in music, you have no future of music in America."

I mentioned Leonard Bernstein as both intellect and musician. Boulez replied: "Bernstein was not there at the right time. When he arrived at the New York Philharmonic, it was too soon for this activity. Then too, such a figure must be personally involved in the advanced creative thinking of the time. You can't introduce a new work to the orchestra, apologizing for it at the same time."

Boulez denied rumors that anyone had ever approached him with the suggestion he take over Bernstein's present job: "But if anyone had, I could not have considered it. The circumstances of directing the New York Philharmonic are such that you are the prisoner of a frame. I am not American enough to be such a prisoner. Nor do I know enough about New York's musical life to bring about the necessary changes. To change bad habits, one must know them well."

Boulez says that—as director—he would require a much larger

orchestra, between 150 and 160 musicians, who would play two different kinds of programs. Boulez would do a conservative series featuring big-name soloists as well as a series of avant-garde concerts. "The same musicians," he says, "should be able to do both. A culture center moves in many directions. The money you make with the 'museum' series you must invest in performing new pieces."

In 1971 Boulez will curtail his extensive traveling to settle not in Germany but in London, where he'll take over as permanent conductor of the BBC Symphony Orchestra: "London is the model of my conception of contemporary musical life with the BBC's regular repertory including many 20th-century works. Today London plays the role of Berlin in the twenties—not only in music but in everything. And with Berlin all cut up, there's no city the size of London left in Germany."

London also offers a swingier life as well as a big prestigious job. With Sir Thomas Beecham dead, Boulez will rule the city's music while Von Karajan is alive and well in Berlin.

The interview enraged America's university composers—there were demands for "equal time" in the *Times*. But it did not appear to enrage anybody else, and when Boulez came to New York and conducted those twentieth-century "classics" which he was then conducting better than anyone in the world, he received only accolades from the press. It is true that many people walked out, particularly the women of the Friday matinees, but the critics were unanimous in their praise. *New York Times* critic Harold Schonberg raved.

The Philharmonic's board of directors was ready to act right away. The late David Keiser, a literate amateur musician who had studied at Harvard and Juilliard in his youth, was in power as chairman of the orchestra's Music Policy Committee. Formerly president of North American Sugar Industries, Inc., Keiser was also chairman of the board of the Juilliard School and a member of the board of directors of Lincoln Center.

Keiser reported the background of the Boulez decision: "In 1967 and 1968, Szell was enthusiastic about Boulez. I went to Cleveland to hear him conduct. I forget the program now but I think it contained the *Sacre du Printemps*. I was terribly impressed. He first conducted our orchestra in March 1969. After the first concert I said to my wife, 'That is our new music director.' You really cannot make such a decision until you hear a man conduct our own orchestra in

184

our own hall. That first concert I was very favorably impressed with him. After the second I knew for sure.

"Then Carlos Moseley and I talked about appointing Boulez. On April 1, after Boulez had conducted several weeks of programs, Alice Tully gave a luncheon for him. About twenty people were there, among them members of the Music Policy Committee. Boulez was charming and likeable, as he always is. After lunch he left and we held a meeting. We decided we wanted him as music director. We checked with those absent and all agreed. Carlos called Boulez to tell him we wanted to meet with him right away. We met at 7 o'clock at the bar of the Essex House where he was staying. Although he had vast commitments he did not say No. Both Carlos and I knew then he would say Yes. The Music Policy Committee presented their recommendation to the board which accepted it unanimously.

"It was clear Boulez was the right man for the job. There were a few old men—Szell, Steinberg, Stokowski—but such a person would come in for not more than two years and also men of that age would find the burden of music director far too onerous. There were, of course, some young men—like Mehta and Ozawa—but they were not old enough for the job. They did not have enough experience.

"As far as all this 'revolution' is concerned, the press has gone much too far with it. To be sure, Boulez let us know from the start that he would not be interested in taking over a standard repertoire and continuing to do only standard things. He wanted to do concerts in Greenwich Village and to lecture on new music. He thought this would be the scene in which he could do all of that."

Boulez reports that when he received the call from Moseley, he anticipated it was due to a snag in the programming for his guest appearance in 1970–71. He says that when the two men arrived and Moseley asked, "How would you like to be music director of the New York Philharmonic?" he first thought that because this was April 1, this must have been an April Fool's joke. It took him more than a few seconds to comprehend that it was a genuine, serious offer.

Boulez returned to London to discuss the matter with Glock who, understandably, was horrified. Glock had planned to have Boulez for ten months a year; in addition he had reservations about Boulez in New York: "The BBC had a background for doing contemporary work. It seemed so much more suitable for Boulez than New York. Why did he want to do both? I shall never quite know that. He loves New York. Partly he hoped to influence musical attitudes in these two super-cities. I thought, then and now, that it would have

185

been more fruitful for him to concentrate his efforts in London. When we spoke in April, he appeared to agree with me. I went off for a holiday in France thinking that the threat had been averted. But when I returned Boulez said the New York problem had come up again."

Indeed it had hardly gone away. In May, Boulez flew to New York to confer with Moseley, who was then in the hospital. Boulez and Moseley agreed on a plan: Boulez would give the orchestra one week of tour and seven weeks in New York during the 1971–72 season. After that the year would be divided in three parts: four months in London, four months in New York, four months for composing in Baden-Baden. Szell, then serving as music advisor and senior guest conductor of the New York Philharmonic, would continue to handle the bulk of the traditional repertoire, allowing Boulez to concentrate on the works he does best. (Szell died on July 30, 1970, one year before Boulez assumed the directorship.)

Glock was not pleased with the proposed schedule. "Being chief conductor," he says, "is quite different from being a guest. One must choose players, sack players, and all the rest. But in late May Boulez reiterated he wanted to do all that so I had to accept him on his own terms." On June 1, 1969, less than six months after his appointment with the BBC was made public, Boulez's post at the New York Philharmonic was announced.

When the news broke, Boulez's father was ill in the hospital with cancer. Léon Boulez died two months later. Jeanne Chevalier says that the Philharmonic appointment brought her father "the greatest joy of his life." Boulez could not be found by reporters on that day for comment. The *Times* front-page story asked why Boulez had gone back on the stand he took in the *Times* interview several weeks before.

In addition to all of the public statements, these more "private" motives emerge: The appointment was strongly promoted by Szell, too ill to assume the post himself, but anxious to have virtually free access to it. The appointment was strongly supported by Bernstein, who sensed that soon into Boulez's cool regime many who had attacked his own expansive ways would long for the panache of the old Bernstein days. The appointment was agreed upon by the board because the members correctly perceived that despite Boulez's iconoclast image he would work in a congenial way with them. Finally, the appointment was accepted by Boulez for the influence and fame it would bring him.

19

In March 1971, Boulez and I met in Cleveland, where he was conducting a Varèse program, to discuss a book about him. At the concert Boulez first talked about "Varèse, the man," then about *Arcana*, *Ionisation*, and *Poème Electronique*. Interspersed with his precise discussions, replete with diagrams, were the performances of the pieces. At the end he opened the floor to questions. The audience was attentive and polite. After the concert many went to the home of Mr. and Mrs. Robert Frankel in suburban Cleveland to celebrate Boulez's forty-sixth birthday. Mr. Frankel is a member of a family business of electrical fixtures and appliances. Mrs. Frankel, then thirty-two, was vice-president of the Women's Committee of the Cleveland Orchestra and a staff writer for the pop music empire, Motown. (Since then she has established her own firm, Music Masters, which writes and produces commercial jingles.) The Frankels had met Boulez two years before, in 1967, when they gave a party after a Boulez concert. On learning that the conductor was scheduled to stop at the local Howard Johnson Motel during his next engagement in Cleveland, Mrs. Frankel invited him to stay at her house instead. Boulez accepted. Mrs. Frankel became to Boulez in Cleveland what Hilda Strobel had been to him in Germany. She selected his clothes, served him good food, and saw to it that he was comfortable and well. She refers to Boulez in correspondence and conversation as "my resident genius" and speaks freely of the gratitude she feels that her young son who takes piano lessons and has begun to compose has grown up in inspiring contact with Boulez.

Boulez's forty-sixth birthday party was an extravagant one, but it was not entertainment à la Tezenas. A blown-up photograph of Carol Frankel and Boulez was mounted in the Frankels' living room. Hand-printed posters proclaimed: "Schoenberg loves Boulez," "Webern loves Boulez," "It's Bartók's birthday too but he couldn't make it." Drinks flowed. The food was generous. "Hot-pants" had just come into fashion, and several of the women were sporting them. The Frankels and their guests called Boulez "Pierre," and, as the women left, most of them kissed him affectionately.

The morning after the party I met with Boulez in Severance Hall. I outlined my purpose in regard to the book. Boulez agreed to cooperate and to waive all approval rights. He said he would be in New York in a few weeks for his second guest engagement with the Philharmonic—he was not to take over as music director until September —and that I could begin to go to work then.

The schedule for his guest appearance in 1970–71 was a particularly heavy one. It included five long programs with the orchestra, one concert for the New and Newer Music series at Alice Tully Hall, one concert for the Chamber Music Society of Lincoln Center at Alice Tully Hall, one article commemorating Stravinsky's death for the Saturday Review, and recordings of Berlioz's overture to Beatrice and Benedict, Debussy's Three Nocturnes and Printemps, and Ravel's Tombeau de Couperin. The New York press celebrated Boulez; his image was that of the disciplined revolutionary who would stop at nothing until he had converted New York. Newsweek's cover story was "Boulez to the Attack."

For the first week of concerts, Boulez programmed Webern's Passacaglia, Schoenberg's Verklaerte Nacht, Berg's Altenberg Lieder, Seven Early Songs, and Three Orchestral Pieces. For some, the concerts proved to be "the revelations" that Glock said they were for Londoners a few years before. For others, that proved not to be the case; those listeners left the house in droves. Harold Schonberg criticized them in his review of Boulez's first concert that spring: "There was nothing very problematic about the program . . . which consisted of early works by the three [modern Viennese] composers. That meant late romanticism and early expressionism. Nevertheless, a good part of the audience fled the last half of the program as though sirens warning of an atomic attack had been set off." Schonberg concluded his review: "The performance was tremendous. Mr. Boulez created the kind of music unity that only a musician immersed in the style could do. The music, which can sound spasmodic and febrile, went with the logic and power of a Beethoven symphony. Is any living conductor superior in this repertory? One doubts it."

For the second week of concerts, Boulez conducted scenes from Berlioz's *Beatrice and Benedict*, Messiaen's *Oiseaux Exotiques*, Varèse's *Ionisation*, and Ravel's *Tombeau de Couperin*. New Yorkers can be a docile lot. Exhorted by Schonberg to remain in their seats, most of them did exactly that. But the Furies were unleashed afterwards. At the Plaza Hotel I was introduced to a group of people who had just come from the concert. One woman, amply decorated with jewels, lashed out at me about Boulez: "That was the most dreadful concert I ever heard. What are those bongo bongo drums doing in Philharmonic Hall? When I listen to music, I am put in another world. I sit with my needlepoint, listening to Mozart, and I am in another world. But with tonight's music I am in Hell! The board of directors will have something to say about this kind of programming."

Other listeners, not decked with jewels, could not tolerate the predominantly modern diet. No Schubert, no Beethoven was in Boulez's programs at that time. Management received many letters of protest, and, for the first time in memory, the perennially sold-out Philharmonic took out ads offering subscriptions for the approaching season. Still, critics continued to rebuke the audience. In a May 1971 issue of *New York* magazine Alan Rich wrote, "If the Thursday night fogies—to say nothing of the dear Friday ladies—find this programming not to their tastes, it is because their tastes have been coddled far too long."

The reaction to the *New and Newer Music* concert moved as predictably in the other direction. The first rehearsal gave a sense of the rapport that prevailed. Boulez was conducting an outstanding group of performers from the Juilliard School in Schoenberg's *Septet*, Stravinsky's *Pribautki* and *Berceuses du Chat* (from Stravinsky's early period), and his own *Marteau sans Maître*. He sat on a stool and appeared relaxed. He worked carefully, taking each of the players separately and then in combination with one another. During the break he bought a Coke from the machine and behaved the way he does when he is around friends: he was cordial, responsive, convivial, good-humored, and had inexhaustible patience with those working with him. The rehearsal lasted more than three hours, and at the end the players wanted to stay for more. The performance was splendid; the audience enthralled.

After Boulez left New York at the end of May, I wrote an article about him for the Sunday *New York Times*. My purpose was to contribute some degree of humanity to his generally austere image and at the same time make clear that Boulez was intransigent in his demands. The major theme of the piece was this: if he did not get his way with programming, if he could not "supply a model of musical life as I conceive it, a musical life that is part of genuine culture," if he did not find a responsive audience for the major works of the twentieth century, he would leave. Such an action would recall one that had happened more than fifty years before: in 1919 Varèse founded the New Symphony Orchestra in New York to bring new music to those "eager to listen and learn." Three pairs of concerts were scheduled, but Varèse conducted only the first. After the initial performance the orchestra's board notified him that he would have to compromise on the programming. Varèse refused and lost the post to Artur Bodansky who took over with the traditional repertoire.

Pierre Boulez is finally making the New York scene but he is traveling light. He rents no apartment, subletting a different one each time he is here, and though he will take over as musical director at the New York Philharmonic in September, he avoids all the props of today's American musical life. With no manager, press agent, secretary, maid or wife—without even a telephone answering service—the 46-year-old Frenchman lives simply and alone. He says that his aim as musical director of the Philharmonic is "to supply a model of musical life as I conceive it, a musical life that is part of genuine culture—not a kind of second-rate enjoyment."

What he's trying to accomplish with his style, with his pace, and especially with his programming may be hard for Philharmonic audiences to take, and many subscribers have written to the management demanding a return to Beethoven and Brahms. If Boulez cannot find a responsive audience for the major works of the 20th century, he says simply: "I will leave."

His output is formidable; between March 15 and May 15 when he returned to Europe, Boulez conducted over 60 different works in Cleveland and New York. The musicians performed most of them for the first time. On Monday of his fourth week in New York we met for lunch. I asked how things were going for him. "Intensely," he replied.

The night before he had conducted the Chamber Society in Mozart, Berg and Schoenberg at Alice Tully Hall. That morning he had rehearsed the next Philharmonic program which included "The Miraculous Mandarin" and the rarely performed Schoenberg Opus 22 Songs. Later, at 7:30, he would conduct the last performance of the Stravinsky Memorial program. Boulez never chooses the easy way out: "Pulcinella" and the "Requiem Canticles" were new to the men and he could have simplified his work by using the 1947 version of "Petrushka," the one they know. But he chose the superior 1911 original. Not all of these are among his favorite works, but Boulez programmed them because he thinks they should be heard.

This refusal to impose his taste on others is consistent with a general sense of mission. During his stay in New York, he rarely was diverted from his work. He attended no films, shows, galleries, or large parties. Here is a typical Boulez day, pieced together by observation and conversation. It is April 27, a Tuesday, traditionally a day off for the orchestra:

In an apartment overlooking Central Park West, Boulez awakens early—about 5 o'clock. Without breakfast, he begins to work. Generally he spends these early hours composing, but this morning he finishes an article on Stravinsky commissioned by the *Saturday Review*. Stravinsky's very recent death does not stop Boulez from criticizing him for using quotations of old music. He concludes with a plea for amnesia in composers. (Later he takes off from Stravinsky's use of the past. "Creators," he says, "must look straight ahead. It is not enough to deface the Mona Lisa because that does not kill the Mona Lisa. All the art of the past must be destroyed.")

At 8:30 he showers—not answering the telephone until he's dry. (He thinks you get electrocuted if you answer when you're wet.) Then he takes calls. Totally unconcerned with fashion—with no trademark like Bernstein's cape, Ozawa's bell bottoms or Stockhausen's pony tail—he puts on blue suit, white shirt and dark tie and walks a few blocks to Philharmonic Hall to make his first record with the orchestra: the overture to Berlioz' "Beatrice and Benedict" and Ravel's "Tombeau de Couperin." Still without breakfast, he steps onto the podium at exactly 10 o'clock. He takes off his watch, places it on the music stand, takes off his jacket, hangs it by the collar on the podium rail, and says good morning to the men. Boulez does not loosen his tie.

From the sound booth, producer Andrew Kazdin says: "This is the overture to 'Beatrice and Benedict.' Insert one, take one." Prefacing each direction with "May I take, please, from bar . . ." Boulez works until 12:50, thirty minutes into overtime, when the telephone next to the podium rings. Kazdin says: "I'm afraid I'll have to stop now." Not yet satisfied with the Ravel, Boulez answers—with intensity—"Please don't." Two minutes pass. Even

191

the usually restless musicians remain still. Then Kazdin gives him the go-ahead. About 1:10 Boulez brings down both his arms (he never uses a baton), puts on watch and jacket and rushes backstage to hear the replay. He and I had a one o'clock appointment. As I wait in the wings for him, the musicians file out. Several discuss the overtime; it means $47.50 for each of the 57 men who played the Ravel.

Boulez is laughing as he leaves the sound booth. Obviously he likes what he heard. On seeing me, he remembers our date and puts his hand to his head in a gesture of shock. It's 1:35; he meets with Columbia Records at 2. "Let's go to La Crêpe," he says. "It's faster than The Ginger Man." As we run down the steps (Boulez never walks), he compares himself to Sisyphus: "I push the rock up and it comes down again."

At La Crêpe he orders a pancake filled with egg, ham and cheese, a half bottle of white wine, and talks of the audience's reaction to his first program of Schoenberg, Webern and Berg. "Can you imagine how it feels to see more empty seats each time you come back out on stage?" I ask if it feels bad enough to persuade him to compromise with the audience's taste.

"A free society," Boulez says, "is not very different from a state society. In one case you are dictated to by subscribers; in another case by the government. I know some subscribers have complained that there is too much modern music in next year's programs. But there is very little and I'll reduce it no further. A few days ago I was at a friend's house for dinner and the guests said they had never been able to buy Philharmonic subscriptions. I told them to buy them now. I'm hoping for a younger audience—by that I mean people in their forties." Boulez adds that he'll leave the bulk of the conventional repertory to guest conductors: "I see no reason why I should conduct Brahms when there are others who do it better."

In front of La Crêpe, he says he loves New York. I ask how he knows because he never seems to go anywhere. "That's true," he answers, "but the streets are enough." Crossing 66th Street, he extends his left hand, bringing an oncoming automobile to a halt. "I love to do that," he beams. "It works—most of the time." After the 2 o'clock conference with Columbia Records—in which scheduling and promotion are discussed for an hour—he leaves the Board Room for the Green Room of Philharmonic Hall. There he coaches the soloists for "Pulcinella" from the piano until after 5. Then back to the apartment to rest.

192

During his five weeks in New York, Boulez spent only three full evenings with friends. This Tuesday was not one of them. At 7, in a rehearsal room at Juilliard, he works with student performers on his own "Marteau sans Maître," part of the New and Newer Music program for that Sunday night. It's the only concert in either Cleveland or New York in which Boulez programmed a work of his own. Later he explains he wants no one to say he is using his position to promote his own work. During the break, he buys a Coke from the machine and talks informally with the performers about Schoenberg's Opus 29 Septet. At 10:15, friends from Cleveland—with whom he stays when he is there—join him for supper at Le Poulailler.

Boulez drives everyone as he drives himself. And, on occasion things break down. Two important instruments dropped out of the last bars of the Requiem Canticles during the Thursday night performance. When the conductor spoke to the players during intermission, one said that his mind went blank. This is not hard to understand. Boulez says he needs 20 hours of rehearsal for the kind of programs he conducted this spring. He gets only 10. The problem of time hangs over everything. All his politeness—the pleases, thank you's, I beg your pardons—cannot conceal the time-pressure he feels. He has suggested a rehearsal storage plan: if one program requires only seven hours' work, can we have 13 for the next? The union says no.

What he does at rehearsal is to clean everything up. The musicians played under guest conductors for two years and that is death to discipline. Bernstein had a whole other way: concerned mostly with sweep and thrust, he allowed the instruments a great deal of leeway. But precision claims top priority for Boulez. He'll say to a violinist, "Your rhythm is wrong," and then work with him until his rhythm is right, while the other men shift restlessly in their seats. He concerns himself with balance, not only the balance within one section so that the one horn doesn't stand out over the rest, but balance among the various sections. Above all, he works for correct intonation. During the course of an orchestral passage, Boulez stops: "Third trumpet, your E flat is too sharp." Then he thrusts his right arm out in front of him and brings down his thumb, ever so slowly, until the instrument hits the exact pitch. To close the issue, he whistles it. The performance that results is crystal clear.

This approach to conducting works miracles for 20th-century music; Louise Varèse, widow of composer Edgard Varèse, told me

193

that Boulez brought out the lyric poetry of her husband's "Ionisation" as no other conductor has ever done. The approach does not always work as well for older music; the sensuous aspects of a melodic line can get lost in Boulez's excessive attention to detail.

Still, at this juncture, there are only two roads for the orchestra to take: it can remain a museum for the presentation of old work, or it can bring to life the music of this century. If Boulez cannot transform the New York Philharmonic into an instrument of "genuine culture," there is little likelihood that anybody can.

The Sunday editor, Seymour Peck, indicated his skepticism regarding Boulez's success in New York with a question mark at the end of his title: "Bringing 'em Back to Life?"

20

Boulez's success in New York is measurable not in terms of curtain calls or sold-out houses but in terms of programming alone. Boulez reiterated to the press that if the Philharmonic had wished to proceed as it had in the past, it would have hired a music director who conducted the standard repertory better than he did. "It is obvious," he said repeatedly, "that the management in New York wants something new."

Indeed, in London, since 1964, Boulez had been doing something new. Between his conversation with Sir William Glock in 1963, when he had twenty pieces in his repertory, and the end of 1972 when Glock retired from the BBC, Boulez conducted 187 pieces with the orchestra, the great majority of them twentieth-century works. On occasion he did intersperse traditional pieces, but he never did much of that. Glock explains: "There are composers with whom Boulez cannot get deeply involved. What Beethoven has to offer him is very little. He speaks with passion about Bach's *Chorale Preludes* but I cannot imagine him conducting the *St. Matthew Passion*, or, for that matter, the *B Minor Mass*. I cannot imagine Liszt by Boulez.

"We had a marvelous time planning concerts together," Glock recalls. "Planning programs became like a game of tennis. I would come with suggestions. He would not want what wouldn't fit. I always tried to make a start so he wouldn't be faced with a blank page. A good program is like a work of art. It's made of works that not only fit but genuinely enhance each other as well. Boulez had the instinct for what was a positive program and what was not. I remember suggesting *Eclat* and Berlioz's *Symphonie Fantastique*. At first he just stared in stunned silence. Then he said, "It's really not so bad. It's a program to show off orchestral virtuosity."

"Boulez is a theorist," Glock went on. "He likes patterns. Concert life is not one good concert after another to him. I'm always looking for the next good thing. He's out to establish attitudes. His approach is more methodical, more intellectual. I was against this idea of a season of people or a season of, say 'Cantatas, beginning with Buxtehude.' I could not do it. It was too systematic for me. I was never enamored of titles and the like and on that subject we disagreed.

"But in the main we worked very well together. Boulez's main idea was to break down divisions in audiences themselves. He wanted to establish a circuit involving St. John's, the Round House, and Festival Hall, bringing people from one house to the other two. St. John's invites chamber music, like the Haydn Masses; we did Stockhausen and Webern there. The Round House had been used for avant-garde theater; we used it for the most contemporary musical events. Festival Hall invites traditional listening; the BBC began to take big risks there. Of course I had my bosses at the BBC, the heads of the administration there. But these men were always my allies; the BBC had a background of doing contemporary work."

The New York Philharmonic had no comparable background, and it depends on the box office, so the orchestra entered Boulez's arena somewhat tentatively. Boulez's first season focused on Berg and Liszt —Liszt, a professed enemy during Boulez's youth, and the composer whom Glock could not imagine Boulez conducting. Indeed, during the first season, Boulez himself conducted not only many major works by Liszt, but also works by Mahler, Schubert, Schumann, and Mozart. Boulez's appointment, then, was less a tribute to the management's faith in the twentieth-century repertoire in which Boulez believes, than to the age and personality factors noted by Keiser as well as to one other exceptionally important fact: the anti-bourgeois attitudes associated with the modernist movement in art had, by the late 1960s, been adopted by the middle class itself. As distinguished professors deferred to impassioned rebels in blue jeans, so the oldest and one of the greatest orchestras in the country elevated to its own helm the most articulate enemy of traditional music in the world.

When Boulez arrived in New York in September 1971, he arrived as music director of the Philharmonic. His plane landed during a driving rainstorm. He said later that the weather "was not very seductive" but that everything else was "perfect." The management of the Navarro Hotel, where he was staying during that visit, had seen to it that he had a good light and a long composing table, and that, he insisted, is all he needs anywhere. Boulez read an advertisement in the morning's *Times* that the first two weeks of concerts were sold out and that information pleased him a great deal.

Tuesday, Frank Milburn, the orchestra's press director, announced that it was "crisisville here today." André Watts, the pianist, was ill with hepatitis and had cancelled the concerts he was to play with the orchestra. Only hours after the news arrived, Boulez was auditioning Jorge Bolet, Misha Dichter, and David Bar-Illan and worked out the following plan: Bolet to play Liszt's *Totentanz* on opening night, Bar-Illan to play Liszt's *Malédiction*, and Dichter to play Bartók's *Piano Concerto No. 3*. The "crisis" did not ruffle Boulez. "All I ask," he said, "is to hear each of them play his piece completely through one time."

The opening, a benefit, was a festive occasion, the men in black tie, the women in formal gowns. Boulez conducted Wagner's *Faust Overture*, Berlioz's *Royal Hunt and Storm* from *The Trojans*, Liszt's *Totentanz* for piano and orchestra, Debussy's *Prelude to the Afternoon of a Faun*, and Stravinsky's *Rite of Spring*, surely a program to warm the hearts of the most traditional audience. During the intermission one gentleman, in a red moiré jacket, said he had decided against subscribing this year "because this guy is supposed to be very far-out." Another commented that "Boulez is in the same camp as Szell, but Szell's academic ways are saved by a certain uniqueness of style that saves it from the lack of incandescence we feel here tonight." His companion asked: "Is Boulez Jewish?" "Heavens, no!" he replied. "I think he must be the son of a Swiss watchmaker."

After the last piece on the program, *The Rite of Spring*, the house was filled with thunderous applause. The Green Room overflowed the way it had with Bernstein. Mayor Lindsay was on hand, posing for photographs along with Goddard Lieberson—president of Columbia Records—and Mrs. Leonard Bernstein. Parties were very much in the air.

The next evening Boulez telephoned me to confirm an appointment and also to talk about the opening concert. He said the orchestra had worked so well, had sounded so well, and that his rapport with the men was so good. I asked whose party he attended afterwards. He replied: "Carlos and I dined at Poulailler alone."

The glitter and glamour were for the occasion, not for Boulez. By then he had emitted the unmistakable sign of compulsive isolation that the astute hostesses of New York picked up. It was that, more than the programming, that lay behind the fact that no Carol Frankel adopted Boulez in New York.

It seemed only right and proper that Boulez's milieu in the United States would not be the social whirl but rather his avant-garde concerts in Greenwich Village. It was at these "Prospective Encounters," held in one of the Shakespeare Festival's complex of theaters, that Boulez was to present contemporary works—a counterpart to the Round House Concerts in London. And it was to the first of these concerts that *Life, Time, Newsweek,* and network TV sent its reporters and camera crews. On the ride downtown in the Philharmonic car, someone remarked on the ugliness of the abstract sculpture in Cooper Square. Boulez said, "It's better than the generals on horseback all over France."

The Encounters had been heralded as informal affairs, with people free to come and go as they chose, with conversation among participants and listeners, with performances repeated as the audience wished. At 7:15 Joseph Papp, founder of the Shakespeare Festival, appeared to introduce Boulez. Papp wore boots and a long suede jacket. Boulez's concession to informality was a blue turtleneck shirt under his dark business suit, the same blue turtleneck shirt he was to wear to each of the Encounters that year.

Boulez came to center stage—it was a theater in the round—and described in a clear and staccato delivery exactly how the evening's program would proceed. He said he hoped to bring the two worlds together, that people from the Village would go up to the Philharmonic and that people from the Philharmonic would come down to the Village. He said the programming for the series was guided by conversations with composers in New York and that the first year would be exclusively American.

Because of the attention that the press and public had focused on the first of the Village concerts, the programming for it was critical. Boulez chose Mario Davidovsky's *Synchronisms No. 6* for piano and electronic instruments—a ten-minute work for piano and tape, and Charles Wuorinen's *The Politics of Harmony*—a forty-minute work with musicians from the Philharmonic and members of the American Mime Theater. Davidovsky and Wuorinen were logical choices: both

198

were members of the Columbia University music department and the Columbia-Princeton Electronic Music Center, probably the most powerful base for composers in the United States. In addition, Wuorinen had recently been awarded the 1970 Pulitzer Prize in composition.

By the time Paul Jacobs, the pianist of Boulez's early Paris days who was then official pianist for the New York Philharmonic, appeared on stage, the house, seating 350, was packed. Every pillow on the floor was taken, "regular" subscribers were sitting on benches, and the press section overflowed. Jacobs was to play the Davidovsky, synchronizing his part with the prepared tape. Boulez explained that Davidovsky was not there because he had hurt his back while moving one of the speakers into place. Boulez quipped that the electronic medium is filled with such unforeseeable dangers.

Jacobs played the piece, then described several sound patterns to the audience. After his exposition, he played it again. Boulez asked for questions from the audience. A man asked if the work were happy or sad. Jacobs replied he found it "engaging." The man said he didn't like it at all and found Jacobs's comment pretty low-key. Boulez stepped in. He said he found the mood contemplative and that, in fact, he liked it very much. Then he invited Wuorinen to say a few words about Davidovsky's piece.

Wuorinen began by dissociating himself from Davidovsky. He said Davidovsky liked to "manipulate substances" whereas he preferred to "work with pitch relationships." As it came out it was a put-down of Davidovsky. At the same time it was useful to make clear that the medium does not dictate the syntax, that a piece for conventional instruments by Wuorinen is more like a computer piece by Wuorinen than it is like a piece for conventional instruments by Davidovsky. Whatever the means, Wuorinen considers pitch the most important aspect of music while Davidovsky concentrates on texture, on sound per se.

There was a twenty-minute break. I walked down from my seat in the bleachers (for that is how the house was set up) and conversed with Wuorinen, who was angry. He said that in our society, it is a question of "either-or," that if an evening is to be informal, "an inappropriate intimacy ensues." He objected, he spelled out, to Boulez's light jokes. Julius Baker, the orchestra's first desk flutist—who was on hand to play the Wuorinen work—said he was sorry he had not brought his eight-year-old son because "the boy loves the kinds of sounds Davidovsky makes." Robert Miller, a pianist specializing in the contemporary repertoire who had given the world premiere of Davidovsky's piece, reported that Davidovsky's bad back was caused by learning that the Philharmonic, which had devoted so many hours to rehearsing Wuorinen's piece, would not replace the small piano in the house with an appropriate concert-size grand. Stanley Silverman noted that Wuorinen had put down Davidovsky and that he himself works like Davidovsky. Silverman said he was distressed and would like to go home but added that if he did, everyone would see him leave. That was a problem of performance in the round.

Teresa Sterne, the volatile director of Nonesuch Records, a company with an excellent history regarding new music, was livid with rage. She said Boulez was on "a big ego trip," that two-thirds of the audience were professional musicians and what the hell is he doing talking to them as though they were kids. Someone noted that not everyone there was professional: what about the man who asked if the piece were happy or sad? Miss Sterne replied, "My God! That was Earle Price of Columbia Records. He was just pulling Boulez's leg." She added that the avant-garde in New York had been knocking themselves out with such concerts for years and now Boulez walks in and capitalizes on it all.

The hall was unbearably hot. Harold Schonberg took off his jacket. Wuorinen walked on to center stage to discuss his own much longer work. He spoke of the ancient Chinese tale on which his piece was based, and he described, in minute detail, the calligraphy on the backdrops that were to act as sets which were not yet before the audience. (At rehearsal that morning Wuorinen complained that the expert calligraphy would be wasted on an audience that knew nothing about Chinese calligraphy.)

The tedium of the piece, set for three voices and chamber instruments, was not relieved by the mimes. But the audience was more imprisoned than any audience uptown. Those who tried to leave were impeded by a door that would not open easily. People pushed and scuffled around in embarrassment with the audience's eyes riveted on them as they tried to make their escape. Afterwards, when the discussion began, there was a mass exodus. Boulez asked Wuorinen to talk about the compositional principles of the work. Wuorinen said he didn't want to "bore" anyone. Someone asked him if it were twelve-tone. Wuorinen replied, "It is at least that."

After the second break, poet-translator-critic Richard Howard, librettist for the Wuorinen work, conversed with Wuorinen and Boulez on stage. Howard said there was generally a fifty-year span between the creation and appreciation of a good work. Boulez said it was not necessarily so, that *The Rite of Spring* was popular immediately and that Schoenberg's *Erwartung* was not. Both, Boulez said, are good works, so obviously there is no rule. Howard continued to plug obscurantism, ignoring Boulez's statements and insisting that if an artist works quietly he will have to wait fifty years for recognition.

In his review of the concert, Harold Schonberg wrote: "The Davidovsky was a rather conventional arrangement of serialized synthesized tape. At least it was clear and direct. The Wuorinen was one of those academic post-serial drags, completely amelodic, awkwardly set for three voices." In his Sunday essay, Schonberg went on: "The Wuorinen work ran some dismal forty minutes with the singers maltreating the English language in extended twelve-tone syllabic extensions, with the usual academic kind of organization, with a 1960s kind of athematicism, with virtually no personality, without a trace of charm." In commenting on the final discussion, Schonberg wrote, "It did not seem to occur to anybody that if a work of art has not established itself in fifty years, it conceivably, just conceivably, might be the fault of the work of art and not the public."

The next morning a member of the Columbia-Princeton group called and asked me what I had thought of the concert. I said the Wuorinen was not one of my favorite pieces. He said it was probably the worst Wuorinen had composed and accused Boulez of selecting it to show American music in the worst possible light.

When I asked Boulez why he had chosen The Politics of Harmony, he said it was because he believed the use of mimes would prove attractive to the audience.

21

On August 23, 1972, the Philharmonic began a tour of the Midwest that was to last until just before Boulez began his second season as music director in New York. Erich Leinsdorf conducted the first week in Rochester, Detroit, Toronto, and Pontiac. André Kostelanetz took over for Madison, Chicago, and Des Moines. Leinsdorf returned for Wichita, Kansas City, Topeka, and Bloomington. The Bloomington performance was on Thursday, September 7, the day Boulez joined the orchestra for his first American tour.

On the seventh, Boulez, Moseley, Milburn, and I flew to Bloomington. I had asked to join them for a few days because I thought that would be the best way to understand the balance of power between Moseley and Boulez and the nature of the relationship between Boulez and the men. In Bloomington we drove to the Holiday Inn which had on its marquee: "Welcome to the New York Philharmonic." Half of the musicians were there; the other half were at the Executive Inn.

That evening the orchestra was playing under Leinsdorf: Brahms's *Variations on a Theme by Haydn*, Gunther Schuller's *Three Pieces: Trio, Devil, Machine*, and the Mahler *Fifth Symphony*. The university auditorium, seating between five and six thousand people, was sold out. Afterwards we drove to a restaurant. The car was air-conditioned, and Leinsdorf asked if the system could be turned off. It struck me then that I had never heard Boulez request even as simple an accommodation as that.

In the restaurant a pianist played pop music loudly. Everyone ordered steaks, Boulez's very rare. Boulez never orders salads, because he believes only Italians and the French make them well. Leinsdorf was in good spirits. The waitress was pretty and he flirted with her. It struck me that I had never seen Boulez flirt with anyone.

During dinner I told Leinsdorf that his former wife had dined at my house in the Berkshires several summers before, and that she had brought along with her a Swiss journalist who was very much in favor of the Vietnam war. I mentioned that the evening had become unbearable because the fighting was so intense. Leinsdorf said his wife had since married the journalist and that despite his unfortunate views on the Vietnam war the marriage was working out. He spoke of his children and their relationship to the man, and it struck me that I had learned more about Leinsdorf in three hours than I had learned about Boulez in almost three years.

We returned to the Holiday Inn after midnight, and Boulez said he would then go over scores that he was to rehearse the following day. Boulez was conducting Berlioz's *Benvenuto Cellini Overture*, Haydn's *Hornsignal Symphony*, Schumann's *Symphony No. 4*, and Ravel's *Daphnis and Cloé-Suite No. 2*.

To say that Boulez does not "give" like Leinsdorf is not to suggest he doesn't talk. Rather he limits his conversation to trivial subjects that reveal very little about him. During the conversations held on that trip he told me that he left the Essex House the previous year because he had asked for a room on a high floor so he could compose without noise from the street and was given a room on the third floor. After that he sublet an apartment from the mezzo-soprano Christa Ludwig, but the maid who was supposed to come in to clean stopped showing up after the first week. Now he was in the Navarro Hotel in a suite he thought was exorbitant at $1,000 a month. He was looking for a furnished apartment near enough to Lincoln Center so he could walk to work. He said he found he needed a valet and that friends had recommended someone working for a family in Aix-en-Provence and that he had gone there and hired him on the spot. Boulez was looking forward to Hans's arrival because then he would not have to dine out all the time.

My first morning in Indiana I found the restaurant crowded with men. The musicians looked like regular people in very casual clothes. Leinsdorf appeared and sat alone. He wore dark glasses and a blue blazer. He is shorter than one would expect from his appearance on the podium, but he has a large voice and a dynamic manner and gives forth a glow of confidence that makes heads turn. Boulez did not appear; he does not eat breakfast.

A few musicians sat with me. They talked about an interview one of them had given an Ontario paper that had caused trouble with the management. "It was a girl reporter," one said, "and the guy was swept off his feet. He complained about orchestra conditions. He told her that in Madison, Wisconsin we had been booked into a motel that was under construction and in the middle of nowhere with no transportation back and forth to town. We thought Herb Weissenstein should have checked it out first." Weissenstein, assistant to the orchestra manager, was on the tour along with production manager Hal de Windt and personnel manager Jimmy Chambers.

The men left and another man sat down. He said I should disregard whatever the first group had said. "Here are 106 neurotic men. Many have been with the orchestra for thirty years. It is *home* to most of them, even if they are married and have families. Beefing is the occupation they like the best. Last night, at the concert, the men were on edge because they knew Boulez was in the audience. Couldn't you see them looking into the audience to try to find where he was? They gave a much better performance than usual because they knew he was there. They are really a bunch of kids. When the boss arrives, they all behave."

Moseley and I chatted briefly. He said he was sorry they had selected that particular restaurant the evening before, because it was noisy, and Boulez cannot stand that kind of noise. I asked why Boulez would not tell us that and suggest we move to another restaurant. Moseley answered, "Because he is terribly polite."

We spent the day in Bloomington. Boulez was rehearsing in the morning and afternoon. Music students at the University of Indiana attended both sessions, and Boulez rehearsed as he always does: in a businesslike way, expressionless, with little talk except his usual, "Can we take, please. . . . Shhhhhh. . . ."

After the morning rehearsal, Moseley, Milburn, and I lunched at the pianist Jorge Bolet's house. Bolet had been touring with the orchestra, playing the Liszt *Piano Concerto No. 1.* A member of the university's music department, Bolet lives in an apartment that looks like Levittown but is decorated to the hilt with antiques, Spanish paintings, and good Spanish rugs.

Conversation centered on music. Every time a performer was mentioned Moseley asked, "How is he good? How does he fail?" Then he took out his notebook and wrote down the name. When Bolet mentioned a twenty-year-old German girl who was an excellent trumpeter, out came the notebook and Moseley said, "I think we can feature her in the Promenades."

Flutist Albert Tipton arrived. He said he had turned away from "cutthroat music" in the northeast in exchange for a pleasurable life in Tallahassee with the symphony orchestra there. Then, in what can only be described as an assault on Moseley, Tipton said that the New York Philharmonic was the only major American orchestra that had not offered him the first-desk flute chair. He said he knew the other first-desk men and got along very well with them and that he was therefore "expecting the offer." Moseley did not appear disconcerted. Leaning far back in his chair with his right ankle resting on his left knee he drawled, "Lenny wanted Julius Baker." Tipton snapped, "That is because they are friends." (A telephone call to Mr. Baker revealed that he and Bernstein had never been personal friends.)

After lunch I complimented Moseley on the coolness with which he handled Tipton's attack. It was not an empty compliment. Moseley was the big surprise for me. I had always thought of him as a courteous man, smooth, charming, but little more than that. I was wrong. A Phi Beta Kappa from Duke and a pianist who plays well enough to have appeared as soloist with the Philharmonic, this slender, light-haired Southerner is a driving man, sharp in his manipulation of men, and unwilling to delegate authority. It is Moseley, not Boulez, who deals with the unions. In fact, the musicians' strike dragged on in the fall of 1973 probably because Moseley was in the hospital recovering from a heart attack.

Moseley spoke of how things had changed since he came to the orchestra in 1955. At that time the season ran only twenty-eight weeks, and the budget was less than $1 million. In 1972 the budget exceeded $5 million and the season was year-round. If the orchestra takes in $3 million a year, it still must raise an additional $2 million, and foundations are not interested in providing it. "They want something," Moseley complained, "in which they can have a guiding hand and a name. They want a one-shot operation."

Moseley said the summer projects require as much planning as the rest of the year and told me of one of his new ideas, which he was then calling "the rugs" because he "couldn't think of a better name." He said he was considering removing the tables after the Promenades and putting the orchestra in the center of the hall. He would try to charge only $2.50. That would create an enormous deficit but he planned to ask Burlington Mills to contribute not only the rugs but $35,000 to publicize them. (Burlington did not come through.) Boulez, Moseley explained, had been anxious to organize a series of concerts comparable to the London Proms. This seemed to be the right format. Moseley was not certain he could pull it off because of the staggering costs. "Do you know," he asked, "that for free concerts in the park it costs $10,000 to move the piano around?"

When we returned to the hall, Boulez had stopped for a break. The concertmaster was consulting him about a problem in the score. Then Boulez went backstage where a dozen people were waiting to greet him. He went through the line stiffly, looking intently at each visitor, and then, when that person finished what he had to say, both stared at each other until the visitor moved on. Boulez never said goodbye or turned and gestured to the next. When I mentioned this, he remarked, "I may not say goodbye but I don't make small talk. I just stand there and finally the person has to leave."

As Boulez went through the line, Moseley talked to me about conductors in general. He said World War II had taken an entire generation away and that what we have now is the very young who are thrown into the ring as soon as they are discovered and then ruined in no time. He spoke of the difference between a Mark Spitz or Bobby Fischer and a conductor. "In the case of Spitz and Fischer," he said, "they are champions and there is no reason to analyze their performances to determine why they won. The winning is the determining factor. That is never so in art." We listened to the second half of the rehearsal. At the end of the Ravel the students broke into applause; Boulez did not acknowledge it.

Afterwards a reporter from the *Indianapolis Star* interviewed Boulez. Something prompted Boulez to say that Verdi was "stupid, stupid, stupid." When the reporter left, a student entered, a doctoral candidate who had written his dissertation on Debussy and devoted a chapter to *L'Après-Midi d'un Faune*. The student wanted to check the metronome markings, and Boulez worked with him carefully. The young man asked Boulez about his subdivision of the beat. Boulez said he did it for technical reasons. The visitor said he thought that made the piece slower. "Subdivided but not slower," Boulez disagreed, and gave a short lecture distinguishing tempo from speed. Boulez pointed out the errors in the student's edition: here was an A sharp instead of an A; here was a dot when there should have been none.

After the rehearsal, we were given a tour of the university's music facilities, then a cocktail party, then a picnic. En route to the picnic ground, Moseley reminisced about entertainment on tours. Generally, receptions are reserved for the high brass, but on rare occasions the musicians come too. Moseley spoke of a time when the soloist was the

206

late Michael Rabin, who had brought his mother along. She severely berated a host for not having provided enough food. Once, in Monaco, Princess Grace was two hours late to a party she was supposed to be giving; on top of that the bar was closed.

Dean Bains of the university's music school was the official host of the picnic. There was food and a good student orchestra. Bains asked Boulez to conduct the fourth movement of Tchaikovsky's *Fourth*. Boulez shook his head. Later Bains made the request again. Again Boulez shook his head.

A large canvas was mounted and the dean invited everyone to paint on it. The first person he addressed was Boulez. Boulez said he did not want to dirty his fingers. Bains said it was only watercolor. Boulez smiled. A half hour later Bains reappeared. By now the canvas was filled with color and must have been, in Boulez's eyes, "a mess." Boulez was such a creative person, Bains said. It would mean so much to the university if he would add his personal touch. Boulez smiled again. At the end of the party Bains returned. "Look how beautiful the painting is now. Surely you will grace it with a stroke or two." Boulez smiled at Bains for the last time: "It is far too beautiful for me to spoil."

After returning to the motel, Boulez, Moseley, and Milburn retired to Boulez's room for a long session of programming that lasted into the early morning. I took a walk and met Hal de Windt.

De Windt told me he had been with Joseph Papp until two years before, but that "the Human Rights Commission then came down hard on the Philharmonic's back so they were forced to hire a black." He said he was lucky. He had gone to Japan with Bernstein and the orchestra. He thought Bernstein combined "commerce, narcissism, and art" and that it was working for him. But he admired Boulez a great deal for his courage in saying what he doesn't like rather than admiring the masterpieces he is supposed to like. De Windt said that he was not invited to the picnic but could not have gone in any case, because he and Weissenstein were always needed by the men: "They ask for money for a poker game or want to know where their trunks are."

The next morning the orchestra was leaving for Indianapolis. At breakfast I spoke to a few more players. Some spoke highly of Boulez's "precise, no-nonsense approach," while others found him "cold and heartless, not a real musician with human feelings." They mentioned that he does not greet the men even after he has been away many weeks. He just steps onto the podium and tells them where to begin. One said that the musicians, on learning of Boulez's appointment as

207

music director, went around saying "The iceman cometh." The rejoinder became, "But he hasn't cometh for a long time."

Despite his coldness, most of the men acknowledged their respect for him, not only because of his professionalism but also because he never humiliated anyone. He would take a performer into a corner, they said, in order to tell him what was wrong. All felt that Boulez was "improving" in the traditional repertoire which, they agreed, he had hardly known at all. "He played the Schubert *Fourth* beautifully," one said. "He even asked us to slow up in one passage. He would never have done that a few months ago. Clearly he is trying to change his image." Another gave Boulez the ultimate compliment: "I swear he sweated in the Mahler *Sixth*."

In Indianapolis, we stayed at a Howard Johnson motel. As always, Boulez had a suite. The sitting room was used for ceremonies and conferences. A woman gave Boulez a plaque and a local photographer recorded the event. Boulez says he has no place for such mementos: "I lose some, I store some, but I don't have an album or drawer for them."

Boulez's program in Indianapolis was the same as in Bloomington. The house, seating 2400, was filled. Moseley and I sat on a ledge at the side. After the Schumann, Moseley asked me why I thought Boulez likes Schumann and despises Brahms. I said Brahms was not the only great composer Boulez detests and told him what Boulez said about Verdi to the *Indianapolis Star*. Moseley winced: "How can he say that?" I remembered then that some people in Boulez's circle have suggested to me that Boulez thinks all Italians "stupid, stupid, stupid." But I believe his distaste is even deeper, that it stems from something visceral: the repudiation of his own libido. Boulez often miscasts singers, selecting muted, restrained voices in place of more appropriate full-bodied ones. It is also a striking fact that Boulez, past fifty, still has not written a single dramatic work.

After the performance there was a reception on stage. Boulez stood alone, shaking hands as he went through the line. Someone asked Moseley if Ravel reminds Boulez of Debussy. Moseley replied, "I rather think he would say no."

At dinner Moseley asked Boulez if he had been friendly with Nadia Boulanger during his student days in Paris. "Certainly not!" Boulez answered. "After the war, Messiaen and Leibowitz were the important figures and no one had any use for Boulanger. I knew only one person who studied with her then and he found her dry and pedantic."

Moseley, in his student days, had been close friends with a number of Boulanger students, Aaron Copland, Samuel Barber, and William

208

Schuman among them, composers Boulez had studiously ignored up to that point in his position in New York. Moseley looked like he had been struck in the face and was wondering where the next blow would fall. On my part I was surprised that Moseley would not have understood—at this late date in his relationship with Boulez—that his music director would have loathed the teacher of the neoclassical Americans and the woman who had proselytized for the "idol/god" Stravinsky. To break the silence, I remarked to Boulez that Moseley would like to know why he prefers Schumann to Brahms. The answer came fast: "Schumann shows invention where Brahms shows none. Brahms was a banal bourgeois. Schumann, on the contrary, was earlier. He was fresher in his approach."

We returned to Boulez's suite and he showed us the interview in the *Indianapolis Star*. The reporter did not quote Boulez on Verdi. All he noted about Boulez's musical tastes was that the composer-conductor of the New York Philharmonic did not consider himself a part of the French tradition of Gounod, Massenet, and Bizet. Moseley was relieved.

I was going back to New York the next day, before the orchestra left for Muncie. At breakfast several players told me that when Boulez arrived for the tour, the musicians did not applaud him at the first rehearsal as they had always done for Bernstein—or even for guest conductors like Barenboim. They don't believe Boulez would respond to such a gesture; in any event, no one was moved to do it. They said that in Boulez's first and only talk with the men, he said he wasn't interpreting music, that he was only there to get everything done exactly as the composer had specified. The men asked me why I thought Boulez had become such a success even though he is a cold man and an unfeeling musician. I talked about Boulez's eye, ear, talent, and energy as well as his skill in managing his career. I added that Boulez's performance of the great music of the past seems to suffer from his insistence on interposing himself, his own exceptional personality, between the listener and the composer. He may acquiesce on minor issues, but he will not surrender himself to a teacher, a beloved, a Mozart, or a Bach.

22

During one of the Rug Concerts, when the chamber ensemble Tashi was playing Messiaen's *Quartet for the End of Time*, Boulez sat next to me in the audience. After the cello movement I whispered, "It is such romantic music." He replied, "It is much less than that."

If Boulez despises the Messiaen quartet, what, then, does he love? He never uses the word love (—except to describe his feeling for yogurt), but if *I* were to assess what he does love, I would include pre-1925 Schoenberg and Stravinsky, Webern, Berg, some Debussy, and some Berlioz. He probably merely *likes* Varèse and some works by Bartók, Ravel, Messiaen, Carter, Stockhausen, Vinko Globokar, and Berio. George Crumb, who presently enjoys considerable success both in the United States and Europe, he finds "cheap—a kind of entropy of serialism."

In general Boulez conducts what he loves magnificently, conducts what he likes very well, and, with rare exceptions, gives stiff performances of the classic and romantic repertoire. After his performance of Schumann's *Rhenish Symphony*, Harold Schonberg wrote in the *New York Times*, "There was no tenderness . . . a brainy orchestral technician at work." Boulez remarked to Milburn that Schonberg was wrong: "I conducted the Schumann freely," he said.

What is free to Boulez can seem tight to others. Boulez's unerring sense of pitch may interfere with his hearing a melody. He is so obsessed with correct intonation—he continually interrupts rehearsals for the musicians to tune up—that the line is often sacrificed in the end. The audience responds accordingly. After a Boulez performance of *Sacre du Printemps* or *La Mer*, where melody does not play the most significant role, the Green Room used to be crowded with fans. After Mozart, Mendelssohn, Schubert, or Haydn, the Green Room was empty; people did not know what to say. (By Boulez's fifth season, the Green Room was empty even for *Sacre du Printemps*. That was partly because of Boulez's personal style in greeting his visitors, and partly because his initial enthusiasm had dampened and he rarely brought to life even those works he admired.)

Columbia Records, which records Boulez and also has the New York Philharmonic as its major contract orchestra, seems to share the public assessment, and herein lies a major problem. Columbia records only what is being performed currently so it doesn't have to pay for costly rehearsal time. When Boulez began to conduct more and more Mendelssohn and less and less of the twentieth-century repertoire, Columbia reduced its recording of him and the New York Philharmonic. In fact, when, in 1975, Boulez recorded the monumental twentieth-century works *Gurrelieder* and *Moses und Aron*, it was not with the New York Philharmonic, because that orchestra had never played them, but with the BBC Symphony.

Boulez began his recording career with CBS-UK in January 1966. Ken Glancy, then chief of the English division, made the deal with Boulez's manager, Howard Hartog. The contract allowed Boulez to record whichever of his own works he wished. (Bernstein's contract allowed him to record whichever of anyone's works he wished.)

Initially, Columbia did not rule out Boulez and the traditional repertoire, but no one in London had heard him conduct it. Then, late in 1966, when Otto Klemperer fell ill, Boulez substituted for him in a Beethoven cycle at Festival Hall. Columbia recorded his Beethoven *Fifth*. Glancy, a first-rate musician, characterizes the performance as "eccentric; it sounds a little like Mahler," and Columbia could not sell that record. Years later, when Boulez conducted the New York Philharmonic in the *Seventh* and *Ninth* symphonies, Columbia did not change its estimate of Boulez's compressed, asensual Beethoven.

Boulez's first project at Columbia was one that was very important to him: the complete works of Webern. Columbia had produced a Webern album under the direction of Robert Craft, but Boulez wanted to do one of his own. Boulez began discovering undiscovered Webern and also started to compose an essay about Webern that would be included in the package.

211

Although he says, "Webern thirty years later is a historical quantity, solidified lava, no longer something directly vital to me," he regarded the essay seriously enough to have worked on it off and on for more than nine years.

Since 1969, when Boulez changed his contract to Columbia New York, he has made about twenty-five albums. Several have been with the Cleveland Orchestra and London Symphony but most have been with the New York Philharmonic. The ones that sell well are very good indeed. The sales of his *Sacre du Printemps* with the Cleveland Orchestra far exceeded any executive's expectations. The complete *Petrouchka*, *The Miraculous Mandarin*, *Valses Nobles et Sentimentales* all sell very well. Of his own works, he recorded *Marteau sans Maître*, *Livre pour Cordes*, *Pli Selon Pli* and his *Piano Sonata No. 1* and *No. 2* and two movements of *No. 3*. Apart from the sonatas, which were played by the American pianist Charles Rosen, all were performed by European groups.

For Columbia Records, all of this amounts to little more than prestige. Only five percent of the record industry's output in the United States is made up of the classical repertoire, and only a small fraction of that is contemporary music. The pieces that continue to sell best are *Scheherzade*, the *1812 Overture*, *Boléro*, and the Beethoven symphonies. Therefore it cannot be said that Columbia hired Boulez as a potential gold mine. It hired him because he was "a bright star on the musical horizon, the great new figure to come out of nowhere," as one Columbia executive put it to me. But because of the skyrocketing costs, Columbia has been reluctant to record anything but the most certified of twentieth-century works. And when, in 1974, Boulez said he wanted to record Mahler, which he does very well, Columbia refused to go along.

Because of Columbia's selectivity regarding Boulez, the conductor left a great legacy with those works he did record. *Gurrelieder* and *Moses und Aron* are extraordinary achievements, both in power of conception and refinement of execution. The same can be said of virtually all Boulez recordings of twentieth-century music as well as the French repertoire. In 1976, after speculating on who would be Boulez's successor with the New York Philharmonic, Peter G. Davis commented in the Sunday *New York Times*: "The most recent Boulez recordings, Stravinsky's *Firebird* and Ravel's *Daphnis and Cloé*, are both brilliant versions of these popular ballets. Every orchestral sonority is superbly tuned, the rhythms are taut and sinuous, the overall shape of the scores carefully plotted but the results always sound fresh and spontaneous. The Philharmonic's new conductor, whoever he may be, will face some very exacting standards when he takes his turn at this repertory."

One man working at Columbia when Boulez arrived in New York was David Kleger, a soft-spoken, low-key publicity agent. Kleger liked Boulez and concentrated on publicizing his records. Because Hurok was then Boulez's American agent, Kleger called to ask if he could work for Boulez for nothing. The Hurok office, delighted, agreed.

Then in a budget squeeze, Columbia fired many of its staff, including Kleger. At the same time Boulez was called by the Internal Revenue Service for his first audit. He was in Cleveland at the time and Hurok did not send anyone to help. Angry, and no longer in need of management now that he had the Philharmonic post, Boulez left the Hurok establishment. It was then that Kleger approached Boulez to see if he could handle his publicity on a private basis. Boulez agreed.

Kleger was uncritical, intensely loyal, even adoring of Boulez, like the Frankels and Jablonskys, the people with whom Boulez spends most of his free time in the United States. But there was still another reason Boulez agreed to Kleger's offer. By then he must have been aware that the publicity issued by the New York Philharmonic and the publicity on which he himself had always thrived were at cross-purposes. The Philharmonic wished to present Boulez as a man for all seasons, as a great conductor of a great orchestra. They were determined not to present him as a composer possessed with a demanding language that most of their subscribers neither wanted nor understood. So Boulez went along with Kleger, probably believing it would offer him the chance to control his own image as "revolutionary."

One of Kleger's early coups was to put Boulez on the Dick Cavett Show. Boulez was enthusiastic. I counseled against it, saying what I still believe to be true: that few serious people can benefit from this kind of exposure. I cut out an article from the *Times* magazine in which the Yale drama professor Robert Brustein claimed substantially the same thing. I showed it to Boulez who made little of it. He said he would have complete control, that he would probably appear with Joseph Papp and no one else for the two hours, and that he was therefore assured of a dignified milieu.

On the afternoon of the taping, in February 1972, Boulez flew in from Cleveland. Jablonsky picked him up at the airport and brought him to the studio in the late afternoon. But that morning the Philharmonic press department got wind of the plans for the first time, so when Jablonsky pulled up on west Fifty-Eighth Street and Boulez stepped out of the car, Moseley and Milburn were waiting for him. Moseley drew his lips back, imitating a smile, and instructed Boulez not to say anything revolutionary on the air.

At the studio Papp was nowhere to be seen. While Boulez waited backstage for an hour and a half, Cavett talked to Leonard Frey, Sada Thompson, and Chuck McCann, all show-business personalities. McCann did a funny vacuum cleaner salesman routine. Boulez was scheduled last. That meant he would appear well after midnight, in the graveyard slot reserved for intellectuals. Cavett began by introducing Boulez as a controversial figure who had caused many subscribers to cancel tickets. Boulez replied, "That is melodramatic. Not so many people canceled tickets." Cavett asked Boulez about the story I reported in the *Times* interview that he had booed Stravinsky in 1945. Boulez replied that other students were booing too and that he was not out to attack Stravinsky but to bring attention to those composers who had been overlooked. Cavett must have been disappointed. His researchers had presented him with the picture of a rebel, and here, instead, was a company man. He told the audience about Boulez's perfect pitch and asked someone in the band to blow a note. Boulez answered correctly; it was a G sharp. Then Cavett informed the audience that Boulez could simultaneously conduct two different beats with each hand. Again Boulez obliged. The audience applauded, as it had with McCann. Cavett asked Boulez what was happening in new music, particularly in regard to John Cage. Here Boulez's congenial manner disappeared: "Cage is not new anymore," he said.

Jablonsky had the car running. At 7:10 Boulez left the theater and at 7:30 stepped onto the podium in black tie. I entered the hall and saw Joe Roddy, a former senior editor of *Look* magazine. (Roddy had written an article on Boulez for the *Times* magazine that had never run. Roddy told me the *Times* turned it down because it was inconclusive: "I didn't know what to tell the reader to think about Boulez. The pieces of the puzzle would not fit.") Roddy had been to the Cavett show and viewed Boulez's appearance as a "fall from grace." He was certain Moseley had compelled him to do it. When I told him this was not true, Roddy groaned, "The virus is the cancer of ambition."

Roddy speculated about Boulez's future in New York. He thought the Philharmonic had made a bold move in taking on Boulez and that it could not back down from it now. He predicted Boulez would be hired for another few years. Neither Roddy nor I knew at that time that Boulez already had signed a second three-year contract in December 1971. Throughout the spring, summer, and fall of 1972 Boulez

Boulez and Stockhausen at Donaueschingen (1963)

The program for a Greenwich Village concert that brought Boulez together
with composers now altogether alien to him

THE LIVING THEATRE PRESENTS A PIANO RECITAL BY
DAVID TUDOR, JANUARY FIRST, 1952, 8:00 P.M., IN THE
CHERRY LANE THEATRE, 38 COMMERCE STREET.

PROGRAM:

2ème SONATE		PIERRE BOULEZ
Extrêmement rapide		
Lent		
Modéré, presque vif		
Vif		
FOR PREPARED PIANO		CHRISTIAN WOLFF
4 pieces		
INTERSECTION 2		MORTON FELDMAN
•		
MUSIC OF CHANGES		JOHN CAGE
4 parts		

THIS IS THE FIRST PERFORMANCE OF THE INTERSECTION AND THE CHANGES, AND THE FIRST NEW YORK PERFORMANCE OF THE PIECES BY CHRISTIAN WOLFF.

Milton Babbitt and Stravinsky at a rehearsal for *Threni*

Boulez with members of Domaine Musical: pianist Claude Helffer is second from left

Boulez in the late '50s

Above, left to right: Nono, Boulez,
Stockhausen. Right, Boulez playing
Structures II with Yvonne Loriod
at second piano. Below, Loriod in
performance of *Structures II*

Above, Sir William Glock in his
apartment on Connaught Place
where Boulez stayed during his London visits between 1973 and 1975.
Below, Boulez as conductor. Right,
Boulez at start of American conducting career in Cleveland

Boulez at his bar in Baden-Baden house

Carol Frankel and Boulez, 1971

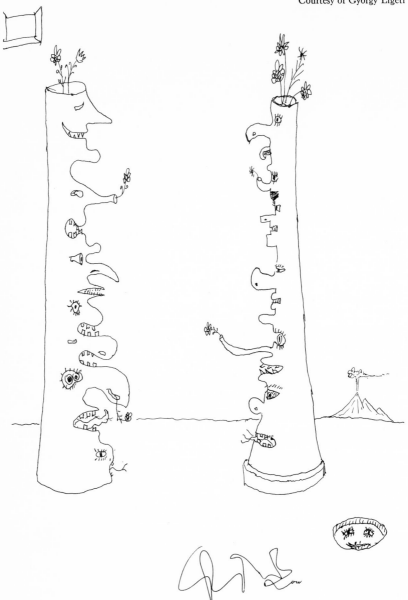

A doodle created by composer Ligeti at IRCAM conference after Boulez denied his request to take the last afternoon of the week-long conference off in order to be free to explore the French Alps, which, Ligeti explained, he had never visited before

Monday, April 22

Appr. 1:35   Arrive JFK
4:30 - 7:00   Rehearsal for Prospective Encounter (Sollberger)
                    (Board Room)

Tuesday, April 23

9:00   Look at apartment with Adele Siegal
10:00 - 12:30   Rehearsal
2:00 - 4:30   Prospective Encounter Rehearsal (Sollberger) (Stage)
4:30   Christoff Wolff

Wednesday, April 24

9:15   Look at apartment with Adele Siegal
10:00 - 12:30   Rehearsal
1:30 - 4:00   Rehearsal
4:15   Piano rehearsal with Philip Sterling, narrator of
                    "Survivor from Warsaw" (Boulez studio?)
5:30--all evening   Max Matthews re IRCAM

Thursday, April 25

10:00 - 12:30   Rehearsal
2:00 - 4:30   Prospective Encounter Rehearsal (Sollberger-Webern)
                    (Stage)
4:30   Edward Downes re program notes
8:30   Concert
After concert   Party for retiring Orchestra members (Board Room)

Friday, April 26

10:00 - 12:30   Prospective Encounter Rehearsal in Village
                    (Sollberger-Webern)
2:00   Concert
4:15   Look at apartment with Adele Siegal
8:00   Prospective Encounter (Loeb Student Center)
Supper   David Noakes, Maison Francaise

Saturday, April 27

9:00 - 6:00   Final auditions (violin and cello) (Stage)
8:30   Concert
Supper   Fischer-Dieskau and Ann Colbert

Sunday, April 28

11:00   Piano rehearsal with Sterling
12:00   Sol Greitzer (Studio)
1:30   Lunch with Louise Varese
6:00   Meeting with Carlos Moseley
9:00   Dinner with Mrs. Pharr and Carlos Moseley

Monday, April 29

10:00 - 2:00   Recording Session (Water Music)
3:00 - 5:30   Prospective Encounter Rehearsal (Ligeti and Wolpe)
                    (Stage)
7:00 - 9:00   Piano rehearsal with chorus at Carroll Studios,
                    351 W. 41

Tuesday, April 30

10:00 - 12:30   Rehearsal
12:30   Lunch with new concertmaster and string principals
                    (Poulailler)
2:00 - 4:30   Prospective Encounter Rehearsal (Ligeti and Varese)
                    (Stage)
7:30   Concert
9:45   Joan Peyser - Poulailler

Wednesday, May 1

10:00 - 12:30   Rehearsal
1:30 - 4:00   Rehearsal
6:00 - 8:00   Women's City Club - Informal Speech (6 W. 48)

Thursday, May 2

10:00 - 12:30   Rehearsal
2:00 - 4:30   Prospective Encounter Rehearsal (Wolpe and Varese)
                    (Village)
8:30   Informal Evening (Alice Tully Hall)

Friday, May 3

9:15   Eye doctor
2:00   Concert
4:30   Audition (Heldentenor) (Green Room)
8:00   Prospective Encounter (Loeb Student Center)

Saturday, May 4

11:00   Annette Michaelson, Art Forum Magazine (Re IRCAM)
12:00 - 3:00 ?   Max Matthews re IRCAM
6:00 - 12:00   Rehearsal (Whitney Museum) (Eclat and Marteau)

Sunday, May 5

1:00 - 4:00   Rehearsal (Marteau) (Studio?)
6:00 - 12:00   Whitney Museum (Eclat and Marteau)

Monday, May 6

11:00 or 12:30   Educational Concert - Leon Thompson conducting
5:30   Dress Rehearsal (Whitney Museum)
8:30   Composers' Showcase (Whitney Museum)
Supper   Lukas Foss home

Tuesday, May 7

12:00 - 1:00   Picture Session with Bernstein and Kostelanetz
                    for New York Times Parks story and Japan Tour)
2:30   Mrs. Elizabeth Sayad re Bicentennial
6:30   Meeting with string principals
7:30   Concert

Wednesday, May 8

Early morning departure for London

Boulez's posted schedule for one New York period
in 1974

Boulez with Carlos Moseley, the president of the New York Philharmonic

told me he would not return to New York unless his programming demands were met. But they were not met, if indeed they had been made. Howard Hartog told me of the second contract in June 1972. Frank Milburn told me about it on November 1. Yet the news was not announced until November 5, the morning after Nixon's landslide. The election news dominated everything else. It is hard not to conclude that the Philharmonic postponed the announcement for ten months and finally chose the day that it did to stave off the negative reaction it anticipated if the news were to be given prominence. By that time the majority of Philharmonic subscribers were turned off by Boulez. They want someone who will reach out to them not only with programming but with a personality that suggests there is a dialogue between them and him.

Roddy's negative reaction to Boulez's appearance on the Cavett show reveals the trouble Boulez had with interviews while he was in New York. As he made his way up the ladder—whether as composer or conductor—Boulez's bold attacks on powerful people brought him attention and respect, particularly among the intellectuals. But it is easier to attack Malraux in print than it is to handle a face-to-face interview, particularly if one is set on hiding many things. One of Boulez's least successful interviews was the opening of John Gruen's series, "The Art of the Live Interview," held at the New School for Social Research in Greenwich Village. Several hundred people were there. Gruen appeared in black velvet; Boulez, as always, in a business suit.

Gruen asked what it meant to be music director of the New York Philharmonic. Boulez spoke of the complications of the post. He said he had to consider guest conductors and guest soloists, what each of them wished to do and how he could integrate their wishes with his theme of the year. He said he had to balance instrumental and vocal music, all the different historical periods, deal with the even and odd subscription series, and then, when he was told a work cost too much, had to substitute another and still maintain all the balances. Boulez spoke of the internal life of the orchestra: of musicians retiring who had to be replaced, of the competition between first desk men, of the preaudition committees and the final auditions—when he and members of the section in question agreed on which of the players to select.

As soon as Boulez stopped for a breath, Gruen popped the big question: "What were you like as a little boy?"

BOULEZ: "All little boys are practically the same. The boy you were does not imply the man you are."

GRUEN: "Well, anyway. What kind of little boy were you?"

215

BOULEZ: "I don't remember."

Boulez refused to give the name of the town where he was born. He spoke only of its provincial quality.

Gruen pressed for details; Boulez answered, this time angrily: "You know by now I am not inclined to give my biography point by point. All I will say is this: I played an instrument and sang in the choir. Neither my family nor my environment was musical. In middle-class families, girls and boys have piano lessons. So by chance I was confronted by the sound of the piano. The most important things need no explanation. It is just a seed."

Gruen: "Do you know you are known as a cold conductor? What do you do when a composer writes 'con amore' in a score?"

Boulez ignored the second question: "There is a kind of legend that I am just caring for structure. I think the form is the feeling and that the feeling expresses itself through the form. Composers work through conceptions. You have to navigate a long work. In *Parsifal* you can't just begin and follow the fancy of the moment. Wagner spent four years writing it. It's not fair to the composer or the score just to follow one's fancy. There's more freedom in knowing than in not knowing."

After the interview someone in the audience asked Boulez what he thought of Copland and Bernstein. Boulez said he would not answer the question because he doesn't like to influence people's reactions. Another asked how he stood politically: "I am personally against making my opinions known, or using the public person to influence things. I prefer to be discreet about this."

The next morning I telephoned Gruen to ask for a transcript of the interview. He said he could not give me one because he hoped to publish all his interviews at a later date. (This accounts for the above quotations being only approximations of what was said.) Gruen complained that his opening event was a dismal failure: "Boulez turned the interview into a lecture. His not answering was unbelievable. He didn't even talk to me on the way downtown in the taxi. He is so noncommittal. Did you ever find out anything about his sex life?"

23

A few incidents in New York reveal a lot about the relationship between Boulez and America.

Just after Boulez began his tenure, I ran into an old friend, the conductor Alfred Wallenstein. I told him I was writing a book about Boulez. He attacked the programs of Boulez's first year, mainly its extravagant dosage of Liszt.

"And do you know the reason," Wallenstein went on, "for all of this Liszt? It's because Harold Schonberg wrote at least three columns complaining about the neglect of Liszt and saying some hero should devote a whole year to him. That's the reason—and the only one. It's not because Liszt deserves it. And it's not because Boulez loves Liszt. He has attacked him all his life."

Whatever Wallenstein's motivation, his perception of events was right. Boulez has never had an affection for Romantic music, and he did not conduct Liszt with feeling. Boulez may acquiesce to Moseley who may acquiesce to Amyas Ames who may acquiesce to the board, but all of them answer to Harold Schonberg—despite Schonberg's repeated assertions that he has no power at all.

When Boulez conducted Berg's *Three Pieces for Orchestra*, he needed a second trombone because the regular man was ill. He himself picked up the telephone and called John Swallow, on the music faculty of Yale. Swallow was moved by Boulez's personal call; that is a rare gesture for a conductor. But what he wished for more than anything else was a personal word of gratitude after the performance—and he was never to receive that. Instead Boulez sent the orchestra's personnel manager, Jimmy Chambers, to Swallow with the message that in general he did well enough but that he missed the entry at bar such and such. Swallow was hurt and furious.

Boulez's display of his ability to spot the smallest musical error is considered by a number of the players to be his most reprehensible trait. Many musicians complain Boulez takes precious time from the rehearsal to point out mistakes and to have the men make corrections in their scores, rather than note them silently and instruct the librarian to make them later—as other conductors generally do.

Boulez himself is not impervious to criticism and, indeed, often tries to give the critic what the critic wants. Unlike many composers and conductors, he admits he reads reviews. When a feature article appears, he goes through it without interruption, as he did at the start of his American career, when Newsweek came out with a highly complimentary cover story. It happened again eighteen months later when The New Yorker ran a scholarly profile. It happened again when the magazine section of the Sunday New York Times ran a particularly damaging essay, attacking Boulez's coldness not only in personal relations but also in his handling of the traditional repertoire. That weekend Boulez was conducting Brahms's A Major Serenade. I did not attend, but Roddy did. He called me to say Boulez was moving all over the stage, swinging and swaying as he never did before. "It was painful to watch," Roddy said, "like a woman faking an orgasm."

When I asked Moseley to cite Boulez's most striking personal trait, he said "his practicality." I would agree with Moseley on that. Boulez was practical in signing a second contract only three months after he began the first. He was practical in agreeing to tone down his advanced stand when he saw people leaving the house in droves. And he was practical in building a research institute in France while maintaining his power and income in the United States. But his strong practical bent can be seen in smaller ways. One evening at Poulailler, Boulez's favorite New York restaurant, Daniel Barenboim, who had just played under Boulez at Juilliard, complained to Boulez about his changing the uniform of conductor and soloist from white tie and tails to black tie. He said the buttoned-up jacket interfered with his freedom of movement. Boulez said he made the change so that he could go straight to a restaurant without changing his clothes. He said it with charm but he was serious. Barenboim told Boulez, also with a laugh, that he exhibited an "elitist" attitude.

Boulez has had little success with either the super-chic or the bourgeoisie. Amy Greene runs the beauty shop at Henri Bendel, one of the most fashionable stores in New York. She is married to Milton Greene, who used to photograph Marilyn Monroe. The Greenes are good friends of the Leonard Bernsteins. One afternoon when I was in her shop, Mrs. Greene told me she had attended a performance of Bernstein's *Mass*. She said it was the most religious experience of her life and added that this was no mean compliment because she had been brought up in a convent. She said she had not been to the Philharmonic since Bernstein left because she heard that "nothing good was going on there." Then she laughed: "Anyway, where's the melody?" A woman from Long Island was trying eye shadow: "I dropped my subscription," she said, "because my husband is tired at the end of the day and he just wants to listen to music he likes."

Boulez has had greater success with many serious students of music. Susan Sommer, a Columbia University–trained musicologist and a librarian in the research music division of the Lincoln Center Library, told me Boulez uses the Library all the time. "It's so gratifying to have one's work applied in this way. Boulez is continually searching out old music: the difficult, inaccessible scores. And I love to go to his concerts. I hear things in the music I never heard before."

When there is adequate rehearsal time, what one hears are the results of Boulez's uncanny ear and the technique he uses to get each note sounding right. But it is never because he is swept away. Several days after conducting Carter's *Concerto for Orchestra* at the Juilliard School, he met Peter Mennin, the school's president. Carter was there. Mennin had not been to the concert and he asked Boulez how it went. Boulez shrugged his shoulders in response. Carter was disconcerted by this and later asked me why Boulez had behaved this way. I put the question to Boulez who said, "Everyone is always asking me how everything *went*. How is it to go? It went, that's all." I asked if he could recall a performance that did more than that, that took off in an unusual and incandescent way. He thought for a moment and said no.

During his first two years as music director, Boulez held annual "composer conferences." He invited a number of New York–based composers and asked their advice on what pieces to perform at the Prospective Encounters in Greenwich Village. Most of them objected to the entire project; they thought their works should not be relegated to a series in the Village but be given wide attention at Lincoln Center itself. Nevertheless, those invited to the conference generally went. One was Lukas Foss, the Berlin-born composer-conductor who came to the United States in 1937 and composed then in Boulez's hated "neoclassical" style. In the 1960s Foss turned "radical," writing music that involved both theater and chance, again an idiom that was anathema to Boulez. Foss was the conductor of the Buffalo Philharmonic from 1963 until 1970. Later he became musical advisor and conductor of the Brooklyn Philharmonia and the Kol Israel Orchestra in Jerusalem.

Foss spoke to me after the first of the composer conferences: "It was nothing more than a public relations maneuver, only the maneuver did not work. Rzewski [a composer] said he heard the Village concerts were costly. Boulez asked him where he heard that. Rzewski said he didn't remember. Boulez mocked him: 'I don't remember. I don't find that answer very interesting.'

"Boulez graded the answers as they came in. 'That's a good point.' 'That doesn't interest me.' 'That is nonsense.' 'That is idiotic.' He was like a party boss with his stooges only there were not many stooges there, only a few composers who do not yet know who they are.

"Boulez's only concern is with power. He lost the leadership of the avant-garde more than ten years ago to Stockhausen. Now others have moved in. With the need for power, where was he to go? So he chose to be a conductor. He is a wonderful musician, a wonderful intelligence. It's a pity there's no humanity there. Does he have sex? I think not. When men have no sex, they go after power in this big, obsessive way."

Stanley Silverman, an admirer of Boulez, reported that at the end of the meeting there was an explosion between Foss and Boulez. Foss asked Boulez why he put Americans in a small chamber series instead of presenting them in the big house. Boulez snapped, "And succeed the way you did in Buffalo?" Silverman laughed at the incident. "They are all the same." he said. "Foss did exactly in Buffalo what Boulez is doing in New York. He gave prominence to Henze and Penderecki and put Americans out in left field. It doesn't matter whether the music director is German or French. They're foreign, so Americans will get the raw end."

Boulez failed in terms of his own promise of "revolution." Certainly he infused the New York Philharmonic with more contemporary music than it had known before he came, and probably more contemporary music than it will know when he is gone. Pitted against performances by a powerful conductor like Szell or a popular conductor like Bernstein, Boulez's performances of contemporary scores remained among the best one could get anywhere. It was precisely because he was capable of doing them impeccably that American composers became angry when he gave them less than that. Davidovsky was unhappy with a small piano; Babbitt thought his instruments were not placed in the right way; Peter Lieberson found his work underrehearsed. Inevitably some accused him of malicious intent.

And they appeared to be on firm ground, for Americans were hardly heard in the big house during Boulez's early years in New York. Even the most recognized received short shrift; Boulez did not program a Copland work until his third season, and first-generation Americans less famous than Copland were virtually ignored until the Bicentennial, Boulez's fifth season in New York, and then they often were not conducted by Boulez. Diamond was one who had been the victim of neglect.

"When Boulez first came to New York," Diamond reports, "Moseley and Bernstein sat down with me and went through my orchestral scores. They decided I should send Boulez my *Sixth Symphony* and my *Elegy in Memory of Maurice Ravel*. They thought these pieces in particular would hold some interest for him. I am certain he never opened them. He is intransigent in his musical views. He will not play a score with octave doublings. That is why he has never programmed Sessions." (Sessions was performed later during the Bicentennial.)

A year after this conversation, Boulez was programming American scores that contained far greater heresies than octave doublings. That was because he did not care any more and was moved by political pragmatism alone.

Such stories suggest Boulez is a monster. But he is not a monster at all. In fact, in day-to-day relationships, he is an extremely decent man—never greedy, vulgar, or phony in any way. A mass of contradictions, Boulez is a man who can ignore David Diamond when he is sent scores, but cables birthday greetings to a secretary an ocean away; who, because he detests "rituals," would not attend his nieces' weddings, but paid for their very expensive honeymoons; who almost never compliments a soloist, but drives two hours in the snow to visit a Philharmonic musician recovering from a heart attack. Alternately aggressive and timid, alternately bold and vulnerable, Boulez can seem a bullying egomaniac to his composer-colleagues, but to others he can appear a generous man: shy, charming, eager to be loved, just somehow incapable of expressing any warmth.

221

On January 5, 1973, the Chamber Music Society of Lincoln Center played Boulez's *explosante-fixe*, his first major composition after becoming music director in New York. During its preparation, Boulez was nervous—a state reserved only for his own creative work. The piece is quiet, unsensational, and the audience responded with polite applause. Schonberg wrote a respectful review. *Explosante-fixe* was to be recorded later that week, but, after the performance, Boulez apparently wasn't satisfied and canceled the recording date.

Scored for vibraphone, harp, violin, flute, clarinet, trumpet, and a number of complicated devices including a giant new electronic instrument, the Halaphone, the work was supposed to have lasted eighteen minutes. But in its first performance it lasted much longer than that. The new instrument—named for its inventor, Peter Haller—was said to have been capable of projecting sounds in various directions and at various speeds. It is reported to have cost Miss Alice Tully $5,000 to bring it here from Germany.

The Chamber Music Society, led by Charles Wadsworth, consists of first-rate, experienced soloists. For the Boulez premiere, none was given his part until the last minute. After that the parts were changed constantly. Boulez invariably works up to the deadline, then revises what he has done.

I attended the first rehearsal. Boulez was concentrating on the exceptional performer, Paula Robison, because the flute plays the most prominent role. "It must be very quick. Can we do it again?" Miss Robison had just been handed a completely revised score, replete with musical notes, and she asked if she could look it over first at home. "Do it," Boulez said, "just for the character of it."

Boulez stood to the right and just over Miss Robison. He would have breathed for her if he could. "Very knopf," he said, "knopf . . . knopf . . ." Then he found the English equivalent. "Tight . . . tight . . . tighter," he went on. Miss Robison was overcome with anxiety. She punctuated her performance with a series of sighs, gees, and oh yeses. She was on the verge of tears. Boulez then reminded her that her part opened the work so her performance had to be "really brilliant."

Then Boulez moved on to the others, working with each player individually. After the opening flute solo, the flutist signals the next instrument when it is to enter. Instruments pile up in this way until the texture is very thick. Then there is a diminution until the flute remains alone. There is no freedom in duration or pitch. Whatever freedom there is lies in the length of the sequences; there are moments when rests can be introduced ad libitum.

Boulez began to work again with the now thoroughly upset Miss Robison. "It must be very uneven," he said, beating in an uneven way. It had to be precise in its unevenness. Miss Robison's eyes were filled with tears. "The notes come so fast one upon the other," she wept. Boulez laughed with false cheerfulness. "The point is to be irregular," he explained. "The point of the piece is to be free."

Before the Friday-afternoon concerts, a lecture series is offered to members of the audience. On September 26, 1975, the start of Boulez's fifth season, he dropped in to introduce the speaker for the day and to give a short talk himself.

He spoke of his experience with Japanese calligraphy. He said that when he was visiting Japan he was struck by the beauty of the characters. But to gain understanding of their meaning he needed someone to translate for him. Boulez mentioned that he wished he knew Japanese so that the perception of the beauty and the understanding of the words would come to him simultaneously.

Then he paraphrased a letter of Diderot, the eighteenth-century encyclopedist, to illustrate his point that in art there is first darkness, then understanding, then one enters darkness again "because finally you do not know why you like a work." He concluded: "To reach darkness after understanding is better—I think—than to be in darkness before understanding."

Boulez's assets and liabilities remained intact in his shift from composer to conductor. His talent and energy serve him as much as his rational intellect serves him little. Again his ambition interferes, but it is his personality that causes the deepest trouble. Boulez's inability to engage in a genuine dialogue with whatever is different from himself—whether people or earlier musical periods—seems to be the flaw that pulls him down.

24

During the reception that followed the concert in Indianapolis in 1972, one young woman asked Boulez why the press represented him as a revolutionary figure when he conducted traditional concerts such as the one he had just done: Berlioz, Haydn, Schumann, and Ravel. Boulez laughed. The woman waited. Boulez smiled. Then the woman moved away. Later I repeated her question to him. He answered, "How many people would have bought tickets tonight if we had programmed contemporary music?"

The core of Boulez's mission lay in his programming, and here I must confess I do not know what went on during those countless private sessions between Moseley and Boulez. On tour Moseley invited me to many social events, but I was never invited to programming sessions, and these sessions occur throughout the year: programming is what Moseley, Milburn, and Boulez do virtually every second of unscheduled time.

The incontrovertible fact is this: within the arena of programming, Boulez deferred to that bourgeois society he had only recently announced he would ignore. He did not leave as he threatened to do, but he retreated from his progressive stand in regard to large audiences, concentrating his efforts on those isolated "special events"—the Prospective Encounters, Mini-Festivals, Informal Evenings and Rug Concerts—which add up to little more than one dozen contemporary evenings a year as against one hundred and twenty predominantly conservative evenings peppered with the twentieth-century repertoire. If Boulez had persisted in his original aim, he undoubtedly would have brought the organization down with him. He and Moseley appear to have agreed as to just how far the audience would move.

Moseley is not a well known figure in New York; he prefers to remain behind the scenes. But foundation executives generally agree that he is a "genius" in arts administration. Moseley began his affiliation with the New York Philharmonic in 1955 as director of press and public relations. He worked his way up through various managerial posts until, in 1970, he became the first full-time professional president of the orchestra. His obligation to the Philharmonic takes precedence over a dedication to any musical "style" or "idea." The Philharmonic was one of the first orchestras to offer full-time employment to its musicians. Unlike other American orchestras which have separate organizations handling summer events—the Philadelphia has Robin Hood Dell managing seven weeks and Saratoga another four—Moseley rules fifty-two weeks of the year.

And his gentlemanly manner covers a will of steel. In confrontations between Moseley and Boulez, Moseley generally prevails. When Moseley learned that Boulez was to appear on the Dick Cavett show, an event not planned by his own press department, he instructed him to steer clear of any revolutionary talk. Boulez deferred. When Moseley read Boulez's reply to Craft for the Sunday *Times*, he was firm in his suggestion that the matter stop right there. Boulez deferred. When Moseley learned that Boulez had agreed to conduct the benefit concert for the orchestra's striking musicians, he conferred with Boulez and a retraction followed. (Boulez gave $1,000 to the musicians' fund and attended the concert conducted by Leon Barzin.)

On each occasion Boulez deferred to Moseley, and he appears to have deferred to Moseley on the programming as well. During the 1974–75 season, Boulez acknowledged that he admired less than thirty-five percent of the works he himself was conducting—and that included not only the traditional but the contemporary repertoire. During that year Boulez presented Wuorinen, Carter, George Crumb, and Jacob Druckman (all certified by having won the Pulitzer Prize); Peter Mennin, president of the Juilliard School; Carman Moore, a Juilliard-trained black composer; and Peter Lieberson, who, among other things, is the son of the man who was then president of Columbia Records, the company that records the New York Philharmonic. And he left unopened on his shelves the bulk of the scores that continued to pour in. Being music director of the New York Philharmonic

225

clearly did not bring to Boulez whatever it was he had hoped it would bring. But rather than ask, "How do I get out of it?" he seemed only to ask, "How do I get through it?"

As president, Moseley serves as liaison between the music director and the board of directors. "Boulez never fought the board," Moseley says. "It is true he had a great desire to bridge the gap between what the mass of people were used to hearing and the contemporary composer. But he is a practical man. He is practical enough to be guided by the subscribers' response."

Boulez reports on the programming sessions: "I propose a theme and then we meet. Part of the problem is with guest conductors. Often those who will accept the programs are not big attractions, while those who are big attractions will not accept the programs. I have never been pushed by Moseley. He is far too intelligent to push against me. I was aware myself that the important thing is not to do too much, for then the people will not come and the organization will be in jeopardy. If you bring down the number of subscribers then you cannot go any further. The point is to attract a number of people and do something of what you want at the same time. It is true that in London I did more British music than I have done American music here. But that is because I played much more contemporary music in London and could do that because of the subsidized BBC."

Perhaps to compensate for the retrogression, Boulez began to spend long hours in the library digging up difficult, rarely performed "older" pieces. During the 1972–73 season, the Haydn he performed was an unhackneyed Haydn: it included the rarely heard symphonies Nos. 28, 31, 49, 60, 75, and 86, as well as the *Theresien* and *Harmonie* masses, and the opera *L'Incontro Improviso*. In a Sunday essay entitled "It's Fun For Boulez—But . . ." Harold Schonberg wrote that he thought many listeners would miss the works they know and love. The essay precipitated a phone call from Moseley to Boulez (then conducting in Cleveland) which was followed by a meeting between Moseley, Milburn, and Boulez as soon as Boulez arrived in New York. Then Moseley spoke to Schonberg. "I told him," Moseley reports, "that the Philharmonic was really doing what he had always wanted it to do: avoiding the war-horses and introducing unfamiliar pieces. The reaction to Harold's article was that some were furious with him but others were furious with the Philharmonic." A letter Stephen Jablonsky wrote to Schonberg attacking his anti-Boulez article provided Schonberg with the opportunity to bring the issue up once again to qualify, to soften his original statement.

Many who work under Moseley report he is "hypersensitive" to the press which he has described as "irresponsible." Moseley says, "The press kept at this business of the Philharmonic doing a courageous thing, getting rid of an old audience for a new one. The people read a good deal about Boulez, 'The Great Iconoclast,' and were prejudiced prior to the time to judge. Many held onto their seats but did not attend in a display of protest. Others left the house before the unfamiliar work was performed."

But Moseley is wrong to blame the press; the reporters were merely loudspeakers for Boulez's ideas. The trouble lay not in newspaper accounts or in magazine articles but in the twentieth-century music of Boulez's early programs. During his first official season, subscriber mail poured in against Berg, and when, in October 1971, Michael Gielen conducted a program of Strauss's *Metamorphosen*, Nono's *Canti di vita e d'amore* and Berg's *Lulu Suite*, very few people remained until the end. The woman in the Plaza who equated old music with heaven and new music with hell was not alone. Boulez says that in his early concerts in New York, when he was conducting much twentieth-century music, he had the fantasy of locking all the doors so the audience would be forced to remain and listen. He says he cannot understand why people would not stay even if made uncomfortable by what they were to hear.

But Boulez could not lock the doors, and his programs became not only less remarkable in terms of rarely heard old pieces; they even began to include "war-horses." The 1973–74 audience heard Beethoven *Symphonies Nos. 3 and 5*, Schumann's *Symphonies Nos. 1 and 2*, Mendelssohn's *"Reformation" Symphony*, Mahler's and Bruckner's *Symphonies No. 1*, Debussy's *La Mer*, and Sibelius's *Symphony No. 2*. All over the United States, orchestras continued to move in the same vein they had moved in before Boulez's arrival in New York. Orchestras like the Chicago Symphony, with a tradition of exploring new fields that went back to Frederick Stock at the turn of the century, continued to move ahead. But the bulk of the other orchestras remained firmly entrenched in the traditional repertoire. On September 24, 1972, music editor Raymond Ericson wrote in the Sunday *New York Times*: "Browsing through the orchestras' schedules does not provide any surprises or suggest any strong trends. The repertory remains basically the same, with the same works as the symphonies of Bruckner and Mahler more firmly established than ever before. Beethoven cycles or festivals have not disappeared by any means." When one critic complained to Milburn, at the start of the 1974–75 season, that the Philharmonic programs were conservative, Milburn replied that other orchestras' programs were even more so.

One would expect Boulez to have felt despair at what can only be described as the failure of his mission in New York and the consequent failure of his larger mission to change the whole direction of American musical life. But Boulez is a very private man, and just as no one in Europe, in the late 1950s, suggests any anguish could be sensed within him then, so no one in New York, in the mid-'70s, could have detected any anguish in his demeanor there. One evening after dinner in 1973, Boulez complained about his recent weight gain. Elliott Carter noted that that was odd, that conducting modern music should guard against that. Boulez laughed. "What gave you the idea I conduct modern music?" he asked. It is impossible to know with Boulez whether indifference or bitterness lay behind that gaiety.

It is a fact that the "wildness" Boulez says persists on his inside is kept under strong check. A not-caring attitude permeates every move in regard to the mechanics of his daily life. Renting an apartment in New York for the first time in the fall of 1974, Boulez asked the Frankels to decorate it for him, noting only that the furniture should be "modern." This was a far cry from the care he took with his Baden-Baden house where he chose each piece of furniture himself, seeking professional guidance only in arranging it. The Frankels worked with Bloomingdale's, a department store on Manhattan's East Side, and in one day put together chairs, lamps, clocks, rugs, tables, glassware, china, and Bill Blass sheets—the sheets to go on a bed almost as narrow as the one in Germany, which is almost as narrow as the one in Paris. The narrowness of the bed was one of the few specifications. (In Cleveland Boulez asked Mrs. Frankel to remove the other twin bed from his room. He gave no reason; he just wanted it out.)

Boulez's indifference extends to clothes. Wherever he is taken he will buy everything he needs. Record executive Ken Glancy brought Boulez to Harrod's in London where he chose a complete wardrobe. When that wore out, the Frankels brought him to a store in Cleveland and he chose a complete wardrobe there. To "select" means to commit oneself as to one's likes and dislikes, and Boulez virtually never does this anymore, not even in regard to people. To christen his New York apartment he gave a party for his "American friends": the Frankels, the Jablonskys, six officials of the New York Philharmonic, two secretaries, and my husband and me, all people who have sought him out or are connected with him through professional affairs.

Boulez's avoidance of choices extended to advice he gave me concerning this book. I told him that for every incident in his life there were as many stories as there were participants. Rarely did other people's narratives coincide with his own. Not whimsically, Boulez suggested that I take my cue from Mallarmé: for each event have a fixed first and last page and place all the variations in between. The idea that statements must be so ambiguous that they shift in relation to one another, that there is really no true meaning of a text, is not, of course, peculiar to Mallarmé. But surely it receives one of its most eloquent confirmations from him.

For Mallarmé was one of the first artists who self-consciously appropriated elements belonging to science into art. In the *Sketches* published in 1957, the Symbolist poet wrote of the "scientific relationships" expressible in numbers which he hoped his own work would embody. "Everything in the cosmos," Mallarmé added, "exists in order to emerge as a Book, a book, perhaps, in several volumes, but, in fact, only one, which everyone has tried to write, the geniuses included, namely the orphic explanation of the earth." Surely Mallarmé's efforts to bring the panoply of science into art, as well as Boulez's own inclinations, play a role in the evolution of his *Institut de Recherche et de Coordination Acoustique/Musique*, scheduled to be in full swing in 1977.

It was during Boulez's fallow period—between 1958 and 1968—that he conceived of a tangible way to incorporate science, or more accurately, technology, into the framework of art. During the winter of 1966, the Max Planck Society in Germany asked him to think about a theoretical basis for a Max Planck Institute of Music. Boulez says, "I had many meetings with scientists and artists. I found these meetings exceptionally interesting and began to work on a theoretical project that was to have been subsidized by Volkswagen. But then there was an economic recession and the Institute did not come to pass. There was considerable hostility towards it. Some scientists were unhappy about spending the money for a musical institute while the music departments of the German schools were equally unhappy about a scientific approach to music. For the first time I thought of the necessity of such a research center to solve many problems. I said so in an interview in *Le Monde* in late 1969. The interview was published in early 1970 and was read by Pompidou who contacted me."

Boulez organizes his career the way Napoleon organized a campaign, and, like Napoleon, he never publishes his plan. More than a year and a half, therefore, before he took over the directorship of the

New York Philharmonic, Boulez was planning what he would do if his aims with the orchestra did not work out.

About the same time, Boulez began to compose again. He says he was brought back to composition by Stockhausen's *Momente* because that piece was so "bad." Stockhausen completed it one year after the release of *Sergeant Pepper*—what one writer has called the "flower-child movement's anthem." As the Beatles appropriated techniques from the musical avant-garde, so Stockhausen, in this particular work, appropriated much of the manner and message of rock.

Momente, which opens with a resounding strike on a gong and a soprano's piercing invitation to "listen to the moments, to the music of love," is scored for brass, electronic organs, and percussion instruments. Bizarrely dressed hippies stream through the theater as they sing, shout, mutter, giggle, clap their hands, and stamp their feet. "*Momente* brought me strongly back to composition," Boulez says, "because it was the cheapest thing Stockhausen had done." As Stockhausen's "good period" had moved Boulez away from composition, Stockhausen's "bad period" moved him back in. For Boulez, Stockhausen's submission to the vulgar and popular undermined the essence of "music" in music.

Since then, Boulez has written *Domaines* for clarinet which he began in 1962 but did not pick up again until 1968 when he wrote it for his composition class at Basel; *Multiples* which he composed in 1970 as an extension of *Eclat*, written in 1965; *Cummings ist der Dichter*, composed in 1970 but inspired by Cage's introduction to him of Cummings' poetry in 1952; *explosante-fixe*, begun in the summer of 1971 but still being revised; *Memoriales*, a commission for the BBC Symphony based on the material of *explosante-fixe* with, in Boulez's words, "lots of brass, percussion, and winds in a number of independent groups all tingling like different clocks." *Rituel*, which has been played both in London and at Tanglewood, is the opening of that series of pieces.

Although many of these compositions have received performances in one or several versions, Universal Edition has published nothing since 1965, when it printed the photocopy of Boulez's manuscript of *Eclat*. Boulez sends his manuscripts in, parts of *Eclat-Multiples* appear in reproduction here, but he advises publisher Alfred Schlee not to go ahead with them as he is continually revising and adding to what he has done. What he is doing may be comparable to Mallarmé's cosmic book *Le Livre*: a great work, composed in fragments, that will one day be pulled together. But Glock reports that Boulez is distressed at

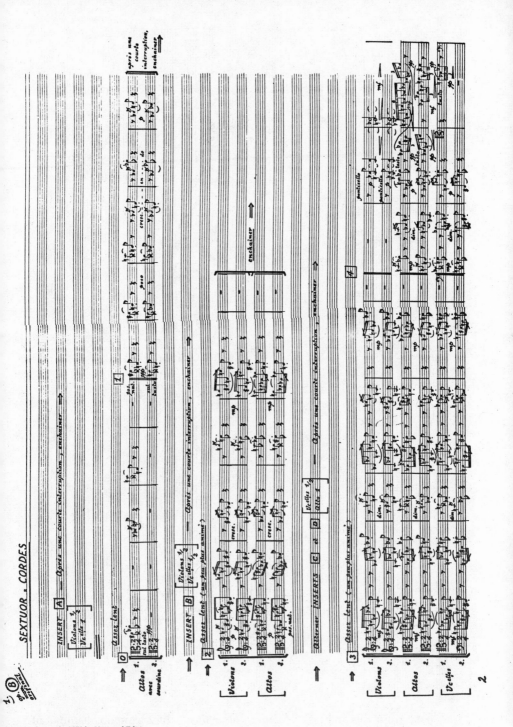

Domaines: music from which the clarinet plays.

231

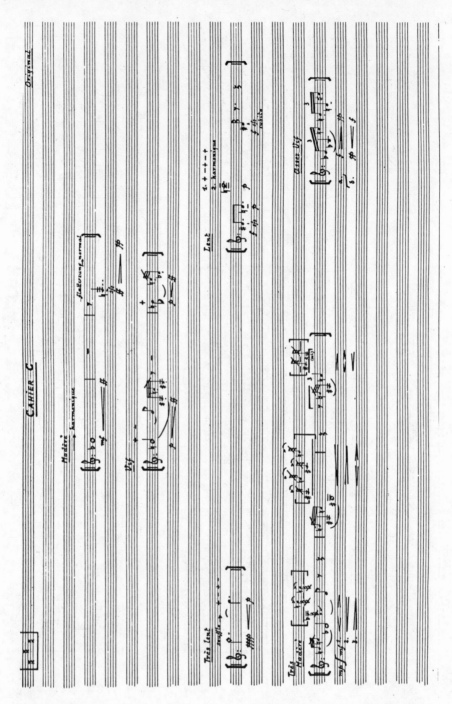

A page from the orchestral score of *Domaines* which contains a moment when the clarinet enters with either material "C" or "D." The clarinetist

232

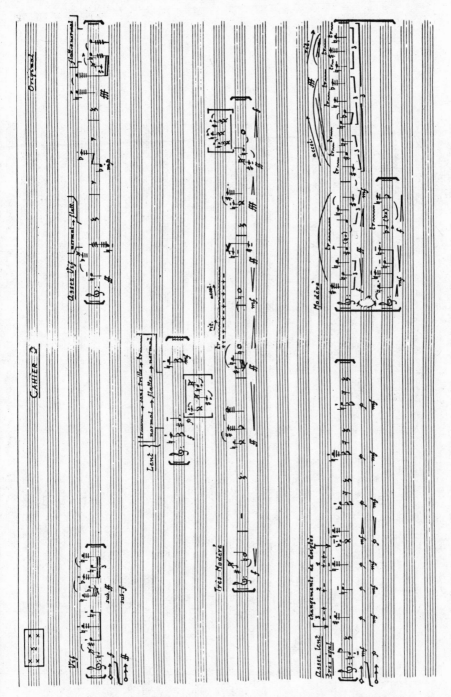

moves from one to another of six groups of instruments; his physical route is a reflection of the complex structure of the score.

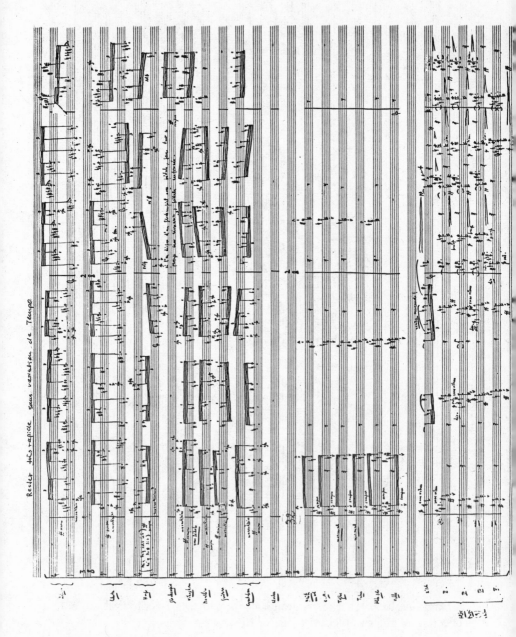

Material Boulez added to *Eclat*, which is written in his own hand and has not yet been published. This excerpt of the new piece, *Eclat/Multiples*, reveals a larger ensemble than used in the original piece.

235

Boulez's manuscript of the first two pages of *Cummings ist der Dichter.*

how things are going. Glock quotes a Boulez letter: "How the years are passing! So many ideas unfulfilled and unrealized and life is passing so quickly."

Boulez explains his ways in precise terms: "I think quickly, but it takes a long time for my thoughts to ripen. I am a long wave reactor. I don't meet things easily, but I don't forget them easily."

Here is the way *explosante-fixe* ripened: *Tempo* magazine, a British music journal, asked Boulez and a number of other composers to write a piece in memory of Stravinsky. The request was for some sort of canon. "Well, if you have to write a canon," Boulez says, "you can do that. Like Bach. And all the other composers did that. But I thought about mixing echoing and canonic writing. You can't have a plain canon in the twentieth century.

"I began to think about the work in August 1971, soon after receiving the commission. That month I visited a castle in Scotland that had once belonged to the Duchess of Argyll. The woman who invited my sister and me was an Austrian woman who lived in France, and she had with her a son who was not very oriented; he did not know what he was to do with his life. Since then he committed suicide. The young man played the flute as an amateur and he improvised in this empty eighteenth-century castle. It was quite impressive. I had the idea then of the work beginning with a flute solo.

"The notes were to provide the basic idea, a kind of ground music. Then I wrote a simple text [Boulez followed two pages of musical notes with six pages of verbal instructions] indicating how to make it more complex. My student, Heinz Holliger, realized the piece but his realization was not sufficient. I wanted one much more refined from this matrix. When I did it myself, I did it in a very complex way, with a definitive form, far too complex to improvise. I have rewritten some parts twice, others three times."

Boulez took his title from *Nadja*, by André Breton. "The line," Boulez says, "was 'la beauté will be explosante-fixe or it will not be.' It was a beautiful poetic image which remained within me—independently floating."

It is also true that as "Poems for Power" revealed a good deal about Boulez in the late 1950s, so "Fixed Explosion" says volumes about the man during his polite and orderly tenure in New York.

Boulez admires the world of Paul Klee because "one can see as many faces in a drop of water as in a large landscape." So the world of Boulez is contained in the smallest segment of his music in which notes are juggled in the most dexterous and complex way. The movement from C sharp to D in one voice is echoed by D to C sharp in another, while a rhythmic group of three followed by two in one part comes on the heels of two followed by three in another. In 1965, in Los Angeles, Boulez discovered 4 x 6 cards with staves on them and has been composing on them ever since. On these small cards, Boulez works out his tiny refinements and then transcribes the final fragments onto the score. There is, therefore, no possibility of grand gesture here, but infinitely and exquisitely worked out small musical worlds.

Boulez does it with language and spoken sounds too. Carol Frankel reports that at a diner in Cleveland a juke box repeatedly blared out a pop record. Finally Boulez asked what it was. Mrs. Frankel replied, "James Taylor, a smash hit." Boulez said, "You mean it's mass shit." Again, before he was to tour with the orchestra, Boulez picked up a book on oral-genitalism that Mrs. Frankel had received earlier. She told him he could not travel with that, that it would not be right for him to be seen with it. Taking the dust jacket off my book *The New Music: the Sense behind the Sound*, Boulez put it on the oral-genital tome and said the subtitle would be "the Sound behind the Scents."

Such intellectual punning might be expected of a brilliant multilingual European, and to say that Boulez delights in it is not to suggest he completely rejects accidents. Many musicians have wondered why Boulez used the German title *Cummings ist der Dichter* for a work based on an English poem. Here is the answer: "I was commissioned to write a piece for the festival at Ulm. I couldn't find a title for the work when they asked me what to print on the program. In a letter in German—my German was not very good at that time—I wrote: 'I have not chosen a title yet, but what I can tell you is this: Cummings is the poet.' A reply came from a German secretary who had misunderstood my letter: 'As for your new work, *Cummings ist der Dichter*. . . .' I found that mistake so wonderful that I thought, well, then, that's a title given by the Gods."

25

Within one year, between the summers of 1969 and 1970, four men who had been important to Boulez died: his father, Adorno, Strobel, and Szell. Reflecting on this series of deaths, Boulez says, "It was a strange configuration. Strobel and I heard about the death of Adorno at the end of July 1969, and Strobel asked me to write a memorial essay for his journal, *Melos*. He came to see me August 15, just after his afternoon nap. That must have made it between 3:30 and 4 o'clock. We worked heavily until 7:30 or 8. Then a phone call came that my father had died. I was working on a memorial for one man when news came to me of my father's death. I knew he was dying, so it was not a complete surprise. But it was a surprise nevertheless.

"Just exactly one year after, as soon as I returned from a trip to Mexico [Boulez went there with his sister and Lawrence Morton], I learned of Szell's illness. He died during a concert I was conducting with the Cleveland Orchestra. Szell had exactly the illness my father did.

"While in Cleveland I heard that Strobel fainted. I knew he must have had some sort of heart attack. I called the Strobels and said I would be home. On the way I stopped at Bayreuth to conduct *Parsifal*. While there I had a call that Strobel had died.

"All of these men were more or less father-figures to me. At one point in your life, you must face the disappointment of such losses and become a father-figure yourself. Of course the loss of Strobel and my father touched me more than that of Adorno and Szell. I met Adorno fleetingly around 1954 and was in close contact with him later in Darmstadt. In the '60s he came to Baden-Baden regularly, but my relationship with him was primarily intellectual. Szell I knew very well but not to the point, of course, of my father or, for that matter, Strobel, whom I had known since 1951 and had been on a day-to-day basis with since 1958."

Boulez's shift from son to father was not accompanied by the lessening of tensions between brothers. One by one the old friendships ruptured. Pousseur, Boulez's first follower into the serial world, describes their estrangement engendered by his own return to tonality:

"In the late 1950s, many of us felt the need for stronger means of characterization. We needed harmony, which was so charged with significance. All the years I had been composing without harmony, I had been playing and listening to harmonic music. The point was to use harmony again but in a still richer, more effective way. I started to work on a piece, Faust, with a libretto by Michel Butor. It took seven years to compose.

"I began to work on Faust in 1961. Boulez planned to do it at the Domaine in 1963. But he became more upset as he saw it. He pulled out of the commitment in 1963. After that we saw each other very little. In the late 1960s I wrote a work, Crossed Colors, based on the Negro spiritual 'We shall overcome.' Boulez conducted it, not only in Europe, but with the New York Philharmonic in 1971. After that performance I gave him an article I had written about Stravinsky in which I discussed Stravinsky's harmonies—being based on polarities as they were. In it I quoted Boulez on Stravinsky but did it in a warm, friendly way. Naturally I quoted the areas in which we did not agree. After that Boulez sent me a letter. He said that for a long time we had had little to say to each other and added, 'Now that you have discovered Agon, there is nothing left. Perhaps soon you'll discover Hindemith. You wrote We shall overcome; I prefer Burn Baby Burn.' Boulez's point was that I was trying to conciliate old and new, black and white, while he preferred to burn everything."

Boulez was never, even in his earliest years, profoundly attached to Pousseur. But the same cannot be said of Stockhausen; yet even here the relationship exploded into a bitter battle culminating around the performance of Stockhausen's Mixtur, a piece in which instrumental sounds are transformed by electronic means. Boulez conducted it at the Round House in London in January 1972. Here is Boulez on what happened then: "Stockhausen was supposed to take care of all the electronics. He said he needed twelve, not six rehearsals. But the piece did not require twelve rehearsals. Stockhausen said he did not want to come to London to supervise the planning of this work. My interpretation of this is that he did not want to be confronted with me on this particular piece. But that may be a psychological excuse on my part. Stockhausen prefers to surround himself with subordinates. He likes feudal relationships.

"So I said to him, 'If you do not want to come, how are we to realize this piece?' In reply he sent inadequate, unprofessional, pontificating acolytes. One of them told the percussionist how to scratch a tam-tam. This kind of pontificating I do not need. The clan of Stockhausen was very hostile. Those in charge of the ring modulators were never on time. I said, 'If you want to do it, do it; if you don't, I don't care.' This was reported to Stockhausen by his Mafia. Then he and I talked. I said to Stockhausen, 'I can talk with you but not with those on a low level with the Lord.'

"After it was over, he told me he heard the work did not receive a good performance. I said it was not a good work in the first place. We have not spoken since then."

As for Boulez's fight with American composers, it has not abated. In the spring of 1970, when Boulez was to conduct a contemporary music festival at Lawrence Morton's Ojai concerts, he programmed nineteen twentieth-century works, not one of which was by an American. A group of composers, very different from each other but related, to some degree, to the ideas of Cage—Morton Feldman, La Monte Young, and Frederick Rzewski were among them—wrote a letter to Morton attacking the situation. Morton was upset about it and spoke to Boulez who waved his hand in a gesture of unconcern. And unconcern was what he felt. Boulez says he took no advice from Babbitt, Sessions, Wuorinen, Rzewski, and others he invited to "composers' conferences" to help determine the repertoire at his Village concerts in New York, because "everyone was bringing in his own little circle." As for the correspondence in the Ojai episode, Boulez interprets the letter writers' silence since then to the fact that "they know they cannot compete with me."

In the fall of 1974, at the start of his second contract in New York, Boulez was as contemptuous of American composers—apart from Carter, of whom he speaks with respect—as he had been more than five years before: "I have not come across a big talent in this country, not even a controversial talent. Here the big disappointment was for me to find no center of interest in New York. There are the academic people on one side. On the other there are those who experiment but are really nothing more than amateurs. They are just playing in the kitchen and there is a great lack of professionalism there."

As for Cage, Boulez's early benefactor, he was not to benefit from Boulez's presence in New York. (A Cage performance during Boulez's last season came about through a Bicentennial grant in which Boulez played no role.) In 1971, at a composers' conference, Rzewski said, "Next year is John Cage's sixtieth birthday. How do you plan to celebrate it?"

Boulez replied, "I shall send him a cake."

Boulez is not alone in suffering from motives that appear less than generous in spirit and heart. Competition pervades every aspect of contemporary life, and music is no exception to the rule. The bitterest fights in university music departments revolve around which professor's book will be used as the "official" text. And instrumentalists in the New York Philharmonic are well aware of the enmity that exists between two extraordinarily talented first-desk men, one of whom sucks on his reed and chats with his colleagues whenever the other performs a solo. If such meanness characterizes relations between professors of music and performing musicians, why should it not characterize relations between Wuorinen and Davidovsky, Feldman and Cage, Stockhausen and Boulez, and Boulez and new music at large? To many listeners, each of these couplings appears to be at one, to share each other's basic approach to art. But on close investigation one finds competition causing bitterness, and in the end such bitterness changes the character of art. For if we live in an age marked by cynicism and rancor, an age in which there are virtually no heroes, would it not follow that art would reflect this and work its will by affirming it?

In *Le Monde Cassé* (*The Broken World*), by Gabriel Marcel, the heroine asks:

Don't you feel sometimes that we are living . . . if you can call it living . . . in a broken world? Yes, broken like a watch. The mainspring has stopped working. Just to look at it, nothing has changed. Everything is in place. But put the watch to your ear, and you don't hear any ticking. You know what I'm talking about, the world, what we call the world, the world of human creatures . . . it seems to me it must have had a heart at one time, but today you would say that the heart had stopped beating.

243

In an essay, *The Mystery of Being*, Marcel quotes that speech and writes:

A broken world? . . . We must be careful here. Certainly it would be rash to put one's finger on some epoch in history where the unity of the world was something directly felt by man in general. But could we feel the division of this world today, or could some of us at least feel it so strongly, if we had not within us, I will not say the memory of such a united world, but at least the nostalgia of it.

In 1943, Boulez told Messiaen, "Musical aesthetics are being worn out," and asked, "Who is there to give it life?" Messiaen replied, "You will, Pierre." Boulez was eighteen at that time. At twenty he discovered the serial idea and has addressed virtually all his actions since then toward using that particular grammar in the service of giving music a new and long life. At first he did it through composing and theory. But that did not work out as he planned. Then he conducted a repertory that he hoped would bring large audiences up to the music of its own time. But once again that did not work. At the end of the Ives Mini-Festival in the fall of 1974, *Times* music reviewer Allen Hughes wrote that Boulez was "far and away the most interesting and creative music director in the world." Few would take exception to that. But what Hughes did not say is this: that on all but the last of the evenings, the one on which the Ives *Fourth Symphony* was played, Avery Fisher Hall was far from full, and that, on the final evening, when the house was brimming with life, it was because the "best seats" were widely advertised at $2 apiece. I asked many people why they were there; none of them replied, to hear Charles Ives. Moseley knows this only too well. Despite the enormous effort that went into this piece, which calls for vast orchestral forces and their mastering massive rhythmic complexities, he did not program it for any subscription audience. The Ives *Fourth* was a one-shot affair.

The denouement was that after three years of backbreaking work, of performing new scores that neither he nor the orchestra had played before—there were ten such scores for the Ives Festival alone which took place on five consecutive days—large audiences for new music were not to be found. New Yorkers were no different in this respect from audiences for the BBC Symphony or the Cleveland Orchestra. In reply to whether Boulez's presence in London made a significant difference in musical habits there, Sir William Glock said, "It must have made a difference to composers who heard crucial works for the

244

first time. But if you ask me if it has changed the habits of people going to Festival Hall, I would have to say No."

As for the Cleveland Orchestra, when Boulez was conducting his special repertory there in large doses after Szell's death—he conducted thirteen weeks during the 1970–71 season—subscriptions dropped disastrously. One might attribute the loss of ticket sales to regrets caused by the death of the much-beloved Szell. But today's programs reveal something more: a rejection of those Boulez introduced. The brochure for 1974–75 states: "The season presents a colorful array of world-renowned conductors and dazzling soloists. Familiar favorites and major masterpieces highlight this popular season . . . Maazel will conduct fourteen subscription programs featuring the music of Rachmaninov, Brahms, Chopin, Liszt, Berlioz, Mendelssohn, and Debussy, plus programs devoted to the music of Mozart, Beethoven, and Elgar." A look at the programs themselves reveals not one work by Schoenberg, not one by Webern, not one, for that matter, by Boulez.

In the fall of 1974, Boulez said he found it disappointing that the two conductors then being considered to replace him at the New York Philharmonic, when he embarks on his Paris Institute full-time, were Daniel Barenboim and Zubin Mehta. "They are both open-minded," Boulez says, "but neither is committed to contemporary music. I wish the board would choose someone to build on what I began."

Boulez still believes in the language he began to carve out in 1945. "It is, he says, "as viable as I thought it was in the 1950s. It must go through this process. Even if Schoenberg at the "Rugs" was not so successful, eighteen hundred people came. And that is twice the size of Alice Tully Hall."

Boulez's "Rug Concerts" take place during one week in June. The tickets are cheaper and the programming more contemporary than at any other time of the year, and the seats on the first floor of Avery Fisher Hall are removed and replaced by carpeting. The Rug Concerts have been widely attended and enthusiastically received by a young and attentive audience. Boulez has interpreted this to indicate that he has succeeded in his mission among the young.

But the size and response of these audiences do not necessarily signify a new and potentially paying public for contemporary music. It seems more likely, in fact, that many of these young people respond to the publicity centered on Boulez as a revolutionary figure (the very publicity that Philharmonic officials abhorred), and attend because of the "Revolution" coupled with air conditioning and an invitation to sit or lie on the floor. That view gains support from an experience in New York in 1972–73. After an expensive publicity campaign, the French pianist Marie-Françoise Bucquet offered four concerts of twentieth-century music at Alice Tully Hall with a top ticket price of $3. The first two concerts were sold out and Mlle Bucquet received not only ovations from the public but rave reviews from the critics, and from critics who specialize in new music. It was only after Paul Jacobs informed those critics and a number of other journalists as well, several of whom printed what Jacobs said, that Schoenberg's *Opus 11* was "unrecognizable" and that the *Opus 23* "contained about ten percent of the right notes" that Mlle Bucquet's third and fourth concerts were marred not only by a plethora of empty seats but also by harsh criticism from the press.

The Bucquet story suggests that only composers who write this particular music, performers who play this particular music, and critics with the scores in their hands can tell when an irretrievable mess has been made of the "classics" Schoenberg wrote almost seventy years ago. As to why young people flock and shout *Bravo!*—"The cult of the new," Jacques Barzun pointed out in discussing today's student generation, "is now the compulsory, the *conventional* thing" in intellectual matters and in art.

The question that follows the Bucquet incident is this: what drew so many in the field to align themselves with new music when they could not make the sense of it that they had always made of other music? My answer goes back to the introduction of this book in which I confessed that my own motive was in large measure ideational and did not reside in the music itself. For I believe the commitment of many came from equally extramusical motives, not the least of which was the fear of repeating the mistake of the official salon which, in the late nineteenth century, rejected paintings by Degas, Renoir, Monet, and Cézanne.

Souvchinsky says he knew Boulez was a genius when he first heard Boulez *talk* at a Paris lecture. He had not then heard a single Boulez work. Suzanne Tezenas acknowledges she was never a partisan of new music; there was, in fact, little new music in Paris before Boulez arrived on the scene. But friends report she was not even an active listener of the standard repertoire. Painting (Nicolas de Staël and Dubuffet) and theater (she provided the backing for early Ionesco plays) were Mme Tezenas's primary interests, as literature was the forte of Paule Tévenin, editor of Boulez's "apprentice" essays. Mme Tévenin helped writers Raymond Radiguet and Michel Butor and is said to have read Gatti's poetry well. But music was assuredly not her métier.

For almost three hundred years France has been more literary than musical. So it might be expected that the success of a musical movement there would depend more on verbal propaganda than in the United States. But that does not appear to be the case. Elliott Carter, at present America's most celebrated composer, has frequently confided to friends that those in responsible positions in universities, on foundation boards, and with prize committees understand nothing of the new music they hear, and that one is therefore obliged to use all the resources at hand to get what every composer wants most: his music performed, published, and recorded extensively.

To say that the people surrounding new music were not initially drawn to it through the music itself is not to suggest that composers were moved similarly. On the contrary, composers were drawn to the language through listening to some particular work. Leibowitz came to it through *Pierrot Lunaire*, Boulez through Schoenberg's *Woodwind Quintet*, Pousseur through Webern's *Second Cantata*, and Babbitt through Schoenberg's *Opus 11 Piano Pieces*. It was the music, above all, that excited them. The performers who delivered the first messages fall into a class between composer and listener. For the most part they were motivated by a deep personal involvement with the composers whose works they performed. Cathy Berberian first brought Berio's work to life during the early years of their marriage. Now, long after a divorce, she still premieres his vocal works. Bethany Beardslee, Miss Berberian's New York counterpart, had been married to Jacques Monod. Monod, who studied with Messiaen and Leibowitz during the period Boulez did, settled in the United States and became an advocate of Babbitt, whom he judges "the greatest composer since Schoenberg." Miss Beardslee carved her reputation singing the exceptionally difficult Babbitt works. Still others were drawn to music through people: Paul Jacobs' early friendship with Boulez, Tudor's affection for Cage, provided the emotional glue that led them to adhere to radical ways.

Of course there are now performing groups specializing in the twentieth-century repertoire; this *is* the last quarter of the century. But even here these groups are generally led by an authoritarian composer to whom the rest of the group is attached. Stockhausen's "Improvisation Group" in Cologne, Wuorinen's "Group for Contemporary Music" in New York are examples of this particular practice.

In fact, musicians with one orientation who are forced into doing something else captivated the interest of a German psychologist,

Eckhard Weisenhutter, who confirmed his prejudice against new music with a study he conducted in 1974. Even allowing for the slipperiness of such a study, the conclusions, as expressed by Cologne director Wolfgang Becker, suggest that something in the Cologne Radio Symphony, that bastion of new music, seems to be happening —or, rather, not happening: "Dr. Weisenhutter interviewed the musicians of the Cologne orchestra and found them beset by psychogenic illnesses. The players are impotent. They hate new music. After playing it they cannot engage in sexual activity. This is understandable, for musicians are emotional people and if a musician is not convinced of the validity of what he does, his sexual life is bound to suffer."

26

The late Theodor Adorno viewed the progressive materialism in society as the archenemy of what he considered to be the only legitimate twentieth-century musical language. In *The Philosophy of Modern Music*, written in the 1940s, Adorno deplored the decline of dodecaphony during those predominantly neo-tonal years. He viewed dodecaphony as an underground language struggling for life in a society in which gross and vulgar values prevail. "The liberation of modern painting from objectivity," he wrote, "which was to art the break that tonality was to music, was determined by the defensive against the mechanized art commodity—above all, photography. . . . Because the monopolistic means of distributing music stood almost entirely at the disposal of artistic trash and compromised cultural values, and catered to the socially determined predisposition of the listener, radical music was forced into complete isolation during the final stages of industrialism."

But Boulez, whose thinking often parallels that of Adorno, took "radical music" out of isolation and plunged it into the New York marketplace. Initially he had considerable help from the press. *Life, Time, Newsweek* celebrated him, not for the traditional values that Moseley and Keiser would have had them celebrate, but for Boulez's particular principles as well as his obsession for realizing them.

Still, his revolution did not work. One evening during Boulez's early tenure in New York, Harold Schonberg commented to me that he could not hear a "cancrizans," a melody that reads backward, from right to left. I wonder how many can hear a cancrizans, except perhaps at that pivotal point at which the row turns back on itself. But if one cannot hear a cancrizans, or the manipulation of intervals within a complex fabric, what is there within a work to hold it together in one's mind, to give a sense of closure to the listener?

There are two fundamentally different approaches to listening to music, as there are to perceiving any art. One is immediately accessible, the other more difficult to apprehend, requiring labor, intelligence and experience. Both can be present in the same work. In Huck Finn's world, Shakespeare was performed throughout the small towns of the South. Coincidentally, in the North, Beethoven symphonies opened each of the three concerts that marked the New York Philharmonic's first year, 1842. Shakespeare was played in the South and Beethoven in the North because that art would enhance peoples' lives, would bring them enjoyment and delight. To say *King Lear* and the Beethoven *Fifth* can be approached on a simple level is not to deny complexity within them. It is rather to emphasize that Shakespeare and Beethoven provide enough pleasure at a first encounter to induce the audience to come back for more.

Neurophysiological evidence suggests that there are two separate modes of viewing phenomena that are related to these two approaches to art. One is holistic: the observer grasps the structure, the shape of the whole. The other is linear-analytic: the observer discerns the "atoms," the substructures of the work. The two are not mutually exclusive. Once the viewer or listener grasps the full shape, he is free to return and absorb the complexity of detail. What separates contemporary "serious" music from the great art of the past is its refusal to give the listener form that is immediately graspable. It is so heavily weighted with detail that it does not encourage the listener to return.

Thus the problem of this music "reaching" audiences appears to lie outside the crude values of Adorno's materialistic society, and outside Boulez's revolutionary programs; rather it lies in neurophysiology. A century ago the English neurologist, John Hulings Jackson, wrote that these ways of viewing phenomena were related specifically to brain function, and more specifically to the two sides of the brain. Recent work at Columbia University seems to indicate that the left brain deals with linear-analytic functions, and the right brain with holistic functions. Experiments reported by Thomas G. Bever and Robert J. Chiarello in the August 9, 1974 issue of *Science* reveal that music specialists—and they are not even dealing with a new language here—hear with the left brain which governs perceptions of the right

250

ear, rather than with the right brain which governs perceptions of the left ear, and which is how the majority of people hear music:

> Confirming the results of previous studies, the musically naive subjects have a left ear superiority for melody recognition. However, the subjects who are musically sophisticated have a right ear superiority. Our interpretation is that musically sophisticated subjects can organize a melodic sequence in terms of the internal relations of its components... Dominance of the left hemisphere for such analytic functions would explain the dominance of the right ear for melody recognition in experienced listeners: as their capacity for musical analysis increases, the left hemisphere becomes increasingly involved in the processing of music. This raises the possibility that being musically sophisticated has real neurological concomitants, permitting the utilization of a different strategy of musical apprehension that calls on left hemisphere functions.

These observations lead one to conclude that the inaccessibility of "revolutionary" music makes that music physically discomfiting to the unspecialized listener who is searching for form, without which he is lost. The most skillful manipulation of atomistic details cannot compensate for the holistic void.

If the "linear-analytic" approach does not necessarily make for great art, neither does the "holistic" approach. It is a fact that a good deal of twentieth-century music which displays the most apparently articulated forms has fallen by the cultural wayside. In October 1974, Harold Schonberg devoted a Sunday essay to recalling the ferment in American music during the 1930s and '40s. He mentioned "Copland, Harris, Piston, Schuman, Barber, Shapero, Berger, Smit, Haieff, Fine, Citkowitz, Virgil Thomson, Randall Thompson, Hanson, Sessions, Creston, Chanler, Cowell, Cage, Diamond, Dello Joio, Mennin, Hovhaness... one can go on and on," Schonberg writes. "Very few had any staying power."

Schonberg attributes the problem to the fact that great music is a function of personality and that there have been no great personalities in composition in recent times. But if that is the case, then one must ask why. And if one asks why, there is only one answer: that this time is different from almost all other times, that we are in the midst of a historical impasse, that a certain kind of cultural synthesis is dead, and with it the high art of our tradition is dead.

Those in the new music market in Europe report there are no composers on the horizon today. Gilbert Amy, who took over Boulez's post at the Domaine Musical in 1967, disbanded the Domaine in

1971. He did it, he says, because audiences wanted first performances and he could not come up with any decent ones. At Universal Edition, Alfred Schlee reports that he knows "no young artists who are anything but derivative of the now middle-aged ones." Otto Tomek, who must come up with pieces for the annual Donaueschingen Festival, says that he finds himself in extreme difficulty: "Everyone says they want to hear from the young. In 1972 I did what they asked. I planned a program of only new and young composers and it was more dreadful than anything you can imagine. The concerts were dead. Every style was represented and each program terribly received. I can't ever do that again. But the fact is there is no style today."

In the United States, where men are more optimistic than in Europe, and where considerably more money is involved, those in charge speak warmly about the young. But little I have heard supports what they say. Lawrence Morton, now retired from the Monday Evening Concerts and free to speak, says: "The great men of the century were the Viennese, Stravinsky, and Bartók. They have not had any real successors. The closest two are Stockhausen and Boulez. Stockhausen seems to have gone off the deep end. Boulez's works are open-ended; we cannot know them complete.

"I go to all the concerts today. The composers are mostly anonymous. Certain idiomatic expressions from Stockhausen and Boulez are repeated everywhere. I don't hear anything that says to me, 'This is the way John Smith composes.'"

In the preface to *The Waning of the Middle Ages*, Johan Huizinga writes: "In history, as in nature, birth and death are equally balanced. The decay of overripe forms of civilization is as suggestive a spectacle as the growth of new ones. And it occasionally happens that a period in which one had, hitherto, been mainly looking for the coming of the birth of new things, suddenly reveals itself as an epoch of fading and decay."

27

In March 1970, eighteen months before taking over as music director of the New York Philharmonic, Boulez was conducting the Cleveland Orchestra in Montreal. The University of Montreal took advantage of his presence to invite him to a long and serious interview in front of an audience of academicians and composers. Boulez's remarks were recorded on tape and published in *Les Cahiers Canadiens de Musique*. Because, in this interview, he touched on matters of great importance to him, it will be useful to quote (in my translation) at least a small portion of what he said. What comes across the twenty transcribed pages is Boulez's analytic, penetrating mind and his repudiation of naturalism and representation in favor of science and technology.

Touching on how the Institut de Recherche et de Coordination Acoustique/Musique would cope with the limitations he found in the present musical situation, Boulez said:

> There are some instruments which should be transformed because we still have instruments that were made for the eighteenth and nineteenth centuries. . . . We are still using half-tone scales because there are no instruments suited to other scales. If you want to write music built on one-quarter or one-third tone scales, there is absolutely nothing available now. . . . We must have a period of research to deal with the transformation of such instruments and for composition and electronics as well. . . .

Another example: the sociology of concerts. We would make sociological studies about different audiences: how to organize a concert hall differently, how to affect an audience [comment toucher un public]. . . . (In this last phrase lies the underlying theme of Boulez, his almost tragically single-minded obsession with making the serial principle work.)

On musical analysis:

We have been prepared for a basic analysis of music, specifically in regard to the Viennese school. Don't forget that the Viennese school and specifically Webern was a sort of very narrow and rigorous transition [une espèce de passage extrêmement étroit et rigoureux] in which each sound was settled by a very decisive logic, and there were not two solutions but only one for each problem. Of course it is very easy to analyze this type of thing, because there is one solution at any given time, and since the principles are very easy, the solutions are very easy. What is more important—and here analysis is almost nonexistent—are the dialectics of composition . . . the processes, how a composer, through such a system, has started his thought. . . . What you have to analyze is not the way you have reached formal structures, nor the way you have reached given musical objects: what is interesting is the analysis of the relationships between those musical objects, between those formal structures and the contents of the composer's mind. . . .

Because if you husk only the vocabulary [si vous arrivez a décortiquer uniquement le vocabulaire], you will fall into mannerism. . . . What you must do is look at the "way of creativity" of the composer in a very deep way. . . . What is interesting is the connection between the events. . . . When I analyzed Wozzeck or Gruppen or a Mallarmé poem in my class at Basel, I did not go into the vocabulary. I would leave it to the students to discover certain details in the vocabulary or style. But I would throw light right away upon the structural form and the reason for it.

On structuralism in music:

When I say music is nonsignifying, I mean it does not transmit information. . . . For example, language can give mere information. "We are here today." OK, it is information. It is not very important. What is important is that the information was given. On the other hand, if I read a poem by René Char or Michaux, it is not the information that is important, but the structure of the language, which is just as responsible as the message itself. What I mean is that music does not have to "say. . . ."

On mathematics and music:

I studied mathematics because I had a gift for it. But musical gift is not necessarily related to mathematical gift. You can have one or both. . . . I tell you frankly that I have a great deal of respect for the "pure" mathematicians. They are the ones with the widest imaginations. They often have entities which are very hard to seize or even understand and they manipulate them with great liberty and inventive capacity.

There is a sort of perpetual game between the scientific substratum and the emotional content. We are now in a period in which we perceive more the functional, structural, and mathematical aspects of music. Generally speaking, we use in music much simpler terms than in mathematics, and we are much behind, since all the mathematical notions used in music are at least one century old in mathematics. . . .

Asked how he planned to persuade New York subscribers into some understanding of new music, Boulez replied:

By exciting the curiosity of the snobs. And I am not against it, I must say. I did it in Paris and it worked very well. To start, you always find two hundred fanatics. They are very easy to find, too easy sometimes. What is important is to raise the number. If you have a few, people will think, "I must go there. I should know about it." I have witnessed cases of people who came out of mere curiosity because they thought, "I've heard about it. I think I must go and see what it is. I don't want to seem backward." And finally, gradually, these people came.

At the conclusion of the interview, Boulez acknowledged he would be conducting pieces in New York that he had previously characterized as "caramel custards":

When I speak of "flans au caramel" I am speaking of the way people see that music, which is very different from the music itself. If you asked them to analyze what they are listening to, most of the time it reminds them of their youth. . . . It is like a reflex of Pavlov: when they hear the music they loved at twenty, they remember the years when their hormones were more active. And finally there are a lot of people who doze, who come to doze, and remember the time they did not doze so much.

This is not the way I personally view classical music. . . . I think, in fact, that with this music you must go beyond memory and see at all times how it was made and if it brings anything new. What is interesting when you face the so-called masterpieces is not to see them as stiff things in the past, but to see their potential for the present. . . . It is the same thing as when you clean a painting. Before we used to look at paintings through a good coat of dirt and we would say, "Look at this chiaroscuro. How beautiful!" Then, when we looked at it closely, we could see there was some red, and it did not go at all with the idea we had of it. What is important in the masterpiece is to take away the dirt.

Boulez did take away the dirt. Under his direction the orchestra became a reflection of himself: a lucid, clean and gleaming instrument. Robert Craft describes Boulez as the "professional musician's conductor. He knows instruments better than the others," Craft writes, "can tell the cimbalon player how to restring his box of wires to facilitate complexities, or show the violist a more effective fingering for a harmonic. Second, he is most fastidious about articulation. Third, he has the keenest ear for balance in the equilibrating of the various components of an orchestra. Finally, he draws the most refined colors from the orchestra. It follows that his performances are clean, clear, intelligent, and supremely controlled."

Boulez's performances are indeed clean, clear, intelligent, and supremely controlled, for Boulez has a composer's ear for structure and a unique conducting technique that illuminates virtually everything in a score. But many concertgoers who listen to old music conducted by Boulez miss the genuine pleasure they associate with it. Harold Schonberg, who at first wrote only positively about Boulez, found his performances of nineteenth-century work "inhibited." The retards were minimal, the phrasing stiff. Harriet Johnson of the *New York Post*, also a fan of Boulez's earlier days in New York, wrote in the fall of 1974 of his performances of Handel's *Water Music* and Schumann's *Symphony No. 1.* "These joyous works were played but not really interpreted. They were not played with style. The result was prosaic."

The musicians talked of Boulez's seeming obsession with intonation. When he first came to the orchestra, Boulez found a sloppy ensemble, made so by bad habits under Mitropoulos and Bernstein. Boulez said, "Trumpet, you're sharp" and "Viola, you're flat," and the musicians regarded him with awe. But in time many complained that under Boulez there was virtually nothing *but* precision. One member of the orchestra's governing committee reports that Boulez "requires only that we play the right notes at the right time. He asks for no sweat, blood, guts, or tone quality. He is very fair to players; he doesn't insult or humiliate them, but there is no robustness in the sound, never any dance feeling in the dances, never any joy in making music."

Boulez steadfastly refused to participate in personnel decisions, referring such problems to management. The raise in salary of a first-desk man was not, by his own choice, influenced by him. The men, therefore, found no tangible rewards in doing their very best work for him.

Nor did many find less tangible rewards. Boulez never complimented them, never saluted anyone for a job well done. His invitation for a soloist to take a bow was, at best, speedy and awkward, and most resigned themselves to a simple, quick nod. In this respect he treated them as he treated himself. He says he cannot imagine why anyone would need outside approval to know if he had performed his part well.

Boulez's isolation and indifference grew on the job. He showed little interest in a repertory as favored by him as the French. Even performances of Debussy began to suffer. Some musicians called his *Ibéria* "Siberia," and spoke freely to the journalist who wrote the *New York Times Magazine* story on Boulez. The article was entitled "The Iceman Conducteth."

Nobody is made of ice, but Boulez certainly strives to give that impression. In his Canadian interview, he used the word "beautiful" only once and then in a context of irony. Immediacy didn't enter the picture at all. Criteria used in the evaluation of art for the past 500 years are not part of Boulez's lexicon. This formidable mind, at one time open to passion and feeling, able to produce one great work after another, has closed himself off from the outer and inner worlds in a manner that is both self-protective and at one with his age. Boulez has always claimed that Stravinsky wrote his greatest works before he was thirty, and now others are making the same claim about Boulez. That Stravinsky should have invested his faith in quotation and Boulez in system—rather than in invention and imagination—says something imprecise about each of the men. But it says something far more precise about this painful era, this period between the natural scientific synthesis and "high art" and a new synthesis and a new art.

I quoted Boulez saying, "It is not enough to draw a moustache on the Mona Lisa because that does not kill the Mona Lisa. All the art of the past must be destroyed." The need to destroy past art has been almost a banal slogan in France since the last decade of the nineteenth century. But it is very difficult to destroy past art, particularly at a time when listeners are exposed to it as never before through live programming, their own record collections, and radio stations' record collections. If a businessman harried by events of the day or a scientist in awe of accumulating data can find the order and significance in a work of art that he cannot find in the stock market or in the ever-expanding universe, why would he seek out music in which he could not find his way? The de-emphasis of meaning in music and the celebration of system and structure may be inevitable in a scientific period devoid of belief. But it leaves man without a shadow of a spiritual base.

The fact is that the modern world has not yet evolved an idea that works for both its listeners and practitioners. Because listeners derive nourishment from a certain kind of art does not mean artists can or should deliver it to them. Stockhausen, at one time rooted in Schoenberg and then in Webern, appears now to have no roots at all. His 1973 *Herbst Musik* (Fall Music) presents a man and a woman in a series of tableaux: (1) the couple nailing wood, (2) the couple splitting wood, (3) the couple raking leaves, (4) the couple in the rain, (5) the couple taking a shower and making love. The music consists of a violin, a clarinet, the sounds of the hammering of nails and the raking of leaves. Tomek spoke of Stockhausen's inventiveness in regard to the premiere of this work: "Everyone was expecting more 'intuitive music' and instead he surprised us with 'reality music.' "

That Boulez did not go as far in the path of artistic abolition as many who have followed Cage's powerful lead does not make him any the less central or striving in this amelodic, arhythmic dance of death. Rather it underscores the fact that Boulez was brought up in a severely Jesuit household and educated in the strict tradition of the lycée, and that heritage confirmed in this way throughout the first fifteen years of a boy's life may cause a striking reaction but is not easily erased from his character. Cage, on the other hand, is American. He did not hear Bach until he was twenty years old. Discussing the exceptionally fertile field for post-Cageians in the United States, Pousseur concluded his conversation with me: "We, in Europe, are much more bound to cultural precedents. We are living in the soil, the very place, where all this richness was fertilized. You live where the Indians lived."

28

I arrived at Boulez's house in the French Alps in August 1973 to attend the last session of a six-day IRCAM seminar. Boulez had invited architects, technicians, musicologists, and composers from at least six countries to the twelfth-century abbey, an appropriate setting, for, in the Middle Ages, music was an intellectual discipline taught along with mathematics in the universities. The abbey was one hour's drive from Boulez's house. As we drove, Boulez said the major point of the Institute was that "every individual must be free. That is not a moral point of view. It is a vital point of view. Stockhausen imposes himself so completely on the Cologne project that no one else has a chance to breathe. I have goals but I allow for a give and take. The Institute has become much richer than originally planned." IRCAM has the money to match Boulez's goals. The funds poured into the electronic studio at Cologne from its inception to the present day do not match one year's budget for the Paris Institute.

The meetings were held in a modern wing of the abbey. There were about twenty participants. The plan was to conduct the sessions in English but as Boulez began his opening address, he decided suddenly to deliver his in French. Other Europeans followed his lead.

The first five days were occupied with strenuous nine-hour sessions during which participants read prepared papers. The title of the treatise delivered by Knut Wiggen, director of the electronic studio of the Swedish Radio, gives a clue to the tone of the conference: "Views on the interaction of our time and space conception and the technical basis for composing computer music." On the sixth and last day Boulez tackled less theoretical issues: division of courses into computer programming, acoustics, and basic electronics; recruiting those trained in linguistics; research into sociology of concerts based on Adorno's views; the number and type of publications; whether to give three or four concerts a year or group them together in one week of such events.

In the afternoon, pedagogy was discussed. Plans were made for the organization of the teaching of Fortran (a computer language), cross-correlation techniques, cybernetics, and pattern recognition. Several of the participants expressed the idea that one could not begin to teach until the computers and equipment arrived. Boulez disagreed: "One must teach the theory first, for unless one understands the theory, one's invention is inhibited. I think if you know something first, you will be much better equipped. I like to have a coherent piece of information. Otherwise I pick up this and that and do not have a solid tool. To project something strongly, you must know it. If you go to a technician and say 'do it,' he will be filled with contempt for you. And he will do just anything. Then we stand in the position of the blind and deaf, and in that position you cannot go very far."

In the afternoon, Boulez asked for comments that could be recorded by Mme Brigitte Marger, the Institute's press representative, and included in a brochure for foundations and friends. Boulez said he thought the emphasis should be that using science in art does not bring music into the arena of inhuman affairs but rather provides tools the composers need. Babbitt said the Institute would have difficulty attracting scientists. "Mathematicians look down on physicists," he said. "And physicists look down on composers. The problem is how to confront an attitude that music does not belong in universities but in girls' finishing schools and that exhausts its cognitive content. At Princeton and Harvard one never finds scientists at contemporary music concerts. Scientists think we take ourselves too seriously; they are equally contemptuous of music and technology. Look at Noam Chomsky. To him music is folkdancing, not Schoenberg. Robert Oppenheimer thought of composers as talented children."

Boulez agreed with Babbitt, noting that Werner Heisenberg had "torpedoed" his Max Planck Institute. But he quickly returned to dictating what was to be included in the brochure: "We must have a new point of view. We must have communication between all of these corners which have remained separate in the hands of specialists. It is necessary to have a team to do research. The Bauhaus is the only model I can think of. The Bauhaus changed absolutely everything. We are still living off the ideas which were explored systematically by a small group of people in an institute where only this type of research was done. IRCAM will provide a 'chair,' a type of thinking, a point of view. For now we find ourselves in a situation where one finds if one uses different intervals or wants different timbres, certain pieces cannot be performed. That can't be very healthy."

Vinko Globokar interrupted: "I don't want to go on record saying the situation is sick."

Boulez: "I didn't say it was sick. I said I want more. I want all the possibilities."

Globokar: "Ah you. Not me."

Boulez: "O.K., then, me. I'm not satisfied. I find I'm against a brick wall I have to push." Boulez slammed his right fist into his left hand.

Boulez's nature is composed of irreconcilable, unharmonized dichotomies. His puritanism fights his violence. His desire to be loved fights the idea that one should not seek love. Women who have become infatuated with Boulez have confided to me that when they have embraced him in a spontaneous and effusive gesture, he will flush and remain in high spirits for some time. But he never reciprocates that gesture or indicates he wants it done again. Similarly, at the Rug Concerts, when Boulez receives bravos and extraordinary applause, he takes the next piece at an exaggerated speed, so intoxicated is he by the extreme heat of the response. Yet he never lingers on stage to enjoy or encourage the audience's applause.

Boulez's behavior suggests that he believes man must be a selfless seeker devoted to truth, without any desires of his own. Yet in defining the "most recent period in the history of art," he limited it to the one "between 1945 and 1958," the period when he feels that he alone led the way, and thus he reveals his very deep wish to be recognized as the originator of all that was significant and good. Only after some pressure on my part did he push the period back to 1910 and concede some priority to Arnold Schoenberg.

Beset by these warring elements, Boulez attempts to resolve them through his art. His extreme asceticism, his heroic devotion to everyday work, is in opposition to imagination and expression, which lie too close to passion for him to bear. Boulez programs every instant of every day and posts the schedule in the orchestra's office so that secretaries can make appointments for him from early morning until midnight. He does not allow an unscheduled five minutes which might permit him to get close to himself. Boulez says, "I am neither reflective nor introspective. I prefer to act."

The condition in which large portions of oneself are inaccessible has been characterized ad infinitum as an "alienated" one and the ultimate condition of modern man. No one represents that condition more eloquently than Boulez who covers any frustration or rage with the most elegant and gracious manners. Only rarely do these feelings come to the surface.

A person so alienated, so divided, must attempt to restore wholeness with what he has at hand. At first Boulez tried system and it worked for a while. But then composers turned against him. After that he made a tentative approach to chance. But immediately he controlled that chance. Then through the direction of two major orchestras, he tried to convert Europe and the United States to his way. But the world did not go along with him.

In 1974 Boulez decided not to seek or consider an orchestral engagement after 1977, the end of his second contract in New York. He regards the period of the 1970s as an "exceptional" one in his life and plans to return to "what is more myself" through his work at the Paris Institute. There he will invest all his cognitive and creative passions in an effort to restore both his own sense of wholeness as well as the era's sense of wholeness. For today's music appears to know no way of integrating the past into the present—neoclassicism and collage pieces did not work—and without a past the era is cut off from itself. If your father's a horse, then you are a horse. And if conditions don't allow you to know you are a horse, then the ground dissolves underneath your feet. Boulez's hatred of the past is analogous to his horror of repetition in music; he even cuts the repeats in Mozart. For him music must continue to move on, always leaving the past behind it. This presents a problem for the listener, for whom repetition provides audible articulation and structure.

Boulez's "past" was the music of Schoenberg; he virtually ingested Schoenberg and only after he had eaten him up was he able to separate himself completely from him. That "Schoenberg is dead!" is the title of an essay in which Boulez celebrates a system ultimately based on dodecaphony reveals how crucial Schoenberg was to him.

If the new language he had built from Schoenberg's had matured gently—as tonality certainly did—and if the times had been such to allow for such gentle maturing instead of rewarding a new gimmick a year, then the current generation of composers would have had something to ingest, to move on from or at least attack. But art in our day is moved by *Time* and television. Each composer is forced to make something new every time he writes a piece and that is a large burden for him to bear; and so composers produce far less than in former times. As early as 1918, in a letter to William Carlos Williams, Wallace Stevens wrote, ". . . to fidget with points of view leads always to new beginnings and incessant new beginnings lead to sterility."

To say the period is bad for composers is not to damn the composers at all. Rather is it to emphasize the gravity of the historical impasse, the bewilderment of a period that has not yet crystallized its own synthesis, not yet come up with a predominating style for a new generation to absorb or rail against. It is precisely to bring into being such a style that Boulez has invested his faith and reason in sociology, anthropology, and computer technology. With IRCAM he strives for the flowering of a new art which he says he will try *not* to control, but which, he hopes in the deepest possible way, will be based on the art that he himself built by composing directly from his own time.

The struggle Boulez lost in New York he had lost in Darmstadt more than a decade before. Now he returns to France with an international staff of musicians and scientists who will probably appreciate him more for what he is than for what he is able to give—which is, in general, what Americans appreciate.

IRCAM is a limb of the great cultural center planned by Georges Pompidou on a site called Beaubourg, just to the east of where Les Halles used to be. The center will include France's gallery of modern art (formerly installed at the Trocadéro), a center of industrial design, a reference library, a variety of eating places, a film theatre, games, and exhibitions. Boulez's institute is the only musical constituent; it is located in a subterranean building half a mile to the north of Notre-Dame. Michel Guy, now Minister of Cultural Affairs, but in Pompidou's time organizer of the Festival d'Automne and a good friend of Mme Tezenas and Pompidou, served as the go-between.

IRCAM is financially independent of the Ministry of Cultural Affairs and enjoys the status of an independent foundation. This frees it from much red tape and, at the same time, enables it to accept whatever money is offered from the outside while receiving a generous subsidy from the State. The building alone cost $12 million. There are laboratories, studios, administrative offices. The main area has movable walls that can be tuned to any acoustical conditions and adapted to any kind of music. It will serve for public demonstrations, concerts and research. Boulez has told me he composes at night, "when there is no visual distraction, not even a bird," and that, as well as acoustical considerations, may have played a role in putting the institute under the ground: it is as free from sensory stimuli as it could possibly be.

Boulez's administrators include Luciano Berio, in charge of electronics; Vinko Globokar, in charge of "instruments and voice"; Jean-Claude Risset, in charge of computers; Gerald Bennett, coordinator of the other three; Jean-Pierre Armand, technical coordinator; and Michel Decoust, in charge of pedagogy. Nicholas Snowman will be artistic administrator, Max Mathews scientific consultant, Yves Galmot in charge of general administration, and Brigitte Marger director of public relations.

Of course there have been many electronic studios, but none as big and powerful as this. Boulez says that studios—like the one in Cologne—are in a "primitive state" because they lack the necessary funds. On the other hand, he finds that research centers of American industry, such as the one at Bell Labs, treat music as a hobby, for they make their resources available to musicians only at night or during vacation periods.

As early as 1975, two years before IRCAM was scheduled to open, Boulez's plans captured the imagination of some of the press. In London's *Observer Review*, music critic Peter Heyworth wrote that if IRCAM fulfills Boulez's ambitions, "it will be a milestone in the history of Western music as crucial as the advent of the airplane has been in the field of transport. IRCAM will probably succeed in pushing out the frontiers of sound as drastically as the great explorers of the Renaissance succeeded in expanding man's knowledge of the Earth."

At the outset of this book I wrote that Boulez's tenure in New York would provide the ultimate test for the highly structured music of the modern period: Is this music just seductive to the eye because of the relations a musician reads in the score, or does it finally appeal to something more that makes it memorable or even moving in some way? The answer is turning out to be that it is seductive to the eye of the musician, for large audiences have rejected it on the basis of listening alone.

In answer to the frequent complaint that his music was "too intellectual," Arnold Schoenberg wrote an article, "Heart and Brain," in which he said that music needed brains. But Schoenberg never went as far as Boulez; he turned back to tonality over and over again. Boulez, on the other hand, never turns back. He cannot find pleasure in Verdi or Brahms. His refusal to "interpret" the music he conducts or to give "expression" a high priority in the music he creates is consistent with the character of a very decent man—where impersonal matters are concerned—but a man who cannot bear a performer's embrace on stage, does not smile when he looks at a child, breaks with "fathers" like Messiaen and Leibowitz, breaks with "brothers" like Stockhausen and Saby, and refuses to take on any "sons" as students except in the public arena of a Juilliard master class. Boulez does not tolerate intimacy. His nephew reports that only once did he speak to his uncle about a personal matter, the selection of his own career, and that Boulez never alluded to the conversation again. Barrault claims Boulez possesses a "secret sentimentality" and that may, indeed, be true. But by now the sentiment is so deeply hidden that it virtually never breaks through.

The institute Boulez is organizing in his native land will give him a place to go where he hopes to create another kind of music. It may also give music a place to go. For finally it is inconceivable that art will turn back, that it will not develop further in some genuinely new, presently unimaginable way.

Poetry Set to Music by Boulez

Note: "Le Marteau sans Maître" by René Char is not included because of the poet's refusal to allow us to reprint.

Le Visage Nuptial

by René Char

Conduite

Passe.
La bêche sidérale
autrefois là s'est engouffrée.
Ce soir un village d'oiseaux
très haut exulte et passe.

Écoute aux tempes rocheuses
des présences dispersées
le mot qui fera ton sommeil
chaud comme un arbre de septembre.

Vois bouger l'entrelacement
des certitudes arrivées
près de nous à leur quintessence,
o ma Fourche, ma Soif anxieuse!

La rigueur de vivre se rôde
sans cesse à convoiter l'exil.
Par une fine pluie d'amande,
melée de liberté docile,
ta gardienne alchimie s'est produite,
o Bien-aimée!

Gravité
L'emmuré

S'il respire il pense à l'encoche
Dans la tendre chaux confidente

The Nuptial Face

by René Char

Direction

Pass on.
The sidereal spade
Once dived and vanished there.
This evening a village of birds
Passes over, exulting.

Your ear to the stone temples
Of presences gone,
Listen for the word that will make your sleep
Warm as a September tree.

See, they quiver, the intertwining
Certainties about us
To their quintessence come,
O Branch of me, my anxious Thirst!

The rigor of living wears away,
Lusting for exile.
In a thin almond rain
Mingled with gentle liberty,
Your guardian alchemy appeared,
O my love!

Gravity
Man Immured

Breathing, he imagines the break
In the soft confiding lime

Ou ses mains du soir étendent ton corps.

Le laurier l'épuise,
La privation le consolide.

O toi, la monotone absente,
La fileuse de salpêtre,
Derrière des épaisseurs fixes
Une échelle sans âge déploie ton voile!

Tu vas nue, constellée d'échardes,
Secrète tiède et disponible,
Attachée au sol indolent
Mais l'intime de l'homme abrupt dans sa prison.

A te mordre les jours grandissent,
Plus arides, plus imprenables que les nuages qui se déchirent au fond
    des os.

J'ai pesé de tout mon désir
Sur ta beauté matinale
Pour qu'elle éclate et se sauve.

L'ont suivie l'alcool sans rois-mages,
Le battement de ton triangle,
La main-d'oeuvre de tes yeux
Et le gravier debout sur l'algue.

Un parfum d'insolation
Protège ce qui va éclore.

Le Visage Nuptial

A présent disparais, mon escorte, debout dans la distance;
La douceur du nombre vient de se détruire.

Congé à vous, mes alliés, mes violents, mes indices.
Tout vous entraîne, tristesse obséquieuse.
J'aime.

L'eau est lourde à un jour de la source.
La parcelle vermeille franchit ses lentes branches à ton front,
    dimension rassurée.
Et moi semblable à toi,
Avec la paille en fleur au bord du ciel criant ton nom,

Where his evening hands imbed your body.

Laurel wearies him,
Privation fortifies.

You are the monotone of absence
Weaving saltpeter,
Beyond the fixed thickness
An ageless ladder spreads your sail!

You go, naked, studded with splinters,
Secret, warm, available,
Held to the indolent ground,
But inmost to the man, standing abrupt in his prison.

The days feed on you and grow—
More arid, more unseizable than the clouds rifting deep
    in his bones.

I have pressed the whole weight of my desire
On your morning beauty,
That it burst and escape.

Then came strong drink but no Magi,
The throb of your triangle,
The day-labor of your eyes,
And gravel upright on the seaweed.

An odor of sunstroke
Guards the coming bloom.

The Nuptial Face

Now, my escort, standing in the distance, vanish;
Delight in number has just been destroyed.

Take leave, my allies, my violent ones, my indices.
All drag you away, fawning sadness.
I love!

Water is heavy a day from its source.
The crimson portion appears through its slow branches on your
    forehead—dimension reassured.
And I, like you,
(The straw in bloom at the sky's edge shouting your name)

271

J'abats les vestiges,
Atteint, sain de clarté.

Ceinture de vapeur, multitude assouplie, diviseurs de la crainte,
　　touchez ma renaissance.
Parois de ma durée, je renonce à l'assistance de ma largeur vénielle;
Je boise l'expédient du gîte, j'entrave la primeur des survies.
Embrasé de solitude foraine,
J'évoque la nage sur l'ombre de sa Présence.

Le corps désert, hostile à son mélange, hier était revenu parlant
　　noir.
Déclin, ne te ravise pas, tombe ta massue de transes, aigre sommeil.
Le décolleté diminue les ossements de ton exil, de ton escrime;
Tu rends fraîche la servitude qui se dévore le dos;
Risée de la nuit, arrête ce charroi lugubre
De voix vitreuses, de départs lapidés.

Tôt soustrait au flux des lésions inventives
(La pioche de l'aigle lance haut le sang évasé)
Sur un destin présent j'ai mené mes franchises
Vers l'azur multivalve, la granitique dissidence.

O voûte d'effusion sur la couronne de son ventre,
Murmure de dot noire!
O mouvement tari de sa diction!

Nativité, guidez les insoumis, qu'ils découvrent leur base,
L'amande croyable au lendemain neuf.
Le soir a fermé sa plaie de corsaire où voyageaient les fusées vagues
　　parmi la peur soutenue des chiens.
Au passé les micas du deuil sur ton visage.

Vitre inextinguible: mon souffle affleurait déjà l'amitié de ta
　　blessure,
Armait ta royauté inapparente.
Et des lèvres du brouillard descendit notre plaisir au seuil de dune, au
　　toit d'acier.
La conscience augmentait l'appareil frémissant de ta
　　permanence;
La simplicité fidèle s'étendit partout.

Timbre de la devise matinale, morte-saison de l'étoile précoce,
Je cours au terme de mon cintre, colisée fossoyé.
Assez baisé le crin nubile des céréales:

Throw off my vestiges,
Stricken healthy with light.

Cincture of steam, tamed multitude, factors of fear, here! touch my
    renaissance.
Walls of my duration, I forego the assistance of my venial breadth;
I prop the makeshift shelter, and block the first show of survival.
Afire with itinerant solitude,
I dream of floating on the shade of her Presence.

The desert body, opposed to being mixed, yesterday came back talking
    dark.
Descent, do not change your mind; let fall your mallet of trances, acrid sleep.
Bareness diminishes the bones of your exile and swordplay.
You refreshen slavery gnawing its own back;
Snigger of night, stop this lugubrious hauling
Of glazed voices, lapidated departures.

Early snatched from the flux of creative lesions
(The eagle's pickaxe spouts high the splayed blood)
Upon present destiny I have led my franchises
Toward the multivalve sky, the dissidence of granite.

O dome of effusion over the crown of her belly,
Murmur of dark dowry!
O sealed movement of her speech!

Nativity, guide the unsubmissive, let them find their foundation,
A believable kernel of fresh morrow.
Evening has closed its corsair wound where vague rockets voyaged
    among the sustained fears of dogs.
Gone are the micas of grief from your face.

Inextinguishable windowpane: my breath was already flush with the
    friendship of your wound,
Arming your unapparent royalty.
And from the lips of the fog our pleasure came down to its doorway
    of dunes, its roof of steel.
Consciousness augmented the trembling instrument of your
    permanence;
Faithful simplicity extended everywhere.

Doorbell of morning's motto, dead season of the precocious star,
I come to the end of my arch, a grave-dug coliseum.
Enough of sucking the nubile horsehair of grain:

La cardeuse, l'opiniâtre, nos confins la soumettent.
Assez maudit le hâvre des simulacres nuptiaux:
Je touche le fond d'un retour compact.

Ruisseaux, neume des morts anfractueux,
Vous qui suivez le ciel aride,
Mêlez votre acheminement aux orages de qui sut guérir de la
    désertion,
Donnant contre vos études salubres.
Au sein du toit le pain suffoque à porter coeur et lueur.
Prends, ma Pensée, la fleur de ma main pénétrable,
Sens s'éveiller l'obscure plantation.

Je ne verrai pas tes flancs, ces essaims de faim, se dessécher, s'emplit de
    ronces;
Je ne verrai pas l'empuse te succéder dans ta serre;
Je ne verrai pas l'approche des baladins inquiéter le jour renaîssant;
Je ne verrai pas la race de notre liberté servilement se suffire.

Chimères, nous sommes montés au plateau.
Le silex frisonnait sous les sarments de l'espace;
La parole, lasse de défoncer, buvait au débarcadère angélique.
Nulle farouche survivance:
L'horizon des routes jusqu'à l'afflux de rosée,
L'intime dénouement de l'irréparable.

Voici le sable mort, voici le corps sauvé:
Le Femme respire, l'Homme se tient debout.

Evadné

L'été et notre vie étions d'un seul tenant
La campagne mangeait la couleur de ta jupe odorante
Avidité et contrainte s'étaient réconciliées
Le château de Maubec s'enfonçait dans l'argile
Bientôt s'effondrerait le roulis de sa lyre
La violence des plantes nous faisait vaciller
Un corbeau rameur sombre déviant de l'escadre
Sur le muet silex de midi écartelé
Accompagnait notre entente aux mouvements tendres
La faucille partout devait se reposer
Notre rareté commencait un règne
(Le vent insomnieux qui nous ride la paupière

The carder, the obstinate carder is subject to our confines.
Enough of cursing the haven of nuptial images:
I am touching bottom for a compact return.

Rivulets, neum of the circuitous dead,
You that follow the arid sky,
Join your journey to the storms of him who could cure
    desertion,
Going against your salubrious studies.
In the bosom of the roof, bread is suffocating to bring heart and light.
My mind, take the flower of my penetrable hand,
Feel the obscure plantation awakening.

I will not see your body with its swarms of hunger dry up, cluttered
    with thorns;
I will not see the empuse supplant you in your greenhouse;
I will not see the approach of buffoons disturb the coming dawn;
I will not see the generation of our liberty abjectly self-satisfied.

Illusions, we have climbed to the plateau.
The flint was shivering under the vineshoots of space;
Words, tired of battering, were drinking at the waterfront with angels.
Nothing fierce survived:
The horizon of roads to the rise of dew,
The intimate undoing of the irreparable.

Here is the dead sand, here is the body saved:
Woman is breathing. Man standing.

Evadne

Summer and life were we in one
The fields consumed the color of your fragrant dress
Hunger and restraint were reconciled
The Chateau de Maubec was sinking into the clay
Soon would subside the rolling of its lyre
The violence of plants made us vacillate
A sculling dark raven who had left the fleet
On the muted flint of quartered noon
Kept pace with the tender movements of our accord
Everywhere the scythe was going to rest
Our rarity was setting up a reign
(The sleepless wind wrinkling our eyelids

275

En tournant chaque nuit la page consentie
Veut que chaque part de toi que je retienne
Soit étendue à un pays d'âge affamé et de larmier géant)

C'était au début d'adorables années
La terre nous aimait un peu je me souviens.

Post-Scriptum

Écartez-vous de moi qui patiente sans bouche;
A vos pieds je suis né, mais vous m'avez perdu;
Mes feux ont trop précisé leur royaume;
Mon trésor a coulé contre votre billot.

Le désert comme asile au seul tison suave
Jamais ne m'a nommé, jamais ne m'a rendu.

Écartez-vous de moi qui patiente sans bouche:
Le trèfle de la passion est de fer dans ma main.

Dans la stupeur de l'air où s'ouvrent mes allées,
Le temps émondera peu à peu mon visage,
Comme un cheval sans fin dans un labour aigri.

Turning every night the consented page
Wishes each part I hold of you prolonged
To a land of famished age and giant tear ducts)

It was at the threshold of delightful years
The earth loved us a little I remember.

Post-Script

Leave me, let me wait unspeaking;
I was born at your feet, but you have lost me;
Too well my fires have defined their kingdom;
My treasure struck your chopping block and sank.

The desert—refuge for the mild lonely firebrand—
Has never named me, never turned me out.

Leave me, let me wait unspeaking:
The clover of passion is iron in my hand.

Like a horse aimless in bitter plowing.
In the torpor of air my ways are opening
And little by little time will prune my face.

Le Soleil des eaux

by René Char

Complainte du Lézard Amoureux

N'égraine pas le tournesol,
Tes cyprès auraient de la peine.
Chardonneret, reprends ton vol
Et reviens à ton nid de laine.

Tu n'es pas un caillou du ciel
Pour que le vent te tienne quitte
Oiseau rural: l'arc-en-ciel
S'unifie dans la marguerite.

L'homme fusille, cache-toi:
Le tournesol est son complice.
Seules les herbes sont pour toi,
Les herbes des champs qui se plissent.

Le serpent ne te connaît pas,
Et la sauterelle est bougonne:
La taupe, elle, n'y voit pas:
Le papillon ne hait personne.

L'écho de ce pays est sûr.
J'observe, je suis bon prophète:
Je vois tout de mon petit mur,
Même tituber la chouette.

Il est midi, chardonneret.
Le sénecon est là qui brille.
Attarde-toi, va, sans danger:
L'homme est rentré dans sa famille!

278

The Sun of the Waters

by René Char

Lay of the Lizard in Love

Do not pick at that sunflower,
Your cypress trees would be most disturbed.
Goldfinch: fly off again
And return to your woolly nest.

You are not a pebble of the sky
Bird of the countryside: the colours of the rainbow
So that the wind has no power over you.
Become one again in the daisy.

Man is out shooting, so hide yourself:
The sunflower is his accomplice.
Only the grasses are on your side,
The pliant grasses of the fields.

The snake takes no notice of you,
And the grasshopper grumbles away to herself:
As for the mole, she can't see a thing:
The butterfly hates no one.

The echoes of this countryside have a safe sound.
I am keeping watch and I am a good prophet:
I can see everything from my little wall,
Even the owl as she staggers forth.

It is midday, goldfinch.
The groundsel is there, shining.
Go on, take your time, the danger is past:
Man has gone home to his family!

Qui, mieux qu'un lézard amoureux
Peut dire les secrets terrestres?
O léger gentil roi des cieux,
Que n'as-tu ton nid dans ma pierre!

La Sorgue (Chanson pour Yvonne)

Rivière trop tôt partie, d'une traite, sans compagnon,
Donne aux enfants de mon pays le visage de ta passion.

Rivière où l'éclair finit et où commence ma maison,
Qui roule aux marches d'oubli la rocaille de ma raison.

Rivière, en toi terre est frisson soleil anxiété,
Que chaque pauvre dans sa nuit fasse son pain de ta moisson.

Rivière souvent puni, rivière à l'abandon.

Rivière des apprentis à la calleuse condition,
Il n'est vent qui ne fléchisse à la crête de tes sillons.

Rivière de l'âme vide, de la guenille et du soupçon,
Du vieux malheur qui se dévide, de l'ormeau, de la compassion.

Rivière des farfelus, des fiévreux, des équarrisseurs,
Du soleil lâchant sa charrue pour s'acoquiner au menteur.

Rivière des meilleurs que soi, rivière des brouillards éclos,
De la lampe qui désaltère l'angoisse autour de son chapeau.

Rivière des égards au songe, rivière qui rouille le fer,
Où les étoiles ont cette ombre qu'elles refusent à la mer.

Rivière des pouvoirs transmis et du cri embouquant les eaux,
De l'ouragan qui mord la vigne et annonce le vin nouveau.

Rivière au coeur jamais détruit dans ce monde fou de prison,
Garde-nous violent et ami des abeilles de l'horizon.

Who better than a lizard in love
Can tell the secrets of the earth?
Oh sweet and airy king of the heavens,
Would that your nest were in my rock!

The Sorgue (Song for Yvonne)

River setting forth too soon, at one bound, without a companion,
Give the children of my country the face of your passion.

River where the lightning ends and where my home begins,
Which rolls the rubble of my reason down the steps of forgetfulness.

River, in you the earth is a tremor and the sun anxiety,
May each poor man, in his night, make his bread of your harvest.

River often punished, river forsaken.

River of the apprentices to the horny-handed state,
There is no wind which does not bend at the crest of your furrows.

River of the empty soul, of rags and of suspicion,
Of ancient misfortune unfolding itself, of elm trees, of compassion.

River of the crazy, of the feverish, of the knackers,
Of the sun leaving his plough to descend to the level of the liar.

River of those better than oneself, river where mists bloom,
Of the lamp which assuages the anguish around its shade.

River of respect for dreams, river which rusts iron,
Where the stars have that shadow which they refuse to the sea.

River of transferred powers and of cries as the waters are entered,
Of the hurricane which eats at the vine and heralds the new wine.

River with an indestructible heart in this mad prison-world,
Keep us violent and friends of the bees of the horizon.

Poesiés pour Pouvoir

by Henri Michaux

Je Rame

J'ai maudit ton front ton ventre ta vie
J'ai maudit les rues que ta marche enfile
Les objets que ta main saisit
J'ai maudit l'intérieur de tes rêves

J'ai mis une flaque dans ton œil qui ne voit plus
Un insecte dans ton oreille qui n'entend plus
Une éponge dans ton cerveau qui ne comprend plus

Je t'ai refroidi en l'âme de ton corps
Je t'ai glacé en ta vie profonde
L'air que tu respires te suffoque
L'air que tu respires a un air de cave
Est un air qui a déjà été expiré qui a été rejeté par des hyènes
Le fumier de cet air personne ne peut plus le respirer

Ta peau est toute humide
Ta peau sue l'eau de la grande peur
Tes aisselles dégagent au loin une odeur de crypte

Les animaux s'arrêtent sur ton passage
Les chiens, la nuit, hurlent, la tête levée vers ta maison
Tu ne peux pas fuir
Il ne te vient pas une force de fourmi au bout du pied
Ta fatigue fait une souche de plomb en ton corps
Ta fatigue est une longue caravane
Ta fatigue va jusqu'au pays de Nan
Ta fatigue est inexprimable

Poetry for Power

by Henri Michaux

I Row

I have cursed your brow your belly your life
I have cursed the streets your steps pursue
The objects your hand grasps
I have cursed the inside of your dreams

I have put a puddle in your eye and it no longer sees
An insect in your ear and it no longer hears
A sponge in your brain and it no longer understands

I have chilled you in the soul of your body
I have frozen you in the depth of your life
The air that you breathe suffocates you
The air that you breathe has an air of cellars
Is an air that has already been exhaled that hyenas have expelled
The dung of this air no one can breathe any longer

Your skin is moist all over
Your skin sweats the sweat of the great fear
Your armpits exhale from afar an odor of crypts

Animals halt when you pass
Dogs howl in the night their heads raised toward your house
You cannot flee
Not the strength of an ant can enter the tip of your toes
Your fatigue makes a lump of lead in your body
Your fatigue is a long caravan
Your fatigue extends to the country of Nan
Your fatigue is unutterable

Ta bouche te mord
Tes ongles te griffent
N'est plus à toi ta femme
N'est plus à toi ton frère
La plante de son pied est mordue par un serpent furieux

On a bavé sur ta progéniture
On a bavé sur le rire de ta fillette
On est passé en bavant devant le visage de ta demeure

Le monde s'éloigne de toi

Je rame
Je rame
Je rame contre ta vie
Je rame
Je me multiplie en rameurs innombrables
Pour ramer plus fortement contre toi

Tu tombes dans le vague
Tu es sans souffle
Tu te lasses avant même le moindre effort

Je rame
Je rame
Je rame

Tu t'en vas, ivre, attaché à la queue d'un mulet
L'ivresse comme un immense parasol qui obscurcit le ciel
Et assemble les mouches
L'ivresse vertigineuse des canaux semi-circulaires
Commencement mal écouté de l'hémiplégie
L'ivresse ne te quitte plus
Te couche à gauche
Te couche à droite
Te couche sur le sol pierreux du chemin
Je rame
Je rame
Je rame contre tes jours

Dans la maison de la souffrance tu entres

Je rame
Je rame
Sur un bandeau noir tes actions s'inscrivent
Sur le grand œil blanc d'un cheval borgne roule ton avenir

Your mouth bites you
Your nails scratch you
No longer yours is your wife
No longer yours is your brother
The sole of your foot is stung by a furious serpent

They have spit upon your progeny
They have spit upon the laughter of your little daughter
They spit as they pass before the face of your dwelling

The world shuns you

I row
I row
I row against your life
I row
I multiply into innumerable rowers
To row more powerfully against you

You feel yourself in a daze
You cannot breathe
You grow tired even before the least exertion

I row
I row
I row

You go away drunk tied to a mule's tail
Drunkenness like an enormous parasol that obscures the sky
And collects flies
Dizzy drunkenness of the semi-circular canals
Beginning of hemiplegia neglected
Drunkenness never leaves you
Fells you to the left
Fells you to the right
Fells you to the stony ground of the road
I row
I row
I row against your days

You enter the house of pain

I row
I row
On a black band your actions are being enrolled
On the great white eye of a one-eyed horse your future revolves

JE RAME

Efficace comme le coït avec une jeune fille vierge
Efficace
Efficace comme l'absence de puits dans le désert
Efficace est mon action
Efficace

Efficace comme le traître qui se tient à l'écart entouré de ses hommes
 prêts à tuer
Efficace comme la nuit pour cacher les objets
Efficace comme la chèvre pour produire des chevreaux
Petits, petits, tout navrés déjà

Efficace comme la vipère
Efficace comme le couteau effilé pour faire la plaie
Comme la rouille et l'urine pour l'entretenir
Comme les chocs, les chutes et les secousses pour l'agrandir
Efficace est mon action

Efficace comme le sourire de mépris pour soulever dans la poitrine du
 méprisé un océan de haine, qui jamais ne sera asséché
Efficace comme le désert pour déshydrater les corps et affermir les âmes
Efficace comme les mâchoires de l'hyène pour mastiquer les membres
 mal défendus des cadavres

EFFICACE
Efficace est mon action

I ROW

Efficacious as coition with a young virgin
Efficacious
Efficacious as the absence of wells in the desert
Efficacious is my action
Efficacious

Efficacious as the traitor who holds you aloof surrounded by his men
    ready to kill
Efficacious as the night for hiding things
Efficacious as the nanny goat for bringing forth kids
Little, little and already forlorn

Efficacious as the viper
Efficacious as the knife sharpened for making wounds
As rust and urine for keeping it
As jolts and jerks and falls for enlarging it
Efficacious is my action

Efficacious as the smile of scorn for rousing in the breast of the scorned
    an ocean of hatred that will never go dry
Efficacious as the desert for dehydrating bodies and strengthening souls
Efficacious as the hyena's jaws for chewing the defenseless limbs of
    corpses

EFFICACIOUS
Efficacious is my action

Translation by Louise Varèse

Sonnets

by Mallarmé

(set to music for three middle movements of Pli Selon Pli*)*

Improvisation I

Le vierge, le vivace et le bel aujourd'hui
Va-t-il nous déchirer avec un coup d'aile ivre
Ce lac dur oublié que hante sous le givre
Le transparent glacier des vols qui n'ont pas fui!

Un cygne d'autrefois se souvient que c'est lui
Magnifique mais qui sans espoir se délivre
Pour n'avoir pas chanté la région où vivre
Quand du stérile hiver a resplendi l'ennui.

Tout son col secouera cette blanche agonie
Par l'espace infligée à l'oiseau qui le nie,
Mais non l'horreur du sol où le plumage est pris.

Fantôme qu'à ce lieu son pur éclat assigne,
Il s'immobilise au songe froid de mépris
Que vêt parmi l'exil inutile le Cygne.

Improvisation II

Une dentelle s'abolit
Dans le doute du Jeu suprême
À n'entr'ouvrir comme un blasphème
Qu'absence éternelle de lit.

Cet unanime blanc conflit
D'une guirlande avec la même,

Sonnets

by Mallarmé

(set to music for three middle movements of Pli Selon Pli*)*

Improvisation I

The virginal, lively and beautiful day,
Will it tear for us with a stroke of its drunken wing
This hard, forgotten lake that haunts beneath the frost
The transparent glacier of flights unflown!

A swan of yesterday remembers that it is he,
Magnificent but without hope of freeing himself,
For not having sung of the land in which he lives
When sterile winter's tedium shone forth.

His whole neck will shake off this white agony
Inflicted by space on the bird that denies it,
But not the horror of the earth where his feathers are caught.

Phantom that to this place is assigned by his pure light,
He stills himself in the cold dream of contempt
That clothes the Swan in his useless exile.

Improvisation II

A piece of lace disappears
In doubt of the supreme Game
Half opening like a blasphemy
On the eternal absence of bed.

This unanimous white conflict
Of a garland with its like,

Enfui contre la vitre blême
Flotte plus qu'il n'ensevelit.

Mais, chez qui du rêve se dore
Tristement dort une mandore
Au creux néant musicien

Telle que vers quelque fenêtre
Selon nul ventre que le sien,
Filial on aurait pu naître

Improvisation III

À la nue accablante tu
Basse de basalte et de laves
À même les échos esclaves
Par une trompe sans vertu

Quel sépulcral naufrage (tu
Le sais, écume, mais y baves)
Suprême une entre les épaves
Abolit la mât dévêtu

Ou cela que furibond faute
De quelque perdition haute
Tout l'abîme vain éployé

Dans le si blanc cheveu qui traine
Avarement aura neyé
Le flanc enfant d'une sirène.

Fleeing on the sallow windowpane
Floats more than it shrouds itself.

But with him who gilds himself with dreams
Sadly sleeps a lute
Hollow musician of nothingness.

Such that near some window
According to no belly but its own,
Filial one might have been born.

Improvisation III

To the overwhelming cloud hushed
A reef of volcanic rock and lava
Even to the enslaved echoes
By a virtueless trumpet

What tomb-like shipwreck (you
Know it, foam, but slobber there)
Supreme one among the wrecks
Abolishes the denuded mast.

Or that which, furious for want
Of some high damnation
All the empty abyss spread

In the whitest hair that trails
Greedily will have drowned
The side-child of a siren.

Index

294

297

300

301